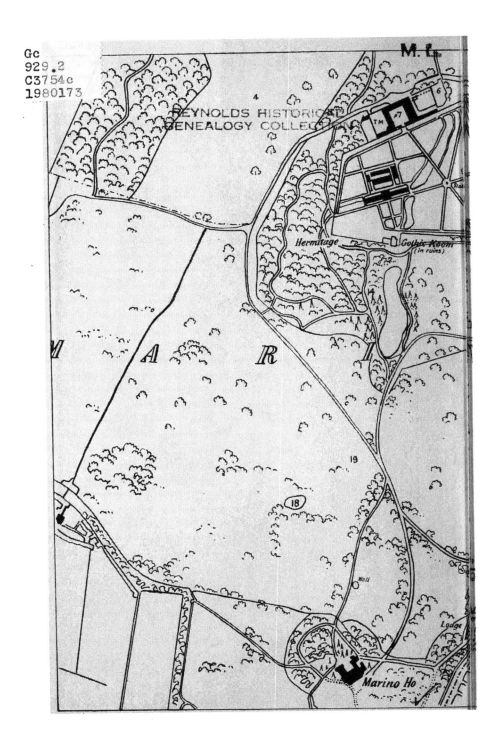

M. L.

Hermitage

Gothic Room
(in ruins)

M A R I

Well

Lodge

Marino Ho.

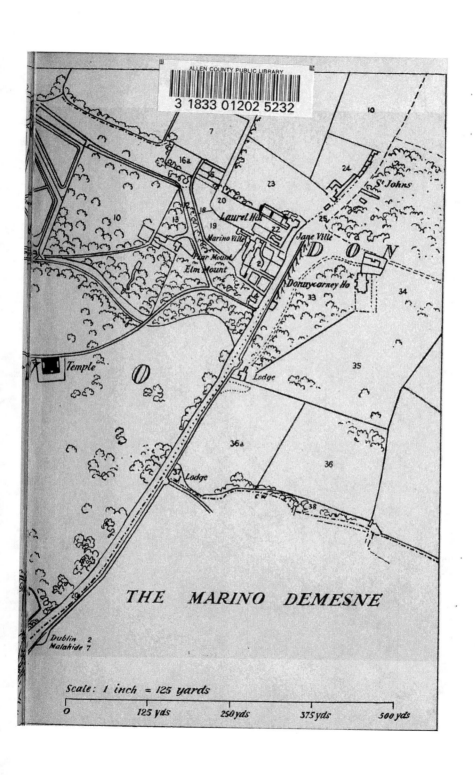

THE MARINO DEMESNE

Scale: 1 inch = 125 yards

0	125 yds	250 yds	375 yds	500 yds

THE VOLUNTEER EARL

Frontispiece

THE EARL OF CHARLEMONT

From a print by J. Dean after the portrait by R. Livesay, 1785

THE
VOLUNTEER
EARL

Being the Life and Times of
JAMES CAULFEILD
First Earl of Charlemont

BY

MAURICE JAMES CRAIG

*'The very rabble grew civilised
as it approached his person.'*

GRATTAN

LONDON
THE CRESSET PRESS
MCMXLVIII

HENRICO AIMERS WHEELER
CVIVS DELICIAE
HAEC OMNIA

First published in Great Britain in 1948 by
The Cresset Press Ltd., 11 Fitzroy Square, London, W.1.
Printed in Great Britain by
Robert MacLehose and Co. Ltd., The University Press, Glasgow.

ACKNOWLEDGMENTS

The author's thanks are due to many who have helped him in various ways. In particular he must record his indebtedness to the present Viscount Charlemont, and to Mr Bruce Boyle, Major Y. A. Burges, Miss Eleanor Butler, Mr Hubert Butler, Mr C. P. Curran, Mr J. E. B. Gray, Mr John Hayward, Mr H. G. Leask, Dr R. B. McDowell, Mr J. Morgan, Mr T. G. F. Paterson, Br. Roche, Mr T. U. Sadleir, Mr Geoffrey Taylor and Mr H. A. Wheeler. To all he is indebted for kindness, patience and the correction of error; but for the faults and errors which remain he is alone responsible.

To the Staffs of the Royal Irish Academy, the National Library of Ireland, the National Gallery of Ireland, and the Ordnance Survey of Ireland, grateful acknowledgments are also due.

The endpapers are reproduced from the Ordnance Survey by permission of the Minister for Finance; Plates III and XIV by permission of the Board of Governors and Guardians of the National Gallery of Ireland; Plate XII by permission of the Trustees of the National Library of Ireland (Lawrence Collection); frontispiece by the kindness of the conductors of the Ulster Journal of Archaeology, who also lent the block for the purpose; Plate X by courtesy of Independent Newspapers, Ltd.; and Plate II by kind permission of the owner, the Viscount Charlemont.

For permission to publish extracts from the Charlemont MSS. and from the Academy's Minutes, as well as for Plates VI, VII and XIII, the author is glad to record his thanks to the Council of the Royal Irish Academy.

M. J. CRAIG

Dublin
June 1947

CONTENTS

LIST OF PLATES

PLANS

BIBLIOGRAPHICAL NOTE

The primary sources of information on the Earl's life and activities are:—

(1) The Charlemont MSS. in the Royal Irish Academy, deposited there by the third Earl between 1882 and 1892. There are 27 volumes in all, including a priced catalogue of the Charlemont House Library Sale of 1865.

> Cited in notes as 'RIA MSS.'. The Volume number which follows is the RIA shelf number. In the case of letters, the letter-number follows; in the case of Charlemont's own journals etc., the page-number.

(2) The first volume of the Minutes of the Council of the Royal Irish Academy.

> Cited as 'RIA Minutes'.

(3) Historical Manuscripts Commission: Twelfth Report, Appendix, Part X, 1891; and Thirteenth Report, Appendix, Part VIII, 1894. These consist of printed extracts from the RIA MSS., edited by Sir John Gilbert.

> Cited, respectively, as 'HMC, I' and 'HMC, II'. The page-numbers, not the letter-numbers, follow.

(4) Memoirs . . . of James, Earl of Charlemont . . . By Francis Hardy. 1 vol., 4to, 1810, and (2nd edition) 2 vols., 8vo, 1812. The second edition is that cited in the notes.

> Cited as 'H, I' and 'H, II'. Pages 113-128 of Vol. II are incorrectly numbered as '131-146'. The citations are by the correct numbering.

(5) Select Sonnets of Petrarch . . . by James, late Earl of Charlemont, Dublin, 1822.

This book embodies most of pages 365 et seq. of RIA MSS., II. It is prefaced by the following anonymous note:

The object of these Translations may be best ascertained from the Introduction. They form a small portion of a work, found, in a state nearly ready for publication, among the author's papers, and intended to illustrate in a similar manner the writings of the great Italian poets, from Dante to Mesastasio. A limited number of copies has been printed, for the perusal of his friends and admirers, at the desire of his nearest relative, to shew that the leisure moments of a life devoted to the cause of his country, were devoted with equal ardour to that of literature, and to teach those who come after, to what a height of elevation rank and talents can raise their possessor, by being unremittingly applied to the purposes for which they are vouchsafed by our CREATOR.

With the exception of the Political Autobiography, printed by Gilbert in HMC, I, and the four papers in the Royal Irish Academy *Transactions*, noted in Chapter X below, this is the only literary work of its author to see the light of day.

The other contemporary and secondary authorities on which I have drawn are too numerous to particularise; they are mentioned where necessary in the notes. The Journal of the Royal Society of Antiquaries of Ireland is cited as 'JRSAI', or, for the earlier period, as 'JRH & ASI'.

For general background and guidance in the intricacies of politics I have found Lecky's great *History* indispensable at every turn. The works of Caesar Litton Falkiner, who wrote later than Lecky and from a more markedly unionist view-point, are scholarly and stimulating. Especially valuable for Charlemont and his times is his *Studies in Irish History*, 1902.

The six great volumes of the *Georgian Society Records* (Dublin, 1909-1914) are in general of very great value, though on Charlemont's buildings they are less informative than one would expect.

It would be ungenerous to omit reference to a modern author who has done more than anyone else to fill in the general background of the Irish eighteenth century. Professor Constantia Maxwell's *Dublin under the Georges* (1936) and *Country and Town in Ireland under the Georges* (1940), have been of constant service, not least by virtue of their admirably full bibliographies. Another modern author whose research, on the purely political aspect, has recently illuminated the period, is Dr R. B. McDowell: *Irish Public Opinion, 1750–1800* (1944).

PROLOGUE

THE CAULFEILDS

On the night of the 30th July, 1920, a party of men roused the caretaker of the Charlemont Fort from his bed. They gave him time to rescue one relic only from the building, a yeomanry helmet of the seventeen-nineties. In a very short time the subtle distribution of petrol-soaked rags and shavings had borne fruit, and by the end of the brief summer night the old building, shaped as it was like a natural chimney, was a gaunt and eyeless ruin. It had been stacked high with miscellaneous effects: nobody seems to have known exactly what was in it. Very likely it contained chestfuls of papers which would throw light on matters which must remain obscure. But the papers, if any, were destined to provide a shorter and fiercer illumination.

Perched on a high bluff over the Tyrone Blackwater, the Fort might have continued to stand indefinitely after the fire, no less picturesque and a good deal less ruinous than the rest of the ruins which dot the Irish countryside. But fate, in the person of the Dowager Countess of Charlemont, thought otherwise. At the Armagh Quarter Sessions in November the Countess sought £5,000 compensation from the British Government. She was allowed £2,023, and she appealed. At the Spring Assizes of 1921 the award was increased to £3,010. This was accepted, and the usual undertaking was given on her behalf that the money would be devoted to the rebuilding of the Fort. With almost incredible promptitude, the Countess sold the building

1

in May of the same year to a contractor for demolition.
The foundations, the gate-lodge and the adjoining
works are now preserved as a national monument by
the government of 'Northern Ireland'.

The Countess, fortified by the court award and the
contractor's blood-money, withdrew from Ireland and
died at Bath in 1925. At her death, all the honours
attaching to the Earldom of Charlemont lapsed. In a
sense, therefore, the end of the Fort marks the end of
the direct line. Its origin marks more definitely still the
beginning of the family fortunes. For the Charlemont
Fort, the first and almost the least interesting of the
long line of Charlemont buildings, was probably the
only one to be directly profitable to its builders. But
for the Fort, there might well have been no peerage in
the Caulfeild family..

It stands, or may still in imagination stand, as a
symbol for the family's place in Irish history, not least
because, as a building, it may fitly set the tone for a
story in which buildings are among the principal characters. It may even be allowed a somewhat wider symbolism. When it was first built, in 1602, the division of
Ireland along the lines of the English Pale was still a
political, and still more a military reality. In the year
in which it was destroyed, the most recent division of
Ireland became a constitutional fact. Its lifetime coin-
cides with that of the Anglo-Irish caste. It came into
being as a military outpost, and it perished at the quasi-
military hands of forces which believed themselves to
be its ancient and natural enemies. But, for two out of
its three hundred years of existence its military importance was, save on one or two occasions, negligible. It can
only remotely be regarded as background to that part of
the Caulfeild history with which we are here concerned.

Charles Blount, Lord Mountjoy, Queen Elizabeth's Lord Deputy of Ireland, was charged with the reduction of Hugh O'Neill, Earl of Tyrone, then holding out in his wild fastnesses of Tyrone 'among the bushes'. Blount's method was to plant a huge ring of forts round O'Neill's territory, hemming in central Ulster from Donegal to Armagh. On the south-eastern border of this area the river Blackwater formed the natural boundary. Here, therefore, in 1602, Mountjoy built a fort facing across the river. He called it 'Charlemount' after his own Christian name and the first half of his title, and he placed in it Captain Toby Caulfeild with 150 men.

The situation of the fort was precarious enough. It lay a good thirty miles from the nearest point in the Pale,[1] over difficult country. A few miles to the rear was the Yellow Ford, where Marshal Bagenal had been defeated and killed in 1598, and only a step to the westward was Benburb, the scene of an equally crushing English defeat fifty years later. Even Armagh City, continually liable to sack and burning by the Irish, was separated from them by seven miles of boggy country to the southward. Today, the position of the fort marks the transition from the fat orchard-country of Armagh to the Tyrone uplands. The Armagh landscape is anglicised and comfortable: Tyrone is dominated by the inaccessible Sperrins and Slieve Gallion, and perhaps in spirit dominated a little by Tyrone himself—the Great O'Neill.

Captain Toby Caulfeild was the son of Alexander Calfehill (or Calfield) and was baptised at Great Milton near Oxford on December 2nd 1565.[2] He served under Frobisher at the Azores, under the Earl of Suffolk off the coast of Spain, and in France and Flanders under

Essex. When Essex was sent to Ireland, Caulfeild came with him in 1599. We hear of him at Downpatrick, Newry and Dundalk, and he took part in the defeat of the Spaniards at Kinsale in 1601. And now, in June 1602, here he is holding the Fort of Charlemont for the Queen.

He must at times have asked himself what in the name of God brought him into Ireland. Even when, in Dublin in 1627, he died rich and moderately full of years, he was not in a position to answer that question to the full. Indeed, we are not in a position to answer it finally yet.

We do not know how frequently or how seldom the name of God was upon Sir Toby's lips. We know, indeed, that his motto was 'Deo Duce, Ferro Comitante', which has been jingled into English as 'With God as my guide, my sword at my side'. But the flavour of this is perhaps misleading. Sir Toby was no Cromwellian, but an Elizabethan; and as such, no doubt, put his powder and his trust in God in that order. But however he may have judged between them, it is certain that together they served him well enough in his time.

It was long traditionally current in County Armagh that you could walk from Slieve Gullion to Slieve Gallion without stepping off Caulfeild land. No doubt this was always an exaggeration, but hardly a very serious one. Slieve Gallion lies near the north-west corner of Lough Neagh, and from there to Slieve Gullion on the fringes of the Pale is a distance of forty-five miles. It is certain that Captain Toby, between O'Neill's submission in 1603 and his own death in 1627, became possessed of some twenty-five thousand acres at least, lying along this belt. King James signalised the downfall of O'Neill by knighting Captain Toby, and making him a Privy Counsellor and Governor of Charlemont in the same year, 1603. Copious grants of land followed, especially after O'Neill's flight to the Continent in 1607. Between the Flight of the Earls and the Plantation of Ulster, he acted as collector of Tyrone's rents, whereby he was probably not the loser. Perhaps more important still, he had the custody of Con, O'Neill's youngest son, from his father's flight till the boy was moved to the English court for safety and sent to Eton.

Before 1611 he had rebuilt the fort as a condition of continuing to hold it. In that year it is described as:

A good fort built, fairly ditched, with a strong palisade and bulwarks. Within the fort are good houses, built after the English fashion, for lodgings, and to keep the King's stores of victual and provision. Sir Toby Calfield, constable there, had 60 l. sterling from the King towards this building. A very fair garden without the rampier, etc. The town is replenished with many inhabitants both English and Irish who have built good houses of coples after the best manner of the English.[3]

Sir Toby knew the virtue of moderation in pressing his claims, for he acceded promptly to King James's request that he should surrender some Abbey lands which, though previously granted to him, fell within the area marked out for a London company of settlers. He was evidently a diplomat, as his patent of nobility recites the fact that his charm of manner had an infectious effect upon the native gentry. Against this must unfortunately be set an ugly glimpse of him intriguing in 1606 with O'Neill's wife, the Countess of Tyrone, against her husband. It was clearly in the interest of adventurers of Sir Toby's type to encourage an open breach between O'Neill and the Crown, in view of the wholesale confiscations of land which followed the Flight. At the same time it should be remembered that

the tortuous tactics of Elizabethan statecraft in Ireland interfered with the simple English-versus-Irish
alignment of forces, then as always. Sir Toby and his
associates cannot be regarded simply as soldiers in a
conquered country. We see[4] him travelling, in the winter
of 1602-3, from Charlemont through Armagh and Newry
to visit friends at Downpatrick. Captain Toby lost
his way between Newry and Downpatrick, and arrived
three hours late at their rendezvous, the house of Sir
Arthur MacGennis. The MacGennises were aboriginal
lords of the district, and Captain Toby's friend (another
English officer) had been happily whiling the hours
away in admiration of Lady MacGennis who was a
daughter of O'Neill. The MacGennises rose in 1641.

If we must call it war, it was at most a war without
fronts, as wars in Ireland so often are. The Englishmen
of that day, more adaptable perhaps than their descendants, seem to have accepted the situation without
question. Almost at the same time as he was building
his fort at Charlemont, and another fortified bawn of
stone and lime at Maghernahely,[5] a manor which he
had been granted in the extreme south of the County
Armagh, he set to work building an enormous and practically indefensible house at Ballydonnelly (thenceforward called Castlecaulfeild), which lay on the north-
west fringes of his dominions. There was no military
reason for his choice of site, for the position was
hopelessly exposed to attack. It was finished by 1619,
and Captain Pynnar, the Commissioner of Survey, describes it as 'the fairest building in the North'. It still
stands as a magnificent ruin, tall and dark grey with
fine clustered chimneys still topping it. Its life as a
dwelling-house was short, for Sir Toby's successors do
not seem to have lived in it, making it over to a tenant

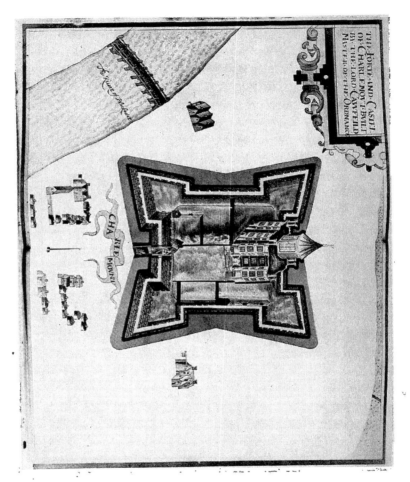

PLATE I   *See page 3*

THE CHARLEMONT FORT

From a coloured drawing by Capt. Pynnar, 1624. Reproduced by
Sir John Gilbert in *The National MSS. of Ireland*, Part iv, 1882

in whose hands it was when it was taken and burned in
the Rising of 1641. It was patched up and the family
lived in it after 1663; but, though details of its history
are scanty, it seems to have become uninhabitable as a
whole by the end of the century. As a gesture on Sir
Toby's part, it was superb and unpractical.

Distinctions came crowding thick and fast upon him
now, matching the swelling of his rent-roll. The lands
of the Abbey of SS. Peter and Paul in Armagh were his.
The site of the Abbey itself in Armagh City became
'Lord Charlemont's liberty'. In 1610 he had been
granted £400 'in harps' for three years, and when that
came to an end he was Master of the Ordnance for three
more. In 1613 he was sitting in the Irish Parliament as
member for his own Borough of Charlemont, one of a
large number created out of hand on a suggestion of Sir
Arthur Chichester, the thorough President of Ulster,
for the express purpose of furnishing 'Protestant Bur-
gesses'.[6] In 1615 he was appointed to the Council of
Munster. His grants of land were made absolute forever
in 1622, and in the following year he was created Baron
of Charlemont, with remainder to his nephew. He was
authorised to hold a court of Pie Poudre at Charlemont, and he paid £400 per annum for the privilege of
farming out King James's penalty on the Irish custom
of attaching the plough to the beast's tail, an enact-
ment, which had probably a financial rather than a
humanitarian reason behind it.

These honours seem to have sat heavily upon the old
man, for in 1625, though only sixty, he is described as
'aged and unwieldy'. He died unmarried, in his town
house in College Green—Hoggen Green as it was then
called—on the 17th of August, 1627, and was buried in
Christchurch Cathedral. He had a sumptuous funeral,

B

but the place of his burial is unknown and he has no
monument. We have only one hint at his character,
other than those furnished by his actions, or the testimony of his patent. In the account of the visit to
Downpatrick, it appears that 'to while away the time
Caulfeild talked of supper, for he was hungry'. Physically speaking, he was more full-blooded than our subject, his remote successor. But there are three points of
his character which are of some significance in this connexion. He claims himself, in a communication to King
James, that he was exceptional for sticking to his post
in Ireland, suggesting that others less deserving had
profited by acting otherwise. His collateral descendant
was to make a similar claim, though to him the virtue
was its own reward. He seems, too, to have been more
of a builder than most of his fellow-adventurers at the
time. More, that is to say, of a builder for pleasure than
a mere military engineer. Finally, his patent commends
him for 'uprooting the barbarous manners and customs
of a rude and savage race; for he had brought many
(and amongst them some of the higher ranks) to civility,
and they had so continued'. It is impossible on
reading this, not to be reminded of Henry Grattan's
eloquent testimony to the eighteenth-century Earl.
Acceptance of Ireland—not Gaelic Ireland nor colonial
English-Ireland pure and simple, but yet a third Ireland; the love of architecture and the instinct to build in
the teeth of time; courtliness and civility and the power
to plaster over the rifts in the political fabric: these are
three of the virtues which the Anglo-Irish caste at its
best moments displayed. Nor is it altogether fanciful to
trace them in Sir Toby, the first Baron, at least in his
better moments. The eighth Baron, fourth Viscount
and first Earl possessed them all in abundance.

William, the second Baron, was the son of Sir Toby's brother George, and of him little is recorded. He seems to have been for practical purposes an Englishman; so the process of acclimatisation had to begin all over again. He died in 1640, in his bed. Not so his son, Toby the second. He succeeded his father as Governor of the Fort of Charlemont, and as such lived there. On the outbreak of the 1641 Rising, the last convulsive struggle of Gaelic Ulster, he, with Lady Caulfeild and his family, was surprised in the Fort and taken prisoner by Sir Phelim O'Neill. One set of partisans allege that Sir Phelim took the Fort by treacherous abuse of Lord Caulfeild's hospitality: the other side alleges with equal warmth that it was a genuine military surprise attack.[7] Every circumstance of the 1641 Rising is still a fruitful ground for controversy, and we may despair of finding out the truth.

According to one usually reliable authority, masquerading parties of the local Irish inhabitants were in the habit of frequenting the Fort on the very eve of the Rising. It would be rash to draw conclusions from this: it may indicate apparent good-feeling on both sides, or the garrison may have regarded these people more or less as 'nigger minstrels'. Sir Phelim, however, can hardly have been of their number.

But two important consequences followed from the capture. The O'Neills held the Fort for nine years. As late as June 1650 a London news-sheet reported in its 'Intelligence from Ireland':

In the Province of Ulster all the places of consequence are in the power of the Parliament's forces, except Charlemont, where are about 6,000 Ulsters, who would fain challenge the reputation of the best soldiers in Ireland. . . . There is a considerable force . . . to endeavour the reduction of that place, which, indeed, is of great strength.

The Dublin government must have wished that Sir
Toby had built somewhat less impregnably.

For the Caulfeild family the results of Sir Phelim's
enterprise were more immediate and more painful.
Lord Caulfeild was held prisoner in the Fort for six
months, and apparently treated with consideration.
But Sir Phelim sent him to his own (Sir Phelim's)
manor of Kynard (now Caledon), and as he entered the
courtyard he was shot. The only certain fact is that Sir
Phelim was not present. The murderer's name is vari-
ously given, and needless to say the views as to Sir
Phelim's responsibility are as widely divergent. The
complicated web of prejudice and suspicion is still im-
penetrably tangled.

Toby the second was succeeded by his brother
Robert, who died within a few months, seemingly from
taking an overdose of opium. The title passed to another
brother, William the second, the fifth baron. William
was more or less of a Cromwellian, and the most unscrupulous character of his line. Perhaps this is unfair;
perhaps he was merely adaptable. There were at least
four sides to the struggle. The Rising or Rebellion in
Ulster was a rebellion only by discourtesy, for it was in
a sense part of an Irish civil war, which was going on at
the same time and largely in the same place as the
English Civil War, which, in its turn, is called by some
the Great Rebellion. There were the Anglo-Irish Royalists, represented by the Earls of Ormonde and Inchiquin. There was the Catholic Confederation of Kilkenny, of which the moving spirit was Rinuccini, the
Papal Legate. Their interests were not the same as
those of the nobles of the Pale, who were more concerned to keep in with the winning side and save their
remaining lands, than to become pawns in the Pope's

game in Europe as a whole. Finally, of course, there were the Elizabethan adventurers, who for the most part threw in their lot with the Cromwellians. But they, too, were actuated not only by political or religious preconceptions. They had their newly-won estates to think of, and titles which would not bear too close a scrutiny might hope to pass muster if their owners had backed a winner. The natural result of all this might be foreseen: an incomparably kaleidoscopic sequence of opportune alliances, secret understandings, desertions, shifting alignments and recombinations of forces, which defies description. Against this background that protean man of war, Edward Wogan, performed his memorable sequence of quick-change acts. Wogan's history and William Caulfeild's impinge at one point. Whereas Wogan deserted the Parliament side for the King's, Caulfeild deserted the other way round. On November 1st, 1649, Caulfeild was on his way from Lord Inchiquin's army to Cromwell's at Cork. He was captured by a Royalist force under Colonel John Barry, and taken prisoner to Clonmel. The Cromwellians, hearing that the Royalists (or the Irish) were intending to hang him, considered him important enough to announce that if he were killed, all their prisoners (among whom were Wogan and Lord Ormonde's brother) would be put to death. Execution of the sentences was stayed on both sides, and Ormonde's brother, after protracted negotiations, was exchanged for Caulfeild and others. Wogan took advantage of this respite to escape from Cork, and so lived to fight another day.

William Caulfeild, too, passed rapidly into circulation again. He had made one not very convincing attempt to escape from Clonmell to Carrick-on-Suir, the nearest Cromwellian garrison. By the time he was delivered into the hands of his parliamentarian friends, Protestant Royalist and Catholic in Ireland were acting as one. Ormonde's diplomacy had succeeded in dissolving the Catholic Confederation, most of whose members accepted him as Lord Lieutenant. An odd result of this manoeuvre was that Sir Phelim, who had been holding the Charlemont Fort for eight years, discovered that he was now holding it for the King, even as old Sir Toby had held it for the old Queen.

It seems certain that William Caulfeild was a member of the Cromwellian force under Sir Charles Coote which laid siege to Charlemont in July 1650. They succeeded in making 'a long-breach in the east side of the wall', but they found themselves 'so paid by shots, scalding urin water, and burning ashes' that they were unable to press home their advantage.[8] By the middle of August, however, Sir Phelim's position had become hopeless. It was doubtless owing to his new status as a King's man that he and his force were allowed to march away with bag and baggage. By the terms of his surrender, he undertook to live at his own house in Kynard. According to another account, he contracted 'within three months to transport himself beyond sea'. Whichever be correct, Sir Phelim did neither. Probably the sight of Lord Caulfeild's face among the besiegers suggested to him that his house would not be a safe place. Possibly the thought of leaving Ireland for ever was unbearable to him. At all events, his racial instinct came uppermost and he went into hiding. The only water that he crossed was the water of Roughan Lake, four or five miles north of Dungannon. In a crannog in this lake Sir Phelim lay low.

He was taken by treachery, but whose treachery it was is not clear. His wife, Lady Jane Gordon, was held prisoner by Caulfeild in Charlemont. A messenger by the name of O'Hugh was the means of Caulfeild getting to know Sir Phelim's whereabouts. Caulfeild may have extracted this information from O'Hugh by threats or trickery. But it is equally possible and perhaps more likely that O'Hugh gave it of his own accord.

The name of Toby the second's murderer, it will be remembered, is in some doubt. According to one account it was Edmund O'Hugh, a foster-brother of Sir Phelim. The same account says that Sir Phelim 'had O'Hugh committed to Armagh Jail for trial for the murder: but he escaped, whereupon Sir Phelim had the sentry hanged for his connivance or neglect'.[9] The first O'Hugh's escape may have been genuine, or it may have been stage-managed by Sir Phelim. In either case the second O'Hugh may have seen his way to getting Sir Phelim hanged for the murder and so vindicating the family honour of the O'Hughs.

The event was ironical, though we may hardly suppose that poor Sir Phelim relished the irony. He was captured at Roughan Crannog by Lord Caulfeild, and conveyed to Dublin. There he was acquitted of the murder, but found guilty of treason and hanged in March 1653.

The restoration of Charles II was remarkable in Ireland for the Alice-in-Wonderland quality of the land settlement. The fantastic four-sided war had partaken of this quality; and so, of necessity, did the peace. Those who had fought for Charles's father might as well have fought for Cromwell, except that, had they done so, there would not have been enough land in Ireland to reward them all. As it was, the English Parliament had mortgaged the lands of the Irish to pay its debts and the wages of Cromwell's soldiers. Charles had no

practical alternative but to honour the bond, if
'honour' be not too shameless a word to use. 'The King',
says Carte in his *Life of Ormonde*, 'considered the
settlement of Ireland as an affair rather of policy than
justice.' There is something to be said for Charles, but
less to be said for Ormonde, who had led the Irish to
Charles's standard and now regretfully informed them
that the King must be served for love.

The next thirty years may be summarised in Lecky's
words:

> The downfall of the old race was now all but accomplished.
> The years that followed the Restoration, however, were years
> of peace, of mild government; and of great religious toleration;
> and although the wrong done by the Act of Settlement rankled
> bitterly in the minds of the Irish, the prosperity of the country,
> gradually revived, and with it some spirit of loyalty to the
> Government.[10]

This lucid interval, astonishing enough in itself, is
only a pale foretaste of the glories of another brief and
lucid interval, a century later. It is fittingly commemorated by Dublin's oldest surviving public building,
the Royal Hospital at Kilmainham, and by the Phoenix
Park—both of them projects of charity and open-
handedness. There was to be little enough charity in
the years that followed.

William, Lord Caulfeild, as an honorary Cromwellian, partook of the rewards of deserting the losing side.
After the Restoration he was called to the Privy Council. In 1661 he was made Constable and Governor of the
Charlemont Fort for life. But the fort had played such
a notable part in the past that the Crown, on second
thoughts, deemed it unwise to allow it to continue in
private hands. Accordingly, on April 3rd, 1664, Lord
Caulfeild conveyed it to the Crown in consideration of

the sum of three thousand five hundred pounds, and relinquished his governorship in favour of Sir Matthew Appleyard.[11]

For the next two centuries the connexion of the Fort with the family was mainly nominal. At the revolution of 1688 it came into the hands of King James II, who visited it twice in 1689. But Teague O'Regan, the Jacobite governor of the Fort, surrendered it to William's general Schomberg in May 1690, two months before the decisive Battle of the Boyne. King William made the Lord Charlemont of the day (the fifth Baron and second Viscount, of whom more presently) Governor of the Fort. But the period of its military importance was, it so happened, over at last though we shall hear of it again in the 1770s. The military governorship was abolished in 1822, though the second Earl, as Lord-Lieutenant of Tyrone, was titular Governor of the Fort as well, and in 1858 it ceased to be a garrison. In May of 1859 the Crown sold it back to the second Earl of Charlemont, for £12,884–5–0. The remainder of its history has already been told.

William Lord Caulfeild was very quickly compensated for the loss of his Governorship. In 1665 he was created Viscount Charlemont, and appointed Custos Rotulorum for the counties of Armagh and Tyrone. Having sold the Fort, he was obliged to find somewhere to live, and it is probable, though not certain, that he put the great house at Castlecaulfeild again into commission. It had been burned by the Donnellys in 1642, and there is some evidence that it was again burned in the Williamite wars. It is also said to have been burned (probably by accident) in the reign of Queen Anne.[12] We may take it that the first Viscount, who died in 1671, lived mainly in Castlecaulfeild,

whether in the Castle itself or another house. He had a
town house in the capital, which seems to have been
the very house in which Sir Toby had died in 1627[12a].
He was the last of the line to live at Castlecaulfeild.
Thereafter the family, if and when they were in Ireland,
lived in Charlemont House, Dublin.

The first Viscount is a difficult character to assess
with any justice. He was responsible for preserving the
peace of the counties of Armagh and Tyrone from the
Tories, not the English political party which later annexed the name, but the political heirs of Sir Phelim
O'Neill. The most conspicuous figure among them was
'Count' Redmond O'Hanlon, whose beat lay miles to
the east and south of Castlecaulfeild, and who suc-
cumbed only to treachery as late as 1681. Francis Car-
lin's memorable ballad[13] springs to the mind:

> On Douglas Bridge I met a man
> Who lived adjacent to Strabane,
>   Before the English hung him high
> For riding with O'Hanlon.
>
> The eyes of him were just as fresh
> As when they burned within the flesh;
>   And his boot-legs were wide apart
> From riding with O'Hanlon.
>
> 'God save you, Sir', I said with fear,
> 'You seem to be a stranger here.'
>   'Not I,' said he, 'nor any man
> Who rides with Count O'Hanlon.
>
> 'I know each glen from North Tyrone
> To Monaghan, and I've been known
>   By every clan and parish, since
> I rode with Count O'Hanlon.
>
> 'Before that time', said he to me,
> 'My fathers owned the land you see;

> But they are now among the moors
> A-riding with O'Hanlon . . .'

Lord Caulfeild's method of dealing with this situation was as much of a patchwork as the situation itself. He had the name of being a notable Tory hunter, but it seems that when hunting them failed, he resorted to bribing them. Peace at any price was a good enough motto for a man who had lived through the past thirty years. The first Viscount is sometimes referred to as 'the good Lord Charlemont', and who shall say, at this distance of time, that the name was not deserved? There is one circumstance at least which stands altogether to his credit. The noble and unfortunate Catholic Primate, Archbishop Oliver Plunket, who was barbarously murdered by the English government at Tyburn, received nothing but good at Lord Charlemont's hands.

As instances of Lord Charlemont's kindness, he said that he had not only given him for his life a fine house, garden, orchard, and two fields, in an excellent position, but on one occasion, seeing the Primate afraid, he said to him, 'Never fear: no one shall touch you; and when you want to administer Confirmation, don't go any more to the mountains, but come to the courtyard of my palace.'[14]

William, the second Viscount, who succeeded his father in 1671, took after his great-grand-uncle Sir Toby, in that he won distinction fighting in foreign parts. He was, naturally, attainted by King James's Parliament of 1689, and King William's parliament of 1692 as naturally reversed the attainder. King William gave him the Governorship of Armagh and Tyrone, and the command of a regiment of foot, as well as the Governorship of Charlemont. Evidently he found tory-hunting in Ireland too tame a sport for his liking, for he was serving in the West Indies in 1702, in Spain under Peterborough in 1705, and had reached the rank of Major-General in 1708. When he died at his house in College-Green in 1726, he was the oldest nobleman in the dominions of King George.[15]

His son James, who succeeded him, made the move from College Green to Jervis Street. The old house must have been of the gable-fronted type—it is more than likely that Tudor's print of College Green in 1753 shows it still standing on the left of the picture. Although it was directly opposite Chichester House in which Parliament met, the district was becoming less fashionable than the new streets to the north of the river. And in Jervis Street 'hanging over St Mary's churchyard' the second Charlemont house was built, possibly before the second Viscount died in the first one. It was in Jervis Street, on the 18th of August, 1728, that the Volunteer Earl was born.[16]

NOTES

1. Ardee, Co Louth.

2. See Prendergast in JRH & AS of I, No. 59, July 1884. See also Gilbert, *Nat. MSS. of Ireland*, 1882, IV, 1; and HMC II, 76 and 205, where John Caulfeild of Clover Hill and Edmund Malone communicate with the Earl on family affairs.

3. Carew MSS., 1603–24, p. 226.

4. Latin narrative of Capt Thomas Bodley, quoted by Prendergast, loc. cit. p. 329. More details are given in C. L. Falkiner, *Illustrations of Irish History*.

5. Lewis: *Topog. Dict. of I: sub voce* Camlough.

6. Carew MSS., loc. cit. p. 136.

7. See Toohall, 'The Fort of Charlemont in Tyrone' in *Ulster Journal of Archaeology*, 2nd series, No. xvii, 1911; and Prendergast, loc. cit.

8. UJA, loc. cit.

9. Ibid.

10. Lecky: 8-volume ed. of 1883–1890, II, 181.

11. For Charlemont Fort, see particularly Marshall: *Charlemont and Mountjoy Forts*, Dungannon, 1921.

12. Prendergast, loc. cit.

12a. From Gilbert, *Calendars of Dublin Records*, iii, 260, it appears that Primate Ussher lived in and added to the house from 1632. When the Caulfeilds again lived in College Green, it may have been in a different house.

13. Which may be read in extenso in Lennox Robinson's *A Treasury of Irish Verse*.

14. P. F. Moran, *Memoirs of Oliver Plunket*, Dublin 1861, p. 186. See also p. 187.

15. Gilbert, *History of Dublin*, III, 19.

16. This fact, previously in doubt, seems to be settled by the entry in St. Mary's Parish Register, which records his baptism there on Sept 2nd, aet. 15 days.

CHAPTER I

CHILDHOOD AND YOUTH

James Caulfeild was born to the purple, but not by any means to the deepest purple that Ireland could boast. The nobility of Ireland could at that time be grouped into three distinct classes. First, in order of antiquity, came such of the Gaelic clan chiefs as remained. A handful of these, such as the O'Briens, Earls of Thomond and of Inchiquin, had contrived to remain noble according to the English dispensation. In practice, this had usually been achieved by timely observance in matters of religion. Secondly came the Normans, whose peerages were on the whole the oldest in the Peerage of Ireland, since that peerage had been called into existence primarily for their benefit. The most conspicuous among them were the Butlers and the Geraldines, the former Earls and Dukes of Ormonde, the latter Earls of Kildare, and after 1766, Dukes of Leinster. The Butlers and the Fitzgeralds are the York and Lancaster of Ireland: when one is up the other is down. The Fitzgeralds (both the Kildare and the Desmond branches of the family) had fallen from grace in the last years of the sixteenth century. They had till recently been Catholic, and had a name among the native Irish for patriotism. During the seventeenth century, as we have already seen, the Butlers were prominent if not always successful. But the opening of the Georgian era had seen their downfall. The second Duke of Ormonde had been, like the second Viscount Charlemont, attainted by James II. Indeed,

20

he had been a trusted supporter of William's, and Viceroy of Ireland under Queen Anne. But in 1715 he had been impeached as a Jacobite, had fled to France and from there sailed to help the Old Pretender. He had been attainted and his estates had been confiscated. The Butlers had a reputation for subtle statecraft; but this time they had showed their subtlety once too often. The old Duke was now living in Avignon. When he died, in 1745, he was, curiously enough, buried in Westminster Abbey. But the attainder on the family was not reversed till 1791.

There were many of these Normans in the Irish Peerage as it stood in 1728. Some of them were of the old religion, but a number of them had turned Protestant to keep their estates. For by 1728 the monstrous edifice of the Penal Laws was practically complete. In Lecky's words again:

In his own country the Catholic was only recognised by the law 'for repression and punishment'. The Lord Chancellor Bowes and the Chief Justice Robinson both distinctly laid down from the bench 'that the law does not suppose any such person to exist as an Irish Roman Catholic'.[1]

The Norman nobility, whether Protestant or Catholic, were in their turn outnumbered by the rest. And the rest were, roughly speaking, the Elizabethans and the Cromwellians. The Boyle family, who in spite of their apparently Irish name were of English origin, are outstanding among the Elizabethans. Between them they possessed no less than three earldoms, Cork, Orrery and Burlington, and they moved from the highest circles in Ireland to the highest circles in England with remarkable freedom. Their services to chemistry, astronomy, and architecture are well known.

But most of the newer nobility were more closely

tied to the land of their adoption. Their interests lay in Ireland, and their careers and marriages tend to bear this out. William, the first Viscount Charlemont, had married the daughter of Viscount Drogheda, whose origins were similar to his own. Of this marriage the second Viscount was born; and he in his turn married the only daughter of James Margetson, Archbishop of Armagh and Primate of all Ireland under Charles the Second, and successor to Jeremy Taylor as Vice-Chancellor of Dublin University. Margetson was an Englishman, but his whole career was spent in Ireland, which he served according to his lights. As Archbishop of Dublin he repaired the cathedrals of St Patrick's and Christchurch, and he restored, partly at his own expense, the Cathedral of Armagh which had suffered at the hands of Sir Phelim O'Neill. The Palace at Armagh[1a] and the buildings at Trinity College, Dublin, were alike beholden to him. As great-grandfather of the Volunteer Earl, he probably contributed some of his love of building.

Margetson's son-in-law, the second and long-lived Viscount Charlemont, chose his bride for himself, as the marriage took place in 1678, after his father's death. He also exercised his wits in seeking a suitable bride for his son. He returned from his foreign campaigns to find his eldest son, by then presumably in his late twenties, still unmarried. He writes:[2]

To the Rt Hon[ble] the Earl of Mount Alexander in Dublin

London *Aug* 16*th* 1707

My Dear Lord

Having a matter of the greatest Consequence in my thoughts, and fitt only to be imparted to my Chiefest friends, I take the Liberty of Communicating what follows to your Lp

I need not dispeir of getting my son Caulfeild a good Wife

PLATE II   *See page 27*

The Viscount Charlemont, *aet.* 13, with his mother, 1741. From a
painting by William Hogarth, in the possession of Viscount
Charlemont

here, where there is so great variety of Choice, but I do own I had much rather have one for him in our own Country, for several Reasons which I need not now give your Lp the trouble of. I remember your Lp once mention'd Mr Charles Campbell's pritty daughter, She was then verry young, but now I believe her father may be inclined to dispose of her. I would therefore beg of your Lp to sound him (as from your self) what he intends to give with her and if my son may be approved of, to be the happy man. One thing more I shall acquaint your Lp with (which I intreat may goe no further) Some of Mrs Campbell's friends has so far encouraged me to think of this matter as to propose it as a thing that may probably not be unacceptable to him.

So soon as your Lp can inform your self of what I desire and know what he may expect should be done on my part, I shall be ready to comply as far as suits to my Circumstances, and what that is you shall know whenever you shall pleas to Hon^r with an Answer

My Dear Lord
Your Lps most
aff^t Kinsman[3] and humble ser^t
CHARLEMONT

My Spouse gives
you her most hearty service.

I need not tell your Lp that (tho Mr Campbell is a Gentleman) some allowances of Portion ought to be made for want of Quality.

We may heartily wish that the old man had seen fit to expatiate on his reasons for wanting his son to marry an Irish girl. It would be rash to conclude that it was patriotic principle, much as we would like to think so. But we may hazard a likely guess. The new Irish nobility in the early eighteenth century were still in part living the life of a garrison; there is some evidence that under these unsettled circumstances they had become boorish and colonial in their manners; their standard of living was only now beginning to rise above

c

the standards of the camp and fortress. The old man
may have wished to spare his son the burden of a wife
accustomed to English comfort and the settled English
landscape, a wife, perhaps, whose English accent would
contrast unduly with his son's.

In the event, the third Viscount did not marry 'Mr
Charles Campbell's pritty daughter'. He married at
some later date—exactly when is not known but it was
possibly soon after his father's death—Elizabeth, the
only daughter of Francis Bernard of Castle Barnard in
the County of Cork.[4] James was the second son, for an
elder brother William died young, and there were two
daughters. The third Viscount, poor man, concerns us
no longer, for he died in 1734, and his son succeeded
him at the age of six.

Charlemont begins his own *Memoirs of My Political
Life* at the year 1755, when he was already twenty-
seven. His first biographer, Francis Hardy, was a politician and wrote as a politician; from him, therefore,
we get little more information on the years of youth.
We have his own account of his travels, fragmentary
in places but very full in others, which carries us back
to 1747, when he was nineteen. But from his birth till
that age, a stray sentence here and there is all we have
to guide us.

It is likely that his childhood was spent between the
town house and Castlecaulfeild, probably not Sir Toby's
great mansion, but a smaller house which is still occupied close by, and which local tradition calls the Join-
ture House. As a small boy, he may have wandered
among the half-derelict courts, and looked up at the
towering chimneys, still blackened by the fire, abandoned to the starlings and the jackdaws. But there

were less melancholy stirrings in the building line to be seen in Dublin. For Dublin was already well set on the road that was to lead it to a proud position among the capitals of Europe. A visitor entering the city by the north road would have passed down the line which a few years later became Dorset Street, and which, still half a mile from the river, was already laid out as Bolton Street. Then, curving gently to the left to face due south, he would have before him the long straight thoroughfare of Capel Street leading to Essex Bridge and straight up the hill to the grim north front of the Castle, and so to the confines of the fortified city. Inside the walls there was, and still is, the tangle of medi- aeval streets round the Castle and Christchurch Cath- edral. But at the end of the Williamite wars, and even earlier, the long straight fingers had begun to point northwards and eastwards; eastwards to Trinity Col- lege with its park in which the undergraduates are still, by an old statute, forbidden to shoot snipe, and north- wards to the open fields. For a hundred years Capel Street was to be in practice, as in logic it should still be, the north-south axis of Dublin. Jervis Street lay near and parallel to it, full in the flow of the rising tide of fashion. The second Charlemont House was demolished in 1803,[5] but for fifty years before that it was in use as a hospital, and by comparison with similar houses still in being, we can picture it as a tall mannerly building, unobtrusively set back from the street, with a garden behind and St Mary's churchyard in front.

The year of Charlemont's birth was pregnant with architectural promise for Dublin. On the third of February Mr Speaker Conolly, the most remarkable self-made plutocrat that Ireland has ever seen, laid the first stone of the new Parliament House in College

Green. By a curious stroke of fate, its life as a Parliament House was to coincide almost exactly with Charlemont's term of existence. After the Union, the building remained for many years a symbol of Irish aspirations; and a crude woodcut, depicting the sun rising due north behind it, figures at the head of many a Victorian patriotic broadsheet. The legend of the Volunteer Earl, too, had a similar, though a somewhat paler, persistence in the popular Irish mind.

Speaker Conolly was of the native Irish in origin, and his father had kept 'a little thatched ale-house' at Limavady in the County Derry, or perhaps at Ballyshannon in Donegal. By the judicious use of a legacy from two ladies for whom he had acted as agent, he was by this time the richest man and the most powerful borough proprietor in the country. His notorious wealth had recently been used by Swift to drive home a point in the *Drapier's Letters*. In 1728 his enormous mansion at Celbridge, twelve miles from Dublin, had already taken on the appearance of a chaster but only slightly less grandiose Versailles. Begun before 1722, it is one of the earliest, as it remains the largest, of the great houses of Ireland. The architect is uncertain. No less a man than the philosopher George Berkeley is said to have declined the honour of designing it, but to have acted 'in a consultative capacity'.[6] The actual architect was probably Colonel Thomas Burgh, a landed gentleman whose daughter was married to a Caulfeild cousin.[7] It is thus likely that Castletown Conolly made an early impression on Charlemont's mind. One other work of Burgh's he must certainly have seen in its earliest years of existence, the magnificent Library of Trinity College, a building which challenges Wren's Library at Trinity, Cambridge.

The year of Charlemont's birth can hardly be passed by without allusion to another birth, at the little village of Lissoy in Westmeath. Oliver Goldsmith, one of the most illustrious of Ireland's expatriate writers, was thus an exact contemporary. Nor can the Dublin of 1728 be thought of without Swift, who, at the very height of his powers, reigned from St Patrick's Deanery over the Liberties of Dublin, and spoke as the only articulate voice for the liberties of the Irish people.[8]

There is no reason to suppose that Charlemont took any precocious interest in the burning issues of the day, or came very closely in contact with the life of the city around him. He was a delicate child, and was never sent to school. The society of his sister and his young brother was probably sufficient in itself. In later life he continued to suffer from shyness, and as a child he was probably inclined to brood by himself. Not that he was studious: we have his tutor's word for it (which he allowed to go uncontradicted) that he found himself in 1744 or so with 'little or next to no knowledge'. At that time he was sixteen. The Hogarth portrait[9] of 1741 shows a swarthy child standing at his mother's knee, with deep-set eyes from which little may be learnt. But that little is all we know about him at that age.

One factor, however, in the family background, cannot have been without importance. His mother, left a widow at thirty-one in 1734, married in October 1740 her cousin, Thomas Adderley.[10] He was a young step-father—for at his death in 1791 we do not hear that he was remarkably long-lived—and from the first it is clear that he was on the best of terms with his wife's children. Lady Charlemont had one daughter by her second marriage, before she died in 1743. To Charlemont, Adderley, his legal guardian, stood for long in the relation of a trusted and generous elder brother, rather than a father.

Adderley is of some interest on his own account. He won the high opinion of Mrs Delany of Delville, and that must count for something. He was a country squire, descended from military adventuring stock. In his village of Inishannon he spent forty years establishing and fostering local industries—linen, carpets and cotton. In this he is a pleasant example of the small improving landlord. It is melancholy and all too characteristic to have to record that by 1837 his industries are reported as being almost extinct.[11] During the parliamentary session of 1755–6 he introduced, without success, a bill to reform the Dublin Corporation. This, as will be seen, sorts but oddly with certain episodes in his subsequent career. His political activities will come into notice later; for the moment he may be characterised as an enlightened opportunist with a knack for connecting himself by marriage with the nobility, not only during his life but after death; for his second wife married the heir to the Earldom of Buckinghamshire. He did not succeed till 1804, by which time the former Mrs Adderley was dead.

In the year before Lady Charlemont's death, the boy came into contact with a remarkable character, the Rev Philip Skelton, who became his tutor in 1742. Skelton was the son of a poor farmer from County Armagh, who in all but his misfortunes resembles Mr Crawley in The Last Chronicle of Barset.[12] A muscular, fiery, learned man, who laboured unremittingly in miserable curacies, and enjoyed the intermittent favour of the great, he did not survive long in his new post. It appears that Adderley was in want of security for a loan, and asked Skelton to find it for him. Skelton applied to one firm of Dublin bankers (the same who afterwards acted for Charlemont himself), only to find that Adderley had got it over his head from another Dublin bank. This, coupled with his having given the young Lord some advice which Adderley did not approve of, provoked a rupture; and the indignant Skelton took himself elsewhere. He had his genial revenge; for in the next year he dedicated his *Truth in a Mask* to Charlemont. The dedication embodied, in printed form, a great deal of sound advice to his former pupil.

Skelton was succeeded by a Mr Barton,[13] and he in turn gave place to another gentleman who remains nameless. Neither of them can have held the office very long, for in 1744 we find him in the hands of the Rev Edward Murphy, who writes himself down as a friend of Skelton. He rapidly became, and to the end remained, a friend of Charlemont's. Murphy, faced with the well-nigh blank sheet which so swift a succession of mentors had necessarily left him, lost no time in filling it up. His immediate and lasting success was owing not only to his abilities as a teacher, but to the fact that Charlemont was by nature the stuff of which scholars are made. There is every reason to endorse the claim made for him by a contemporary: 'As a general scholar, he has not his equal in the Irish Peerage'.[14] And if this testimony be insufficient, there is the fact that he associated and corresponded with the first scholars of his age, English as well as Irish.

Charlemont and Murphy between them laid the foundations in 1744–5. Murphy, writing later to his friend, says:

... you had for two years so applied yourself to your studies that, considering the little or next to no knowledge with which you set out, you really did wonders, not only as to the quantity you read, but as to the manner in which you understood it, generally equalling and sometimes even surpassing men of celebrated learning and great penetration. Beside this, you had upon public and (what is often more) private occasions discovered very generous tendencies. Your abilities deserved admiration; your application and goodness, admiration and love[15] ...

This may be relied upon, for Murphy was not one to shirk the task of pointing out the failings, even of a lord. Rightly or mistakenly, Charlemont was wont in later life to attribute the weakness of his eyes to prolonged study by candlelight during these early years.

Murphy is one of the most lovable characters in the Charlemont circle. A writer of long rambling letters, as conspicuous for their frankness as for their shapelessness, he signed himself sometimes 'The Hermit', and sometimes 'Edwardus Rex'. He encouraged Englishmen to call him O'Murragh, in honour of his supposed descent from the Kings of Leinster. He had been headmaster of a school before becoming tutor to the young Viscount, and he published in 1744 a volume of 'Select Dialogues of Lucian', with Latin translation and English notes. It seems likely that he could have dedicated it to Charlemont had he wished, but wisely refrained from doing so. From his first association with Charlemont,[16] he became attached to him alone; he was with him all through his travels, and on their return it is pleasant to record that Charlemont pensioned him handsomely, and that he survived till 1774, if not later.

Charlemont's adolescent friendships are known only by implication. One, with whom he must have been nearly of an age, certainly shared his tastes for literature and scholarship. This was Richard Marlay, son of

the Chief Justice of the Irish King's Bench, and afterwards Dean of Ferns, Bishop of Clonfert and finally
Bishop of Waterford. It is safe to assume that Charlemont became very attached to Marlay before he left
for the Continent, for he expressly singles Marlay out
in his autobiographical fragment as his only Irish friend
of the period.[17]

There does exist a roughly shaped quatrain alleged
to be by Charlemont, expressing his admiration for two
famous beauties of the day, Fanny King and Eleanor
Ambrose. The latter, who was a Catholic, is so happily
celebrated in Chesterfield's epigram extempore on her
appearing at a 12th of July Ball which he, as Viceroy,
gave in Dublin Castle, that to quote Charlemont's halt-
ing verses would be no tribute to anybody concerned.
Chesterfield's lines are:

> Say, lovely Tory, why the jest
> Of wearing orange at thy breast,
> When that same breast betraying
> shows
> The whiteness of the rebel rose?

Swift's friend, William Dunkin, thus describes Charlemont in 1744:

> When he should shew his early Skill
> At Ombre, Whist, Basset, Quadrille
> You find him sitting among Sages
> Or poring over musty Pages . . .
> When he should pay his Tea Devoirs
> And talk of Family-Memoirs
> To shew he would be of a Piece
> His Fancy runs on *Rome* or *Greece* . . .
> Nor thinks it to his Birth a Brand
> To take a Curate by the hand . . .

The poetry is poor but the description convincing,

particularly as, four years before the event, he fore-
casts Charlemont travelling and writing

> Accounts of Lakes, Volcanoes, Grottoes,
> And Monuments, with ancient Mottoes[18] ...

While Charlemont was abroad, his friends and relatives were apt to end their letters with complaints that
he never wrote to them. We, with the voluminous and
meticulously written volumes of his journal in mind,
can perhaps understand the neglect. Yet the fact remains that the only letter of which we know, was
written to Marlay from Constantinople, on the author's
twenty-first birthday. Murphy's testimony to his
scholarship is borne out by the fact that it is a graceful
adaptation in verse from Horace. 'Tis past three years
—'twill soon be four', he writes, 'since first I saw my
dearest friend.'

But all was not as well to the benevolent but anxious
eyes of Murphy, as the mention of Marlay alone would
seem to indicate. Those in charge of the young viscount
came early to the conclusion that something must
quickly be done. Possibly Murphy, with a humorous
self-importance which it is easy to forgive, over-stressed
his share in the decision. But it is more likely that he
talked Adderley into the idea, in itself conventional
enough, of taking his charge abroad. Later he took care
to let Charlemont know the reasons in his own mind,
in such a way as to lay the responsibility for his judg-
ments on himself alone. Part of the letter has already
been quoted; but the remainder, as the only reliable
account of Charlemont's behaviour as a youth, is so
interesting that it must be given at some length. In
this particular case, the fact that it was written for the
eye of the person to whom it refers, detracts less from
its reliability than it would in most cases.

You absolutely and in very fact [says Murphy] became, at the
age of 17, the very first character of a peer in Ireland; so
that no less than the eyes of a nation were turned upon you
with pride and expectation. In this situation were you (as
you still are) when—when—(come, my lord, if this honest
truth will not come forth of its own accord, I'll drive it out,
for I mean you well,) when your love of cards and sitting up
to late hours was noticed and sorely regretted by every one
that kept your constant company. Strong expressions of their
fears and concern for you have I had from their mouths, and
more than once. I softened the thing by urging that you were
unwell and wanted amusement, and defied cards or dice ever
to get the better of such sense and caution as you were master
of (which prediction I am, this day, overjoyed to see so likely
to be fulfilled). But cards and late hours were not all that gave
us trouble at this time. For not only all thoughts of the university were laid aside but, what was worst of all, books began to
be entirely neglected. I began to repent of my undertaking, but
bethought myself that vexation was but an additional evil,
and that I had better consider what was best to be done.
Whereupon, revolving the matter in my mind, I quickly fore-
saw that, having quitted your studies, you must soon inevitably be snatched up by the young profligates of your country
at their plays and assemblies, and so get a seasoning in tav-
erns, stews and gaming-sets; whereby all your modesty, fine
parts, fine character and worth of various kinds must soon
end in the nauseous dregs of riots, revels, idleness, stupidity
and nonsense. This made me anxious in myself and importun-
ate with you to come away: for nothing in truth was left for
your safety, but flight. Had you remained at home but to this
day, [two years later] even in the innocent play and indolence
with which you have spent your time here [i.e. at The Hague]
your character were, even this day, gone.—For, my lord, you
cannot abroad, much less at home, escape the busy, sharp
looks of men. A little man may, for a while, but you, not possibly. And the very companions of your idle sports (if in any
you indulged yourself) would pride themselves in divulging
your weaknesses, in order to make their own the less notorious . . .

And the good Murphy concludes his letter:

I had a letter the other day from Ireland that assures me that your health begins to be commonly drank there by way [of] a public toast, 'twas this made me dirty this Paper.

And the Tutor, as he signed his name in his lodging at The Hague, no doubt drained his glass to the apple of his eye.

There are several remarkable features in this passage. The statement in the last and first sentences seems difficult to fit with what little we know positively of Charlemont's actions to date. It is echoed by Adderley seven years later, when Dublin had not seen its darling for eight years: 'We are in high spirits at the thoughts of seeing you here this winter, where you are wished for by thousands.'[19]

There is nothing for it but to take these flourishes at their face value. Dublin had seized on the young Charlemont as a symbol of promise: in some sense he had already become an embodiment of the hopes of Ireland.

But there is something else which calls for explanation. A course of Continental society is not, least of all was it in 1746, the obvious prescription in such a case as this. For boorishness of manner, yes; for narrowness of views, by all means; for native limitation and angularity nothing could be better devised. But for a tendency to even a mild dissipation?

But this is to miss the point. For us, Mr Addison's *Letter from Italy* has been eclipsed by Xanadu. To see the shores of the Mediterranean, to tread on classic ground, to look for streams immortaliz'd in song—Murphy knew that the bait was all-powerful. He knew his pupil: he knew that the remoteness and the urgency of the appeal would easily outbid any social opiate.

Charlemont had fallen or was in danger of falling a victim to Dublin, to Dublin's gentle rain and to the humid air that has dissolved so many cores of well-intentioned will. The temptation to juggle with conversational balloons in Daly's Club, to fritter away initiative in pipe-dreams on the Beaux-Walk in Stephen's Green under the enormous Irish skies, must be supplanted by a more powerful lure. The young man's mind was stocked with classic images: the example of antiquity alone could bring them to life.

Grattan, whose gestures, whose eloquence, whose very conception of his own function on the political stage, was saturated through and through with an ideal of the 'high Roman fashion', told Samuel Rogers that he 'was shut up when a boy to read Plutarch's lives, and could not bear the confinement—used to read five pages, and doze away the rest of the time. Thinks now, however, that Brutus' life is very affecting towards the end'.[20] One wonders whether Charlemont, under such a regime of republican severity, would have found it 'very affecting' even towards the end of his own life. But the spirit of the time takes on many guises, and the middle-class politician and the great lord found their paths converge on common ground. Charlemont's sentimental education was pleasant to undergo: it was now to begin; and the horizons of space and time extended rapidly during the next nine years.

NOTES

1. Lecky: op. cit., I, 284.
1a. Not, of course, the present Palace.
2. RIA MSS., IX, 1.
3. 'Kinsman' because both Charlemont and Mount Alexander had married into the Moore family (Drogheda).

4. She was born in 1703, of another family of Elizabethan settlers. At a much later date the family was dignified with the Earldom of Bandon.

5. Warburton, Whitelaw and Walsh, *History of Dublin*; see also Evans in *Irish Builder*, March 15th, 1892.

6. Hone and Rossi: *Berkeley*, p. 108 n. For the Conollys generally, see Macdougall: *Irish Political Characters*, 1799, and *Georgian Society*, Vol. V, 1913, article on Castletown. There are two excellent articles on Castletown and the Conollys in *Country Life*: August 15th and 22nd, 1936, by Christopher Hussey.

7. James Caulfeild (son of Rev Caulfeild rector of Donaghenry, who d. 1768 and was 5th son of 2nd Visc Charlemont) married Catherine, daughter of Thomas Burgh of Oldtown, Co Kildare. It is of some interest that Edmund Burke dates a letter to Charlemont in 1786 from Oldtown (HMC, II, 42). The family of Hussey de Burgh was connected.

8. On Sept 29th, 1728, Swift was made a freeman of the Borough of Charlemont (UJA, 2nd series, Vol. XVII, p. 73).

9. The existence of this portrait indicates at least one visit to England. From other indications it appears that there were probably more (HMC, I, 14).

I have seen only a photograph of the portrait. Its present owner, the eighth Viscount Charlemont, has kindly furnished me with the following note:

'I would say that the portrait showed a determined expression, for the rather full lips are tightly closed and the jaw is firm. This would agree with his being a shy and reticent child—he looks, in fact (and his mother looks too) as if he had been well kept in order but that nevertheless he was able to keep his thoughts to himself and knew it. There appears to be a certain consciousness of power and it is altogether rather an unusual face for a boy of 13 which was his age when the portrait was painted. It is the face of a man of thirty except that it has the rounded outlines of childhood.'

Another portrait of Charlemont was painted by Hogarth, apparently before 1753, as appears from HMC, I, 383 n. It may be found engraved in Nichols & Steevens edition of Hogarth's *Works*, 1818.

10. For whom see R. Elrington Ball in *Journal of Cork Hist. and Arch. Soc.*, II, iii, 50.

11. Lewis: *Topog. Dict.*, *sub voce* Innishannon.

12. See his *Life* by Burdy, reprinted 1914 from 1792. The Dedication of *Truth in a Mask* runs to 17 (small) pages.

13. H, I, 11.

14. The anonymous author of *Public Characters of* 1798, Dublin, 1798, p. 184.

15. HMC, I, 178.

16. From UJA, 2nd series, II, 143, it seems that he was appointed Rector of Tartaraghan (in south of Co Armagh) 'about the year 1735' by the Lord Charlemont of the day—perhaps the 3rd Viscount?

17. HMC, I, 14.
18. Dunkin's *Epistle to the Right Honourable James Lord Viscount Charlemont*, Dublin, 1744. RIA Haliday Pamphlets. Not included in Dunkin's *Collected Poems*.
19. HMC, I, 192.
20. Samuel Rogers: *Recollections*, 1859, p. 96.

CHAPTER II

TRAVELS: I

The Europe in which this young man of eighteen now found himself was recovering from a prolonged series of dynastic wars. The traveller of 1946 would certainly devote more attention to the effects of the war on ordinary people, than the traveller of 1746. Nor is it likely that he would be content, as Charlemont was, to leave the journal of his travels in manuscript till after his death. We first hear of him at the Hague in the autumn. He was present when a popular revolution reinstated the house of Orange as hereditary Stadtholders of Holland, and we are told that he used often to relate his experiences. Unfortunately he left nothing in writing which has survived. No Irish Protestant of the period could feel quite a foreigner at any scene which concerned the House of Orange. It is unlikely that Charlemont, however little he may till then have thought of politics, was altogether unmoved by these events.

The faithful Murphy was with him at the Hague, and it appears that when Charlemont went on to the English camp in Germany, he stayed behind. We know little of what passed in Germany. But we are told that the Duke of Cumberland, fresh from his exploits in the Forty-Five Rebellion, and still fresher from his crushing defeat at Lauffeld by the French, 'was not only extremely kind to him, whilst there, but through life'. While making due allowance for the fact that in eighteenth-century politics men who would not vote together might still dine together, we may yet observe that in later life Charlemont was not fond of consorting with those who bore an illiberal political reputation.

The letter from Murphy which we have already given, was written to Charlemont while he was still at the camp. In it, among other things, he reminded Charlemont that no less a personality than the wicked Earl of Sandwich, then in Holland on diplomatic business, had dropped him a broad hint that one did not go to the Continent to waste one's time in an English officers' mess: 'Turin', said my lord Sandwich, 'is the best place you can now go to. There you have a polite and friendly court, where both French and Italian are well spoken; and there you have good academies of all kinds. I have spent 12 months there and am well acquainted.' Charlemont took the hint, and set off through southern Germany, in May or June of 1747. We may guess that he was well enough pleased to go.

One vivid picture has survived of his journey south. Years later, in a letter to Edmond Malone, he wrote:

Travelling through Germany, I went three days' journey out of my way to visit the source of the Danube . . . My road lay through that immense tract of wood known by the terrific name of the 'Black Forest', at the extremity of which the capital of the landgrave is situate; and as I approached his residence, I was surprised and shocked to observe that most of the trees bordering the highway were hung with human limbs, so as to have the appearance of a shambles in a country of cannibals. Hands, feet, arms, legs, and even heads were everywhere to be seen; and my first idea was that some numerous gang of robbers had been there taken and executed. I stopped the chaise, and, enquiring of the postilion into the nature and circumstances of these supposed banditti, was thus answered: 'No, sir; here have been no robbers; those limbs once belonged to certain desperadoes who were audacious and wicked enough to kill the prince's game.' And upon farther enquiry, I soon

D

found that the hands and arms had murdered partridges and
pheasants, that the legs had feloniously followed hares, and the
heads had been so abominably impious as to plot and execute
the assasination of wild boars. On this fact I shall make no
comment, but shall only say that such atrocities invite rebellion, and that the true means to prevent conspiracy and revolution is to govern so as to make the people happy. We, thank
heaven, are far removed from the possibility of such horrors[1].

That letter was written from Dublin. The date is
October 1797.

In due course he reached Turin. We may presume
that Murphy rejoined him here or earlier, for from now
on they are constantly together. From the summer or
autumn of 1747 till the end of October 1748, he attended the Royal Academy there: to what effect we
have no direct knowledge. His biographer speaks of a
lost account of his Italian residence and travels, but it
is unlikely to have chronicled anything so undramatic
as his academic progress at Turin.

He did, however, leave a fortunately full account of
some other aspects of a young man's education. Among
the foreigners at the Piedmontese Court was David
Hume, who enjoyed at the time a diplomatic status.
The acquaintance of great men is a necessary stage in
the education of a young nobleman of parts, and
Charlemont, fortunately for us, felt himself bound to
chronicle his dealings with Hume at some length. It so
happens that, Hume's proclivities being what they
were, we also get a glimpse of the tenderer and no less
essential aspect of polite education.

He begins,[2] after some philosophical preliminaries,
by observing that Hume's works, 'both as a Philosopher and as an Historian, are so wonderfully replete
with genius and entertainment, that we are almost in-

duced to pardon their evil Tendency for the sake of their Ingenuity'. Having clarified his position thus, he goes on:

With this extraordinary man I was intimately acquainted. He had kindly distinguished me from among a number of young men, who were then at the Academy, and appeared so warmly attached to me, that it was apparent he not only intended to honour me with his friendship, but to bestow on me what was, in his opinion, the first of all favours and benefits, by making me his convert and disciple . . .

He waxes eloquent on Hume's personal appearance:

His face was broad and fat, his mouth wide, and without any other expression than that of imbecility. His eyes vacant and spiritless, and the corpulence of his whole person was far better fitted to communicate the idea of a turtle-eating Alderman, than of a refined Philosopher . . .

It happened at this time that I was intimately connected with a Lady of great Beauty, Sense, and Spriteliness—the Countess of —— was about four and twenty, and had been married for some years, tho' hitherto childless, her Husband being an old decrepid Man, whom Family Convenience had compelled her to espouse— . . .

She was, moreover, as learned as she was attractive, and in Charlemont's opinion was 'far from incurring any of those disgusting Defects which Study usually produces in the female Scholar . . . and her Hearers, who were always the wiser for what She said, far from being lessened in their own Opinion, were induced to believe that They were teaching her, when in reality They themselves were taught'.

She had been united in her earliest Youth to a Man whose Person, Age and Character were compleat Antidotes against every tender Inclination, and her Heart was consequently left unoccupied, unguarded—Yet, tho' She had too much sensibility to be incapable of Passion, her Choice was however so guarded by Good Sense and Judgment that her Nicety and Discernment rendered her Conquest almost as difficult as if She had been naturally, or rather unnaturally, insensible— . . .

We may well wonder whether the corollary was as apparent to Charlemont as it is to us; namely that in pitching his tone so high he has paid himself as great a compliment as he intended for the lady. In general, he had a high degree of self-awareness, and was prompt to deflate his own pretensions to himself and to his friends. There is no direct evidence as to when this account was written; but various things suggest that it may have been soon after the events in question. 'Such', he observes at last, 'was the Woman to whom I had the Honour of paying my Court, and in whose Company I regularly spent my Evenings.'

But now begins the mischief.

Charlemont, with a young man's innocent enthusiasm, had sung the lady's praises to Hume, who in due course asked to be introduced to her. 'I had no more ardent Wish than that the Choice of my Heart should be admired by a Man whom I so highly esteemed . . .' and accordingly he complied with the request. Hume became as frequent an attendant upon the Countess as Charlemont was himself. One day, when Charlemont was alone with her, she examined him minutely on his feelings towards Hume. His replies were frank and unsuspecting. Finally, after some hesitation, 'I must inform you', she said, 'that I have made a compleat Conquest of this great Philosopher.'

However this may have struck him, he was prompt with a courtly rejoinder: 'Of all Men, Madam, I have no reason to Doubt the Power of your Eyes.' But the situation, it seemed, was not to be dismissed with a phrase, however graceful. In the course of their conversation, the Countess convinced the incredulous Charlemont that Hume was in earnest. She even managed to persuade him to play the part of a Polonius.

At his next Visit, which will probably be this Evening, only take the Trouble to hide yourself behind the Curtain; and you shall be Witness to a Scene, which, if it does not make you angry, as indeed it ought not, will at least make you laugh ... Give me however your Word that you will on no Account discover Yourself, as that might not be to my Advantage ...

'I had too much Vanity', Charlemont observes with engaging frankness, 'to be jealous.' He took up his station behind the curtain, from which, if we are to trust his own account, he was able to see as well as hear. The illustrious philosopher lost no time in preliminaries. No sooner was he in the room than he plumped down on his knees before her. The violence of his passion was equalled by his want of a language in which to express it. 'J'étouffe avec l'amour!' is a specimen of his amorous utterance. 'Silenus', says Charlemont, 'on his knees to one of the Graces, or a Bear making love to an Italian Greyhound woud be Objects rediculous enough—But neither Silenus nor the Bear are Philosophers.'

As the lady had hinted, Charlemont was suspended between anger and amusement. He contrived, however, to remain undetected in his hiding-place. 'We are seldom angry', he observes, 'with an unsuccessful Rival.' After several minutes of Hume's love-making, the Countess decided she had had enough of it, and gave him his marching orders. Charlemont emerged from his hiding-place, and he and the lady talked the situation over. The upshot of their conference was that 'at his next Visit the poor Philosopher was discarded for ever'. His rival, we must suppose, was thenceforth alone in his enjoyment of the lady's favour.

The incident remained closed, till the eve of Hume's departure from Turin. Charlemont, too, had been there for a full year, and having finished his academical course was also on the point of departure. The countess suggested that he should make a clean breast of the business; and the obedient Charlemont took his friend aside and told him the whole story. Hume took it very well indeed, and acknowledged the justice of the treatment he had received. Whatever his private opinion of Charlemont's part in the affair, he never afterwards allowed it to interfere with their friendship. But he did allow himself to offer his young friend a few words of philosophic advice. 'You are young', he said, 'You are aimiable—You are beloved—All that is precisely as it ought to be—Yet let me make one short Observation—in French also, tho' that you will know is not my Talent—Cueillez, Milord, les Fleurs—Cueillez les Fleurs—Mais ne vous faites pas Jardinier.'

The identity of the Countess remains in doubt, unless, as seems likely, she was the 'Madam Duvernan' mentioned in letters from friends in Turin as being 'very well but very sorry to part with you' and later as intending to write to Charlemont by the next post.

He left Turin at the end of October, and spent the winter and early spring of 1748–9 in Rome and Naples. So far he had done nothing very adventurous in the way of travelling. But in April 1749, he, with Francis Burton, Murphy, a Mr. Scott, and Richard Dalton, set sail from Leghorn for Constantinople. It is probably largely accidental that every member of the party was an Irishman,[3] for apart from Murphy, they seem all to have made Charlemont's acquaintance in Italy.

Francis Pierpont Burton was a native of Co Clare, and nephew to Mr Conyngham of Slane, a considerable Irish landlord. Mr Conyngham was at this time married, and in any case he was not raised to the peerage as Baron Conyngham of Slane until 1753, so that Frank Burton was in 1749 a private gentleman with no apparent prospect of elevation to a higher grade in society.[4] But it is clear from Charlemont's account of their travels that they associated as equals. Indeed, it must have been difficult to meet Frank Burton on any other terms. He was a young man of Falstaffian figure with an inexhaustible fund of animal spirits, and some inability to conceal his emotions. If the Italians, Turks and Greeks considered him to be an Englishman (as they presumably did) it must have been more on the score of evident madness than phlegmatic taciturnity. The taciturnity, if it was evident at all, was supplied by Charlemont himself, or by Mr Scott. Mr Scott we know to have been of the party, and beyond that we know nothing, for he is never alluded to by Charlemont. It may safely be assumed that he was a nonentity.

Richard Dalton, who with Murphy made up the party, was a professional architectural draughtsman. He studied at the Dublin Society under West, and later at Shipley's Academy in London, where he met Gandon.[5] He was now in Rome on his own account. On his return he became Librarian and keeper of Antiquities to George III, and one of the founding committee of the Royal Academy.

The journey which these five men made together is of interest not only as an episode in Charlemont's life, but also as furnishing the first important contributions to knowledge in England of Greek antiquities. The journeys of Stuart, Revett, Pars, Chandler and finally of the Adam brothers, exercised in time a profound influence on the decorative arts in England. It would hardly be an exaggeration to say that it was this initial journey which started the revolutionary process in motion.[6] Dalton's membership of the party makes it clear that the journey was undertaken with a purpose. It is curious that out of these five Irishmen, three should find honourable mention in the life of James Gandon, the architect who, more than any other single man, is the author of the splendour of Dublin's public buildings. In one case, indeed, the personal influence may have been decisive. Burton, who in his later years as Lord Conyngham does not bulk large in Charlemont's circle, invited Gandon to stay with him at the very moment when Gandon, fresh from London and faced by obstruction at every turn in Dublin, was beginning to wonder whether he should not pack up and go home. By this politic and kindly act, Burton was indirectly responsible for a great deal of enduring beauty which might well never have come to the birth.

In May of 1749 the party arrived at Messina, which was just beginning to recover from the effects of a plague which, a few years before, had made the whole city a charnel-house. Sailing through the Straits, Charlemont was dutifully attentive to the classic Scylla and Charybdis. While the eye and ear of Faith recorded the 'romantick perpendicular Rock' and the 'horrid Roar', the factual pen did not omit the local inhabitants fishing for sword-fish.[7] At dawn on May 6th they entered the harbour. The splendidly laid out quays and waterfront unfolded themselves; then on a nearer view came the realisation that this city of the dead was almost entirely tenantless. Suitable sentiments did not fail to offer themselves to Charlemont's mind, and

were duly retailed by his pen. But there was some comic
relief. On landing, they were detained for three hours
before being required to produce their bills of health.
After this formality they were all made to jump over a
bar three feet high. All passed this test easily, save
Burton, whose 'corpulent unweildiness was ill-adapted
to the exercise of leaping.' At length even Burton satisfied the medical examiners, and after much striking of
groins and armpits, they were allowed to pass.
Charlemont, with that indefatigable lust for facts
and instances which the reader of his journal comes to
know so well, collated every scrap of evidence he could
come by, on the origin, symptoms and course of the
plague. Hardy's life transcribes many of his observations: we may be content to draw attention to one or
two of his comments on them. Always alert for the
classical parallel, he notes[8] that Thucydides' account of
the plague at Athens tallies in that here, too, the plague-
madness took the form of an urge to throw oneself into
the sea. For some of his facts he relies on a poem by the
Abbate Enea Melani, 'entitled La Peste de Messina, in
which, as there is little or no Poetry, We may fairly
permit ourselves to expect Truth'.... Not a very philosophical attitude of mind, one might say; and yet,
what could be more philosophical than his reflection
that the violence of the plague was largely due to
the fatalistic outlook of the local population? In a
footnote he recommends carelessness as a defence
against infection, in which, from a psychological point
of view, he is probably not altogether wrong.
Their next port of call was Malta, which they
reached on June 20th. Thence, via Smyrna, Tenedos,
the Troade and the Dardanelles, they made their way
without recorded incident as far as Constantinople. Of

his sojourn in the capital of the Ottoman Empire he
left an account over a hundred pages long, covering a
period of a month. Both this, and the accounts which
cover later parts of his journey, are governed by a very
strict theory which Charlemont held on the subject of
travellers' tales. His title-page reads as follows: 'An
Essay / towards a new Method of Travel writing / Being a succinct Relation / of several / Miscellaneous
Occurrences / during my Travels / principally relative
to the Character of the / several Nations with whom I
have had / Intercourse. / with some Observations. /
Homo sum, humani nihil a me alienum puto! / The
proper Study of Mankind is Man! / Haec olim memin-
isse juvabit.'[9] In intention at least, he took the implications of all this very seriously. His 'plan', to which he
refers more than once, did not allow him to indulge in
sentimental flourishes about his feelings towards the
landscape, it ruled out anecdotes about himself and the
other members of his party, it did not even allow him to
treat of well-known buildings from a merely apprecia-
tive angle. Above all, it did not allow him to write
with a view to publication at any time. The title-page
of the Greek volume of travels describes it as 'A
Traveller's Essays / Containing an Account of Manners
/ rather than of Things / . . . Written for my own Amusement / And for that of my Friends / Only / . . .'[10]

  We cannot regret that Charlemont often broke his
own rules, and gave us some of those touches which he
so sternly determined to exclude. Least of all can we
regret that the manuscript has survived to make its
appeal to a wider circle than he intended. He could
write so vividly and so well that there would be little
excuse for breaking his narrative up and serving it
piecemeal, were it not that for most of the time he does

indeed keep to his plan. There is an enormous amount
of scholarly commentary, sociological comparison and
conjecture and archaeological material, which today
has an academic though real interest. The personal
touches sprout like wild-flowers from the cracks in this
objective frontage.

Charlemont approached the Turk, who was already
a byword in Europe for despotism and luxury, with a
remarkably open mind. He blames the evil reputation
of the Turk on Christian missionaries, especially the
Catholics, on Greeks, Christian merchants, European
ambassadors, travellers and other irresponsible folk.
His reflections on the question 'Who are the real Barbarians' lead to memories of the compulsory drinking
at Dublin dinner-parties, and the fact that fashion
requires him to powder his own hair with flour.[11]

Apparently out of pure mischief, he disguised himself in a Greek dress and so gained admittance to the
Grand Vizier's levée and a court of Justice. 'It was
already noised about the Porte', he remarks, 'that a
Stranger of Rank was there in Disguise.' He found himself treated very politely; was offered 'perfumed Mar-
malet' and iced sherbet, and burnt his fingers by mistake on a censer. He even managed to penetrate as far
as the Grand Vizier's kitchen. An astute decision by a
Turkish judge, given in Charlemont's presence, satisfied him that the wisdom of Solomon was not yet lost
to the Orient. He noted with particular satisfaction
that there were no barristers in Turkish courts.

'I was only a month at Constantinople', he relates,
'and a great part of that Time was necessarily, tho'
foolishly, taken up with ceremonious Visits to Ambassadors etc . . .' But he managed to work in a great deal
else all the same. He buttonholed a 'sensible Turk'

called Mustapha Efendi, who was 'Turkish Secretary
to the English Nation'. He catechised him closely on
religious matters,[12] and wrote down a summary of their
conversation. He discovered that, as he had suspected,
many educated Turks were little more than Deists.
The discovery that Mustapha was reading Seneca
awoke in him the eighteenth-century scholars' dream,
the possibility of finding in Turkey a Byzantine manuscript of the lost books of Livy and Tacitus.

Turning from theology to practical religion, he accompanied Frank Burton to a mosque. Burton, 'the dear
and agreeable companion of my travels, who was en-
dow'd by Nature with every [excellent attribute] . . .
was also possessed of a Quality, which was sometimes
exceedingly dangerous, tho' never more so than on the
present Occasion.' He was above all an 'animal risibile',
and some passages in the religious ceremony provoked
him to untimely mirth. Charlemont was naturally
alarmed for their safety as unbelievers in such a place
and at such a time. Between his spasms of laughter,
Burton urged Charlemont to pinch him. Again and
again he did so, 'But alas, I pinched in vain!' Only one
circumstance saved them from disaster.

'By the greatest good Fortune however the laugh of
Burton was totally dissimilar and different from that
of either Turk or Christian.' The worshippers assumed
that Burton was having a fit, perhaps even a religious
ecstasy. Charlemont, with tears streaming down his
cheeks, adapted himself swiftly to the situation, and
allowed the tears of laughter to be taken for those of
grief. Calling on the bystanders to help, he contrived
to have his unfortunate friend carried bodily out of the
mosque. It was a very close shave.[13]

Charlemont procured from a French resident literal

translations of three Turkish love-songs, which he gives in his text. Turning, again, from theory to practice, Burton proposed to Charlemont and a Mr Falkner an expedition to a 'modern Temple of Venus'. They set out by night, and losing their way, were gradually aware that they were being followed by a large number of people. Finally they were surrounded, and in an instant a large number of dark lanterns were uncovered and shone full upon them. When the watch (for they it was) saw who they were, they allowed them to pass. Ultimately they reached their destination. Many of the 'Ladys' here to be obtained, he records, 'are extremely beautiful, and well skill'd in all the necessary Arts and Allurement of their Calling. As it is the Duty of Travellers to leave nothing unseen, our Curiosity, and perhaps something more, has sometimes enticed Burton and me to these hospitable Receptacles.' Nothing could be more characteristic of Charlemont than the admission: 'perhaps something more'.

On another occasion they paid a visit to a bagnio or Turkish bath 'pure and unmix'd with any foreign Refinement'. Charlemont found the experience rather trying, and Burton, from whom we have learned to expect it, 'roared like a Bull'. But both of them enjoyed the last stage of the treatment, when they were put into beds to keep them warm, and plied with 'excellent Coffy'.

In regard to religion, Charlemont found the Turks tolerant of other faiths. He noted the usual evidences of superstition, he commanded Dalton to draw a sketch of some dervishes in the street, and in particular he has an amusing description of a saint who ran about the streets naked, followed by women who desired to be cured of sterility; and, 'happy was She who cou'd con-

trive to kiss that Part of him, which was likeliest, if
properly applied, to perfect her Cure.'[14] But in general
his opinion is that he has seen nothing in Constantinople which could not be paralleled and even exceeded
in Naples and Rome. 'The Catholicks', in his opinion,
'far surpass the Turks in such Absurdities as are
adopted by Superstition or devised by Policy.'[15]
He takes care to absolve himself from the imputation
of admiring the political side of Turkish life. But, as he
points out, 'these very imperfect Essays were designed
to vindicate a Portion of my Fellow-Creatures from
Crimes of which they are falsely accused, rather than
to add to the tedious Catalogue of human Frailties'.
Accordingly he concentrates on the good points. 'I do
not find', he says, 'that Tortures, or cruel Punishments
of any kind, are common among the Turks.' On one
occasion his sense of duty as a traveller made him
follow in a procession for half a mile to see an execution.
But he turned sick and came back without seeing it.
In any case such sights were by no means confined to
Turkey. The notorious corruption of Turkish officials
is, in his view, partly to be explained away as a convention of behaviour. The Turks, he points out, are an
oriental people, and there are plenty of allusions in that
compendium of oriental literature, the Old Testament,
to the social necessity of exchanging gifts. While he was
in Constantinople, the Kisler Aga, that 'odious person-
age' was also at the Sublime Porte. He was the Turkish
overnor of Greece, which Charlemont describes as 'an
appanage to provide him with pocket-money' . . . 'a
vexatious and Heart-wounding Circumstance'. But, as
will appear from his Greek travels, he did not consider
that all the right in the Turco-Greek question lay on
one side. For the moment, he is concerned to vindicate

the Turks from the charge of wanton vandalism. 'We',
he says, 'in the pride of our Wisdom, are not content
with declaring them ignorant and unlettered.' He
points out that Athens, under Turkish rule, has been
better preserved from an antiquarian point of view
than Rome under the Popes. As for the bombardment
of the Parthenon, which was at the time recent history,
that was done by the Venetians 'with a complication of
Gothicism and cruelty'—Gothicism for obvious reasons,
cruelty because the Turks had sent the women and
children into the building for safety. Perhaps, he admits, it may have been a chance bomb. 'I sincerely
wish that it may have been so. Yet their having pre-
sumed to profane by one single Gothick Shell, the
Acropolis of Athens, that favour'd Seat of Minerva,
that Nursery of the Arts, that Treasury of the Muses,
where not a Bomb cou'd fall without destroying some
Masterpiece of Art, is such a Crime against Taste and
Literature, as no excuse can palliate, no Time can
efface, but the Memory and Infamy of it will remain
while a single Ray of Knowledge enlightens the
World.'[16] A few pages later he observes in a note:
'N.B. This was written in the Reign of George the
Second, when England was a free Country.' Happy the
days in which one could feel so strongly about what
has, alas, become in retrospect so little. The passage on
which this is a commentary is a rhetorical appeal to the
Isles of Greece, which so closely anticipates Byron that
it even invokes the identical shade of Miltiades.[17]

There remains a topic which no traveller, then or
now, could leave untouched—what would now be
called the 'love-life' of the Turks. On the subject of the
making and employment of eunuchs in the harem, 'that
abominable custom', he observes that the Pope,

with his *castrati*, is as bad an offender as any Turk. 'The Love of Musick is a ruling Passion in Italy, as the Love of Women, a Taste far more natural and more rational, is in the East . . .' But he goes on to say that owing to their holding 'the injurious and absurd Opinion, that Women have no souls', they are strangers to 'all those endearing Arts, those nice Attentions, by which mutual affection is cheaply and deliciously purchased . . .' The place of love, in his view, is taken by fear, 'their only Engine of Government'. But he adds a significant rider to the verdict:

> We are apt to measure their Sufferings by what we conceive our Women would suffer under similar circumstances. But in this We err . . . In a word, They cried out against our Customs, as our Women wou'd do at the naked Simplicity of the Indians, or at the Liberality of Love, which the discovery of Otaheite has lately disclosed to us.[18]

He traces the institution of the harem, and also the Turkish tendency towards pederasty (which fills him with revulsion) to the Greeks. In his view, the Turks are a northern invading people whose institutions are partly Hellenic and partly Semitic in origin.[19] He explains the misrepresentations of travellers by their failure to understand this basic fact. Whether correct or not, his treatment of the subject shows a detached analytic faculty of no mean order.

One final observation he made which pleased him greatly. The Turks, he found, were fond of animals, and 'many of them made a Merit of feeding Cats and Dogs'. Admittedly, this might be a nuisance at times; but the nuisance was more than compensated for by the pleasure afforded by the beneficence which caused it. There were so many tame sea-birds in the harbour quarter of Constantinople, that 'At his first Entrance into the Bason . . . [the traveller] is led to imagine that the golden Age is restored.'[20]

NOTES

1. HMC, II. 308.

2. The quotations are taken from Hardy, I, 13 sqq. and 230 sqq. Hardy omitted many touches which are in the MS. (RIA MSS., VII, 497 sqq.). I have accordingly restored them, and reverted to the original order of the MS., which Hardy had re-arranged.

3. Gandon's *Life*, by Gandon & Mulvany, Dublin, 1846, p. 210, says that Dalton was an Irishman. But the DNB assigns his birth to White-haven, Cumberland, which is more probably correct.

4. For the benefit of readers who welcome a readily recognisable land-mark, George IV's Lady Conyngham was, of course, of this family.

5. Gandon, op. cit. But he spells Dalton 'Datton' and qualifies his details with 'is said'.

6. According to the DNB, Robert Wood (another Irishman whom we shall meet later) made a similar journey to the Levant in quest of ancient buildings before 1749, or early in that year. He is said to have been accompanied by a 'Signor Borra'. Can this be the 'Squire Dorra' whose 'Constantinople projects' is alluded to in a letter from George Douglas at Turin to Charlemont in Rome(?) on March 5th, 1749 (RIA MSS., IX, No. 7). If so, it would indicate that Charlemont and Wood's party had some thought of joining forces. The exact order in which the journeys took place is of little importance, as Wood did not publish any results till his volumes on Palmyra in 1753 and on Baalbek in 1758. The order seems to be:

before 1749 A journey by Wood.
     1749 Journeys by Charlemont and Wood.
     1753 Wood's *Palmyra*.
     1757 Adam's journey to Spalatro.
     1758 Wood's *Baalbek*.
     1762 Stuart & Revett's *Athens*, Vol. I (Vol. II, 1787, III, 1794, IV, 1816).
     1764 Adam's *Palace of Diocletian*.
     1764 Chandler's journey (under auspices of Charlemont and the Dilettanti).
     1769 Chandler, Revett & Pars *Ionian Antiquities* published. (Vol. I: Vol. II did not appear till 1797).

7. RIA MSS., VII, 464. See also H, I, 20 sqq.

8. RIA MSS., VII, 474.

9. RIA MSS., V, 1.

10. Ibid., VI, 1.

11. Ibid., V, 9.

12. Ibid., 28 sqq.

E

13. Ibid., 37 sqq.
14. Ibid., 93.
15. Ibid., 84.
16. Ibid., 35 n.
17. Ibid., 49 n.
18. Ibid., 64.
19. e.g. ibid., 65.
20. Ibid., 103.

CHAPTER III

TRAVELS: II

On the 18th of August, 1749, while he was still in Constantinople, Charlemont attained his twenty-first birthday. The adaptation of Horace's 'Eheu fugaces' which he wrote and despatched to his friend Marlay in Dublin, is perhaps the best of his 'original' poems, and may be given in full:

MY BIRTH-DAY ODE, WRITTEN AUGUST 22, 1749

To Richard Marlay

My Marlay! see the rolling years
    With certain speed, our lives devour;
Each day its due proportion bears,
    And nearer brings the fatal hour.

'Tis one-and-twenty years, this day,
    Since first I drew my vital breath;
So much the nearer to decay,
    So much have I approached to death.

He well has liv'd, who, when the sun
    Departing yields to silent night,
Can say, my task this day is done,
    And let tomorrow seize its right.

How many minutes, days, and weeks,
    My soul recalling finds mispent;
T'excuse the loss, in vain she seeks
    Of time, for other purpose lent.

O! could I but recal that time!
    Could I but live those years again!
What then? Perhaps the self-same crime,
    Regret again, and double pain.

The price of time, like that of health,
　　Is seldom known till each is lost:
By want, we learn to value wealth,
　　And wish for summer, chill'd by frost.

'Tis past three years—'twill soon be four,
　　Since last I saw my dearest friend:
So much is lost! and now they're o'er,
　　Who knows if fate three more will lend?

Cease! reason, cease! This festal day
　　In harmless pleasure let us pass:
One bumper toast—I'll shew the way;
　　'Tis Marlay's health—fill up the glass.

Charlemont later did a verse translation of the
Horatian original.[1] In this version, as the reader conversant with the classics will recognise, the correspondence
is very slender. The poem shows a thoughtful moralistic
strain somewhat remarkable in one so young. As
moralising verse it is well above the average,
and in places it rises into poetry, faint but genuine. It
was not the only poem which he wrote during his
travels, for a year earlier we hear that the Dean of
Down, Dr Delany, was 'much pleased' with a poem
which Charlemont had sent him.[2] 'Many things in it
appeared to him new, and the image of the moon was
worthy of any one.'

During the next two months the party travelled to
Egypt by sea, by way of the Greek islands of Lesbos,
Chios (Scio), Myconos (Micone) and Delos. The very
opening sentence of his account bears witness to the
enchantment which this sacred region held and kept
for him:

If I cou'd be content to live, as I trust I never shall be, for-
getting and forgotten, Oblitus meorum, obliviscendus et illis,
there is no Country I have ever seen, no Climate I have ever

experienced, to which I shou'd not prefer the Islands of the
Greek Archipelago, and more especially those on the Asiatick
or Eastern Side.[3]

The pioneer quality of his journey really begins here.
From now on he and his friends were well off the beaten
track, savouring the remote and perilous regions of pure
adventure. At times, when the world was circum-
scribed by the sky, the deck under their feet, the sea
and perhaps the half-mirage of a distant island, the
illusion of having escaped into the Homeric age must
have been well-nigh complete. Their first night on
Lesbos they slept on a 'Bed of dry Seaweed'.

'Metelin, the ancient Lesbos' where 'Love still lingers
in his favourite retreat' was their first stopping-place,
and Charlemont declares his absolute preference for it
above all other places. He quotes Milton:

> . . . airs, vernal airs,
> Breathing the smell of field and grove, attune
> The trembling leaves, while universal *Pan*
> Knit with the *Graces* and the *Hours* in dance
> Led on th'eternal Spring.

The Town, and the whole Country round it [he wrote]
is full of broken Basso Relievos, mutilated Inscriptions,
Marble Columns, and Capitals of different Orders, wrought in
the best Taste. Some of these Columns are regularly fluted,
while others are worked spirally, in the manner of those which
still exist in the small Temple on the Banks of the Clitum-
nus[4] . . .

There was nothing he liked better than broken Basso
Relievos, unless perhaps unbroken ones. He observed
the architecture minutely, and kept a book for recording inscriptions. But he is stern with himself, declares
his main purpose is to treat of 'singular Customs' and
spends pages in historical research and conjecture

about the matrilineal society which still flourished in
Mytilene. Half a century later he worked the material
into a paper for his newly-founded Royal Irish Academy.[5] But he found that he had no monopoly of the
spirit of enquiry. He and his party, all being men, were
frequently stopped in the streets by the masterful
women of Mytilene, who examined them, looked closely at their dress, and generally appraised them with
the air of Oriental potentates at an auction of slave-
girls. He notes, however, that he soon became quite
accustomed to such treatment. This island, like many,
lived in fear of the ruinous annual visitation of the
Turkish Bashaw.

Scio, another of the larger islands near the Asiatic
mainland, had a mixed population. Many Turks, he
found, seemed 'to live with the Inhabitants upon a
Footing tolerably equal and Friendly'. The Greek inhabitants, however, dissuaded him from going to visit
the Captain Bashaw. 'We walked to a Palace belonging
to Mustapha Bashaw, a Bashaw of Rhodes, whom we
had seen and known at Malta . . . at which Place was
then lodged the Brother of the present Cham of Tar-
tary' living in 'honourable Exile.'

In one of the villages they found

a Convent of Nuns, the jolliest girls of the kind I ever met
with—They make a vow of Chastity, which they are supposed
to keep as Oaths against Nature usually are kept, yet have
they a better Chance of adhering to their Profession, as they
are not confined, but are at Liberty to go where They please—
They are dress'd in Black, and wear Head Dresses of the same
colour, which are by no means unbecoming—With these
Ladies We pass'd an hour or two very agreeably, and, for the
small Reward of a Sequin, They chanted for us their whole
Service most angelically—Their Church is small, but very
pretty.[6]

Among the hazards of the islands were the 'Levantis', a class of men whose exact status is obscure, but who seem to have been a cross between the naval body-guard of the Turkish Bashaw, and free-lance pirates. At all events, they were much feared. 'Yet', says Charlemont, 'did not this prevent us, on the Eve of our Departure, from getting together a Parcel of pretty country Girls, with whom we danced greek Dances on the Shore for a couple of Hours.' Close by was a small amphitheatre known locally as the 'School of Homer'. Charlemont notes that the girls had high waists, short skirts, and thick legs.[7]

They had already embarked for Micone when they received an invitation to go on board a Turkish man-of-war. They were courteously received by the Commodore, and the usual ritual of coffee, sherbet, perfumes etc. was gone through.[8] The ship was one of 74 guns, and in describing her Charlemont, rather surprisingly, shows himself conversant with the technicalities of nautical equipment and usage. The ship carried four Christian slaves, an Italian, a Spaniard, a Frenchman and an Englishman. Getting into conversation with them, Charlemont found them well contented to stay where they were. The Turks, it appeared, made a point of insisting that Christian slaves should not be slack in the performance of their Christian religious duties. In this, it seems, the Turks are very different from the inhabitants of the 'Piratical States' with whom the ignorant confuse them, and who are 'almost as bad . . . as our Guinea Traders, or our West-India Planters'.[9]

Charlemont gave the captain 'a silver étuyé made in Birmingham', and they were favoured on their departure from the ship with a salute of three guns, 'the utmost compliment' as he observes with some satisfaction, 'ever paid by the Turks'. 'The Imperial Pride of the Turk', he remarks later, 'seldom answers any Salute with more than one Gun.'[10] Charlemont's ship on this latter occasion had fired nine and been answered with three.

They seem to have given up their immediate intention of leaving Scio, for they visited the Convent of Neamone, where Charlemont, already a lover of old books, was excited at finding the eight great folio volumes of St Chrysostom, printed at Eton in 1612. They visited the 'Mastick Villages' which were occupied in the cultivation of a gum which was used as an ingredient in bread and also as a perfume. There was a local scarcity here of ancient remains, and Charlemont thought they had probably been pilfered by the Venetians during their occupation. The Aga of the garrison, a handsome young man, gave Charlemont a sword 'which is still in my Possession, and presenting it to me, told me that it had already kill'd two Men, and that He was well assured it wou'd not be idle in my Service—the Sabre has however been perfectly at Rest ever since; but in return I gave him a Pair of English Pistols'.

Their next port of call was the island of Micone. Here they found themselves again on the track of a Dr Askew, whom Charlemont had already mentioned[11] as a recorder of ancient inscriptions, who erased the originals after copying them, in order to keep the credit to himself. 'Many of these erased Inscriptions I have met with', says Charlemont, and adds: 'But every soil produces Barbarians!' Askew, however, had other interests; and in pursuance of the high opinion of the women of Micone which he had left on record, Burton and Charlemont became involved in an episode of heroic farce, which can be fitly told only in his own words.[12]

He seems to have emerged none the worse from his amorous exploits in Micone. But so great was his interest in the dress of the Miconians that he refers to 'a Baby in my Possession dress'd in the Garb of Micone'. After the first slight shock on reading this, one concludes that he must mean a doll. An old Greek priest, Papa Liniotissa, told him that, when young, he had heard a tradition which Charlemont, to his delight, was able to remember having read in Pliny. Certainly, he reflected, he was treading classic ground from which even the spirit had not altogether departed.[13]

The small island of Delos, adjoining Micone, had perhaps the most sacred associations of all. But he says of it, 'an uninhabited Land can never be brought within the Compass of my Plan'. The marble fragments were being used as a quarry, and the Fountain Inopus was 'scarcely drinkable'. Gallantly he professed himself more interested in a musician from Tenos who danced with their crew. In the island of Rhenea, close to Delos, he found the 'Colossal Body of a Lyon' in stone, and detected the ancient geographer Strabo in an error of fact. Again his crew danced on the shore, and Charlemont tells us that he liked the music, which mingled with the 'Contemplation of those venerable Ruins, which raised in our Minds the most awful and painfully pleasing Ideas'. As background to it all, there was 'the solemn Buzz of the still Sea'.

Some of the smaller islands, it seems, escaped the annual visit of the Captain Bashaw. Naxos was one of these. Twice on one page[14] he speaks, first of the 'romantick beauties of these enchanting Scenes' and then of a 'romantick cave'. Naxos was full of recluses and refugees, for all the world like a Greek island of the nineteen-thirties. Chief among them was an individual who bore the remarkable name of the 'Baron Vigoureux de la Stike'.[15] He was from 'Gascogny', and was guide, philosopher, friend, doctor, midwife and what not else to the islanders, by whom he was much beloved. He had given his son in marriage to one of the principal women of the island. The night of their arrival 'closed with Greek Dances'; and in this Phaeacian paradise Charlemont and his party spent a whole week. He found the 'other Hermits' of the island to be 'Men of Sense and of Breeding'. As for the Baron Vigoureux, Charlemont considered that he was 'doing more real good than all the Potentates of Europe can boast to have done in a Century'. When they left the island, their felucca was laden with 'Sheep, Bread, Wine, Lemons, Oranges, and every kind of the best Fruit'. Listening to the bleating of the sheep, he may well have wondered how long it would be till they met the monster Polypheme.

From Naxos they doubled northwards again to Tino, 'anciently Tenos'. This island was also free from the Bashaw's judicial depredations, in this case because it was the last Venetian possession to come into Turkish hands, and had surrendered on its own terms. Apropos of the Venetian government of the island, Charlemont's opinion is that 'the Despotism of a Republic is by far the worst of all Despotisms'. The inhabitants he found 'industrious, well-clothed, happy and lively'. They grew mulberry-trees for silk-worms, and the 'wonderful beauty of the Women' was, in his opinion, greatly helped by the costume they wore. They danced Greek dances, and also minuets.

Of Syra, the ancient Syros, he has little to say, 'only

that it is the most Catholick, and the dirtiest of all the Islands'. 'Pigs and Capuchins are indeed in such Abundance here that one can scarcely walk the Streets without stumbling over one or other of them.' But he found the view of the town 'singular and romantick' and the people good-natured.

Southward again to Paros,[16] where they found that their ship, being above 200 tons' burden, could not make the harbour. They accordingly changed to a Greek felucca, and left their 'Treasure' on board the larger ship. From Paros they went to Antiparos, and there, having 'view'd with astonishment the famous Grotto', they found to their horror that they had only 1½ guineas between them, which amounted to three sequins. What was to be done? They decided to pay at Antiparos and trust to obtaining credit at Paros. 'With aching Hearts We paid our Bill.' There was half a sequin left; and this, with bold foresight, they changed into smaller coin and distributed at large. 'Our Cloths, which had never been splendid, were dirtied and torn by climbing Rocks and creeping into Caves.' Charlemont's own 'Hussar Jacket' was in rags, but Dalton was the most squalid spectacle of the party.

On their return to Parechia they were put up by the Vaivode, a local official. Later they found a 'dear fat Landlady'. Their lack of means did not seem to interfere with their enjoyment. They became friendly with the Archbishop of Naxia and Exarch of the Aegean, a dignitary blessed with a string of other titles which Charlemont made him rehearse and himself transcribed in full. In the Archbishop's honour a homeric dinner took place, at which they ate kid to the accompaniment of a harper. The wine, according to Charlemont (who always makes a note of this point) was 'incom-

parable' and the harper proposed their healths, crying
'Chaire! Chaire!'[17] Burton in particular found himself
much celebrated for his extraordinary size. Later they
were present at a Greek christening, and Charlemont,
like a true Protestant, thought the priest's manner of
performing the ceremony very offhand.

All this was very well, but they began to be anxious,
and to fear that their captain had absconded with the
treasure. No doubt their situation, had he done so,
would not have been as bad as they feared, but it
might have been awkward enough. However, after
eight days the ship appeared, and Charlemont, to his
immense relief, was able to distribute presents to his
benefactors.

Every cottage in Paros had a 'Doorcase of the finest
Marble, the Remains of ancient Architraves and
Freezes'. He thought the Parian marble well worthy of
its reputation, and went to look at the ancient quarries,
which he found more like mines than modern quarries.
Here, as everywhere, there was a monastery, and
Charlemont's opinion of its architecture was low, but
no lower than his verdict on the inmates. Monasticism,
indeed, is generally a subject which inspires him to
irritation and impatience.

Leaving Paros, they sailed direct to Alexandria. If
he ever wrote an account of his Eyptian experiences,
it has not survived, and all that remains is a handful of
reminiscences here and there in his other accounts.[18]
We catch a glimpse of him chewing water-melons en
route between Alexandria and Rosetta, while their
Arab guides were observing the fast of Ramadan. He
became acquainted with a 'gentleman of Cairo, Hadgia
Mahomet', but in general he found the ruling class of
Egypt an ignorant crew by contrast with the Turks

proper. The Firman or safe-conduct from the Porte
was almost useless to them in Egypt. They had, however, a number of janizzaries attendant upon them.
Charlemont tried to persuade one of these to show him
his wife, but though the man was devoted to him, his
pleadings were without success.

On October the 22nd they sailed from Alexandria,
and again traversed the Archipelago, 'having thus left
no Part of it unseen'. They set their course for Cyprus,
and 'came within Sight of this Isle of Venus'. But contrary winds prevented them from being able to land.

The Papian Goddess, whose Power is equally felt

—per Maria, ac Montes, Fluviosque rapaces
Frundiferasque Domos Avium, Camposque virentes,

angry perhaps that during our Abode in the inhospitable and
ungallant Regions of the Nile, few or no Sacrifices had been by
us offer'd to her Divinity, forbad our Entrance . . .[19]

They arrived at Rhodes on the 30th. They managed
to 'contract some Degree of Intimacy' with the Archbishop of Rhodes, and they found the island full of
'conversible' Turks, whose affability Charlemont a-
scribed to the climate. But, though they waited upon
the Mazulheim, and he in turn visited their ship, they
were unable, for reasons of military secrecy, to examine
the ruins of the old citadel of the Knights Hospitallers.
He thought Rhodes remarkably beautiful, but was
forced to exclaim: 'Yet Alass, beautiful as She now is,
How is She changed!' He goes on to mention Strabo,
'whose Words are so expressive that I cannot avoid
copying them'—and he does so, for nine lines of very
beautiful Greek script, and then translates it into
English. One of the salient features of these travel-
journals is the tireless devotion with which he trans-

cribes long passages—often very long indeed—from ancient authors whose writings bear on something he has seen himself.

The strain of his interests against the strait-jacket of his system now becomes unbearable, and he bursts his bonds, with apologies to the reader:

And now [he says] as I am about to deviate from my original Plan by entering into a Detail which will contain little more than a Description of Ruins, being the venerable Remains of two ancient Citys of very considerable Note, and as I shall also take the Liberty of transporting my Reader from those Islands, which are the immediate Subject of this Part of my Essays, to the Continent of Asia Minor, I think it necessary to apologise for such Transgression, assuring him that his Voyage shall be as short as possible, and that my Reason for thus transgressing is my Hope of contributing to his Amusement by leading him into Scenes of historical Notoriety, which have not, that I know of, been as yet described, and one of which was now, I believe, for the first time discovered and visited— The City to which I now bend my Course is no other than the famous Cnidos, the favour'd Seat of that universally adored Divinity

Quae Cnidon
Fulgentesque tenet Cyclades, et Paphon
Junetis visit Oloribus—

The Queen of the Loves and Graces, Regina Cnidi, Paphique, was now at length propitiated—Our Sacrifices were accepted . . .[20]

The omissions of Eyypt were presumably repaired in Rhodes, which they left on November 7th. At Cnidus, on an isthmus of the mainland, they identified to their own satisfaction the temple in which the Aphrodite of Praxiteles had stood. Temples, theatres, terraces and a fortress, were minutely examined by Charlemont, who concluded that 'There can, I think, be no doubt that the Ruins, which We have now described, are the Re-

mains of Cnidus . . .' There seems, indeed, to be no
doubt but that he was right, though whether he was
first in this particular field is another matter.

They stood out to sea again and put in at the island
of Stanco or Stanchio, which he identifies (again correctly) as the ancient Cos or Coos. The inhabitants here
put them on the track of a ruined city on the mainland to the north-east, in response to their enquiry
after 'old Marbles, as was usually our Custom'. They
landed near the town of Bodromi, and 'pass'd the Evening in rambling about the Country, and finished by
drinking the King's Health, this being his Majesty's
Birthday'. They found some local fishermen and with
them ate fish which Charlemont thought were the
Greek 'polypi'. In the meantime they had sent servants
to the Mazulheim to obtain permission to pursue their
researches. They were told that they might inspect the
ruins and make drawings, but another Turkish official,
the Cadi, who was, it seems, largely a spy on the doings of the Mazulheim, demanded to see their firman
which they had left in the ship. While they were waiting for the firman to arrive, they explored the outer
ruins. When the document was brought back, they
judged it prudent to disburse four sequins by way of
lubrication, and were admitted into the Castle. 'Our
Eyes were immediately attracted and fix'd by several
Basso Relievos set in the inner Walls.' After minutely
examining the remains, he came to the conclusion that
they might well be part of the celebrated Mausoleum.
But the moment they started to make drawings, they
were turned out. They tried in vain to get back, and
the Mazulheim, to whom they appealed, said the Cadi
was a rogue but he himself could do nothing to help.
Burton, Dalton and Charlemont stayed the night in

the village looking at 'Indications of Ancient Magnificence'.[21]

By the 12th of November they had arrived at some arrangement, for while Dalton went to the Castle to work on the sculptures, Charlemont wandered about the hills, tracing the circuit of the ancient walls. After a long review of the literary and archaeological evidence, he decided that the evidence for identification with Halicarnassus was 'incontrovertible'. As for the Mausoleum, he wrote:

We have Reason to suppose that the World is still in Possession of a Portion at least of those Masterpieces which have been the Admiration of all Antiquity; and We can not but flatter ourselves that we have had the Glory of being the Discoverers of this inestimable Treasure—A Pride, which even our faint and inadequate Copies, to which I refer my Reader, will, I doubt not, in some degree justify.[22]

Here and elsewhere, there are references to drawings which should accompany his text. The originals have disappeared, but Dalton, who made them, published in 1751 a miscellaneous collection of engravings under the title *Musaeum Graecum et Aegyptiacum*, one plate of which is dedicated to Charlemont. The Halicarnassus reliefs are not among them, though they are announced in the prospectus. They can be found bound up with[23] a second and enlarged edition not collected till 1791 which Dalton called *Antiquities and Views in Greece and Egypt*. Dalton's draughtsmanship unfortunately lacks what Charlemont's scholarship so conspicuously displays, precision and wealth of detail. Such was the aristocratic attitude that it apparently never entered Charlemont's head to publish his discoveries. Halicarnassus was again 'discovered' by Sir Charles Newton in the eighteen-fifties, though the marbles which Charle-

PLATE III

See page 79

'THE SCHOOL OF ATHENS' PAINTED BY SIR JOSHUA REYNOLDS

at Rome in 1751. In the National Gallery of Ireland. The composition of this picture is based on Raphael's picture of the same name in the Vatican. The seated figure in the left foreground playing a clarinet is Lord Charlemont

mont saw had been rescued by Lord Stratford de Red-
cliffe in 1846, and sent to the British Museum. In
particular, Charlemont lost all credit for his conjectural synthesis of Pausanias' famous description, Wren's
hypotheses,[24] and the actual remains on the spot. As
late as 1862 Fergusson could describe it as 'recently
discovered'.

On the 13th of November they sailed west. After a
nasty night of sailing through narrow straits between
rocks, they ran into a thunderstorm on the 17th and
made for the port of Thermia (Cythnos) in the western
Cyclades. They missed the entrance and lay to on a lee
shore, and there for three days they remained, in a very
precarious situation. But on the 20th they managed to
row ashore and walk to the town of Thermia. The
Vaivode received them 'with great State and Ceremony'
but Charlemont was impatient to push on to Athens.
He stood on deck, contemplating the coast of Attica
'by the uncertain Light of the Moon' and giving free
rein to his mood of moralising meditation.[25] On the
23rd of November they passed the island of Aegina
and were towed into the Piraeus.

Charlemont's keen eye noted the remains of ancient
moles in the harbour, and the sun, he says 'gilded the
truly classic scene'. But, so far from attempting to rise
to the subject of a first view of the Acropolis, he wisely
passes it over almost in silence. He did not think much
of the Athenian people. Their 'subtle and penetrating
Wit' had degenerated into 'low Cunning and Knavery
. . . The countrymen of Aristides are now perhaps the
keenest and the most accomplished Rogues upon the
Face of the Earth.' Though they were not without the
power of defending themselves against rapacious governors, they still did not realise the uselessness of address-

F

ing their appeals for justice to a higher external
authority. 'A Wisdom however of this sort is scarcely
to be expected from any People whatsoever, as We
Irishmen have long known to our Cost.'[26] In that sentence, perhaps for the first time, we hear the voice of
the future leader of the Irish Volunteers.

The schoolmasters of Athens he found 'profoundly
ignorant' except a Father Paeseus, Abbot of a monastery on Mount Hymettus. Charlemont and his friends
got to know him well, and fell to talking about Homer.
The Abbot maintained that no 'foreigners could appre-
ciate him to the full.' Charlemont, 'a little piqued' at
this, begged to differ. So the Abbot challenged him to
read Homer aloud, and began by doing so himself.

... the Effect it produced upon Him was indeed astonishing—
He seem'd in Exstacy—totally enraptured—His Eyes roll'd—
His Features were changed, and in every Particular He ap-
pear'd like Virgil's Sibyl, full of the God![27]

Charlemont considered the performance substantially genuine, and observed that he read entirely by the
accent. Greek accents, Charlemont observes sadly (and
who will not endorse his sorrow?) are 'a Difficulty after
which the Learned seem to labour in vain'. There is
sadness, too, in the tone in which he records that the
women of Athens are very reserved. The very mind-
fulness of their former glories rendered the Athenians
rather pathetic in his eyes, particularly as he thought
them to be, on the whole, the same people as of old, in
character at least.
The friendship of the Governor of the Acropolis
Charlemont found 'absolutely necessary to us'. In spite
of obtaining this, they found themselves regarded with
suspicion. Murphy's measuring-instruments were re-

garded as conjurer's properties or something worse,
and they were turned out. But difficulties of this kind
were got round by giving presents.

We have already found Charlemont anticipating
later archaeology. Here we find him anticipating a
famous passage of Macaulay:

How melancholy wou'd be the Reflection shou'd we suppose,
what certainly must come to pass; that in a few Ages hence,
London, the Carthage, the Memphis, the Athens of the present
World, shall be reduced to a State like this, and Travellers
shall come, *perhaps from America*, to view it's Ruins![28]

Charlemont with his Americans was nearer the mark
than Macaulay with his New Zealanders.

From Athens they went on a tour[29] through Corinth,
Thebes and Negropont. They had a Janizzary and two
Albanian guards. Soon after starting Charlemont was
nearly killed when a vicious horse ran several miles
with him, 'stopping at length on the Edge of a Preci-
pice.' But in general the journey followed the now
familiar pattern. The people of Thebes he found 'sensible and polite, Lovers of Feasting, and not a little
addicted to Drunkenness, holding their Countryman
and tutelar Divinity, Bacchus, in as high Estimation as
ever They did—Indeed He Might have afforded them
better Wine, but such as it is, they drink it plentifully'.
These Boeotians (whose ancient reputation was for
dullness) he notes as now the most sprightly of the
Greeks. He obtained 'a most noble and poetick View of
Parnassus and Helicon cover'd with Snow'. From
Negropont (the ancient Euboea) they embarked and
sailed through the Euripus, landing at Aulis. Thence
on horseback, past a site which he identified correctly
as Delium, and so back to Athens, which they reached
late on the night of December the 14th, safe, to the

surprise of the Athenians, and thanks to their Albanian guards. Everywhere they had met with great civilities from the French Consuls. The British Consuls, he complained, were usually Greeks. He had afterwards a low opinion of Frenchmen,[30] but was quite prepared to give credit where it was due. In Mitylene he was told a story about a town three days from the capital where strangers were obliged to exercise the *jus primae noctis.* Charlemont was very doubtful about the truth of this, as the French Consul had never mentioned it to him. Clearly he was becoming experienced in the ways of the world, and had made some progress in the art of judging by appearances.

NOTES

1. RIA MSS., I, 171. The poem to Marlay is taken from H, I, 27.
2. HMC, I, 181.
3. RIA MSS., VI, 1.
4. Ibid., 3, 4 n.
5. RIA *Transactions*, Vol. III, 1790.
6. RIA MSS., VI, 14 n.
7. Ibid., 15.
8. The Commodore, he notes, kept on board a number of 'handsome Boys' for 'no honourable purpose': ibid., 16.
9. Ibid., 22.
10. Ibid., 29.
11. Ibid., V, 36.
12. As his account occupies four folio pages of his manuscript (RIA MSS., VI, 29 sqq.) and cannot be shortened without serious mutilation, it will be found in an Appendix.
13. RIA MSS., VI, 36.
14. Ibid., 39.
15. There seems to be no doubt about Charlemont's singularly clear orthography: ibid., 40.
16. Ibid., 53 sqq.
17. Χαιρε! Χαιρε!
18. Notably RIA MSS., V: 59, 101, 110, and VI: 21–22, 62, 65.
19. Ibid., VI, 62 and 62 n.
20. Ibid., 73.
21. Ibid., 88.

22. Ibid., 91. On the same page and that following will be found conjectures concerning the 'infamous Fountain Salmacis'.

23. As in the Trinity College, Dublin, copy.

24. From RIA MSS., VI, 191, we gather that not only was he familiar with the paper printed in Wren's *Parentalia*, but that he also possessed Wren's 'original sketch' of the Mausoleum 'in the State He left it'.

25. Ibid., 101.

26. Ibid., 111.

27. Ibid., 121.

28. Ibid., 141.

29. The account of which begins on p. 199 of RIA MSS., VI, as a separate section of the work.

30. See H, II, 443, and HMC, I, 325 middle of page.

CHAPTER IV

ROME AND PIRANESI

They left Athens early in January 1750, with the
intention of visiting Malta on their way home to
Italy. The account of the storm which they encountered
occupies nine pages of Hardy's Life[1]: here it will be
sufficient to say that they were very nearly lost. The
ship's cannon came adrift, and she lay helpless on her
side. Charlemont confesses to having been thoroughly
frightened: but his terror was shot through with admiration for British sailors, and with irrepressible amusement at Frank Burton's behaviour. The captain had
told them that he had never seen such a night, that the
ship might possibly ride it out, but that they should
prepare for the worst.

How this sentence was felt, may be easily judged. A dead
silence ensued, which lasted for some minutes, but was finally
broken by my friend, Frank Burton, who lay next bed to me.
'Well', exclaimed he, and I fear, with an oath, 'this is fine indeed! Here have I been pampering this damn'd great body of
mine, for more than twenty years, and all to be a prey to some
cursed shark, and be damn'd to him!' . . . in the midst of our
fears, we burst out into a loud laugh. Neither let this incident,
this comic break in our tragedy, appear unnatural. Nature and
Shakespeare both inform us, that character will prevail in the
midst of distress.[2]

There was worse to come. The lamp swinging in the
narrow cabin put him in mind of a tomb, and he and
his friends fell to their prayers. But when the storm
abated and they reached Malta in safety, he confesses
that he had grown so fond of the ship that he preferred

forty days' quarantine on board her, to the lazaretto on shore. The time was occupied pleasantly enough in writing up his journals.

The Grand Master of the Knights was a courteous host, but the Knights in general he found, as he expected, to be corrupt beyond words. 'The town of Malta', he reports, 'is one vast brothel'—the necessary consequence, in his view, of their celibate rule. But Charlemont and his party made a thorough survey of the island, making daily excursions from the capital. In due course they took their leave and landed in Italy without further incident.

For the next three years Charlemont lived at large in Italy, based, it would seem, principally on Rome, but spending much of his time in other cities, notably in the North. The Crown-Prince of Piedmont, Victor-Amadeus, was a contemporary and friend, and Charlemont attended his wedding to a Spanish princess.[3] In Verona he was singled out for attention by the Marchese Scipione Maffei, Lady Mary Wortley Montague's friend. The Palazzo Maffei was a noted literary salon, and here and elsewhere Charlemont was free of the highest circles of informed society. We hear of him in Florence, Venice, Lucca, Siena and every centre of cultural interest.

He was certainly not afflicted with any undue solemnity. At Lucca, September 26th, 1751, he and Lord Bruce put their hands to an indenture which was nothing more than a wager in legal form. If Sir William Lowther were to die before John Martin, Charlemont would lose fifty pounds to Bruce, and vice-versa. If General d'Olloune were to survive Lascelles Raymond Iremonger, Charlemont would be ten pounds to the good, and conversely. After signing together a codicil to the effect that 'This indenture affects the parties concerned during their natural lives only and not their heirs and successors', they added a further clause involving the lives of General Sallia and the Duc d'Invernois (whose name is otherwise given as de Nivernois[4]). The flippancy of this is set off by the fact that some of the lives in question were, or afterwards became, personally dear to Charlemont himself. Another indenture, made at Rome in April 1752, between Charlemont and Sir Thomas Kennedy, provides for a race between two horses, bought for less than forty pounds each, to be run on the first Tuesday in July 1755, for stakes of a hundred pounds.[5]

Lord Bruce and Sir Thomas Kennedy were young men of fashion, and it is reasonable to suppose that Charlemont in one aspect appeared much the same. The role of a punter on horses is an unfamiliar one to most of his admirers. Lord Bruce later became Earl of Ailesbury, and was an associate of Charlemont's in later London days. He had literary interests, and was of the same family as Lord Elgin of the Marbles. Among Chambers's designs for *Casini*, there is, in addition to Charlemont's, one for Lord Bruce. Whether it was ever built I do not know, but the motif was certainly used in extensions by Chambers to Marino House.[6] Sir Thomas Kennedy became Earl of Cassilis, an obscure Scotch peerage, and he is depicted, with other of Charlemont's friends and with Charlemont himself, in Reynolds's *School of Athens*, painted in Rome in 1752.[7]

As for Frank Burton and the shadowy Mr Scott, they had both returned to Ireland immediately, where they both married very soon afterwards. In politics, Burton pursued an inglorious career as a government place-

man. In due course he succeeded his uncle as Baron
Conyngham, and died in 1787.

Among those who figure in the *School of Athens* are
Lord Mayo, Mr Henry of Straffan, and Joseph Leeson,
the son of a wealthy Dublin brewer.[8] Leeson had already
begun Russborough House in County Wicklow, and his
family name is commemorated in Leeson Street. When
he was advanced to the peerage as Baron and Viscount
Russborough and Earl of Milltown, he was not to be
the last Dublin brewer to be so honoured. Reynolds, in
his caricature group, has contrived to make his noble
friends appear clowns and zanies. Evidence of the kind
of life they lived, and the pursuits they followed, is not
otherwise forthcoming. It is most probable that they
were dilettanti, in the widest and most generous sense
of the term. They sketched and played the flute, they
patronised artists, architects and no doubt musicians.
If their way of life may not altogether be held up for
emulation, it did at least produce results, and those
results are still present for our refreshment.

Charlemont became a fluent Italian speaker, was
elected a member of most of the academies in the cities
of Italy, and did not lack for acquaintance in purely
Italian circles. The ruling Pope in particular, Benedict
XIV, was on cordial terms with him. Charlemont's
friend, the Duc de Nivernois, was succeeded as French
Ambassador by Choiseul; and when the latter behaved
discourteously towards the Pope, he forfeited Charlemont's regard for good. In Cardinal Passionei, the
Vatican librarian, the young man found a kindred
spirit.

In Rome, he regarded himself so much as a fixture
that instead of living in lodgings, as most foreigners
did, he kept house for himself. The faithful Murphy

acted as major-domo, and every morning Charlemont
and he read together, or explored the ancient remains.
In the evenings Murphy generally stayed at home with
some learned friend, while Charlemont did the round of
the theatres, concerts and conversaziones. With his
memory running, perhaps, on this period of his life, he
writes nearly fifty years later to his son:

. . . if I have not lived irreproachably, I have not, however,
been either useless to my country or dishonourable to myself
or to my family. Though erroneous and imprudent, I have
been able to withstand criminal seduction of every kind. With
David Hume for my early friend, I have preserved my religion
unperverted. With Jack St Leger for my early companion, I
have kept my principles of morality unchanged . . . I have also
laid up for myself a fund of rational amusement independent
of all external pleasure, without which, believe me, man must
be miserable . . .[9]

This Jack St Leger was apparently a County Cork
gentleman, who is sometimes credited with the author-
ship of Lord Chesterfield's epigram on Miss Ambrose,
already quoted. He must have been older than Charlemont, and he must have had a name as a rake. The
presumption that Charlemont's association with him
dates from the early Dublin period, would involve the
conclusion that Charlemont emerged from his shell
rather earlier than we have any sound warrant for
believing. St Leger was certainly in Rome soon after
1750.[10]

In this connexion, one of the few scandals which ad-
here to Charlemont's name must be summarily examined. It is said that his homecoming from the Continent
was 'hastened by a disorder contracted from poison
administered by the jealousy of a woman with whom
he was acquainted'.[11] In some versions the 'poison'
becomes a love-philtre, and the whole train of his sub-

sequent ill-health is imputed to this. The story has presumably some basis in fact; but how much, and to what extent it would affect our estimate if we knew the truth, it is idle to conjecture. From his own admissions regarding his doings in Greece, we are justified in taking recourse to the proverb that there is seldom smoke without fire. One thing is certain: now and for some years to come, he had a strong determination not to marry. He may indeed, as an innocent but imprudent agent in the affair, have been affected by some poison. Late in 1753, and again in the early months of 1754, he was ill: the first adult occurrence of a series of indispositions which were to make much of his life a penance.

He left a full account of one Roman acquaintance of this period, an immortal in spite of himself, that disappointing son to whom Lord Chesterfield wrote the *Letters.* He might 'have passed well enough through life', wrote Charlemont, who liked him and voted him a 'pleasant fellow', 'if his father had not insisted upon making him a fine gentleman . . .'[12] There arrived in Rome an elderly lady and her supposed daughter, Mrs and Miss Eugenia Peters. The latter was, according to Charlemont, the natural daughter of an Irish gentleman, a Mr Domville. But her equivocal status seems to have been no obstacle, for Stanhope, Charlemont, Bruce and others frequented the Peters' lodgings. 'Some of the unoccupied among us' (a phrase which may include Charlemont himself) '. . . persuaded themselves that they were smitten by the accomplishments of the amiable Eugenia.' Young Stanhope married her, and after his death she was responsible, from motives economic rather than literary, for giving the famous *Letters* to the world. He tells a number of amusing anecdotes about Stanhope.

He came into contact with a number of English political personalities who were in Rome at this period. Several acquaintances among the great Whig families, such as the Cavendishes, date from this time, as does his most steadfast English political connexion, the Marquis of Rockingham, and his friendship with Joseph Baretti.

But his main object in Italy was never lost sight of. He had come to Rome in search of art, and it is a little ironical that the most important artistic association which he formed there, was with a Scotchman. Mr William Chambers, as he then was, had indeed been to China and back, on two occasions, but his presence in Rome was a matter of necessity rather than of caprice. He was a hard-working young man, two years Charlemont's senior, and determined to rise to the top of his profession. It argues some degree of insight in Charlemont to have marked him out as an architect of genius. Chambers was not well off, and at the time when Charlemont first met him, he did not know many people. Though no tangible results followed from their association for ten years to come, he saw to it that the young architect became known in profitable circles. He presumably also helped him with money, and it is even possible that the design for the Clontarf Casino was bought, and in part paid for, as early as this; for it appears in substantially final form[13] in Chambers' *Civil Architecture* of 1759, long before the building itself was begun.

Chambers, we are told,[14] lived at Rome with Clérisseau and Joseph Wilton, the sculptor; and when he returned to England in 1755 he brought Wilton and Giambattista Cipriani with him. Chambers, Wilton and Cipriani were all concerned in the works at Marino, and

so was Simón Vierpyl, sculptor and architectural car-
ver. Vierpyl also was in Rome in 1750, employed by
Charlemont making copies from the antique. In 1756,
at Charlemont's request, he settled in Dublin,[15] and
built the Casino which Chambers had designed. The
presumption that the building already existed in Charlemont's mind, if not on paper, is greatly strengthened
by the fact that all its authors were assembled together
in Rome before 1753.

There were many other artists in Rome who were
indebted to Charlemont. As the Earl-Bishop of Derry
was later to do with such éclat as to become a legend
to this day, he bought statues, pictures, *objets d'art*
and all the accepted paraphernalia of culture. Murphy,
with his sound knowledge of antiquity, was able to
render him service as an agent, and no doubt saved
him—so far as any nobleman of the time could be
saved—from falling too easy prey to the astute purvey-
ors of the Eternal City. Vierpyl, in addition to his work
for Charlemont, modelled for Murphy 22 statues and
78 heads of Roman emperors from the real or reputed
originals in the Capitoline museum. Twenty years later,
when Murphy was an old man, he wondered what
should be done with his treasures. After consulting
Vierpyl as to their probable market value, he decided
to give them to Charlemont, who had, directly or indirectly, paid for them in the first place.[16] They were
gratefully accepted: they adorned the large library in
Charlemont House, and in 1868, when the third Earl
decided to give up the house, they came to the Royal
Irish Academy, where they may still be seen. They are
more interesting than beautiful. Murphy, indeed, seems
to have been almost as much of a collector as Charlemont. The latter, after his return, put the Jervis-Street

house at Murphy's disposal as a dumping-ground for his baggage. In 1755 Murphy writes from London to Charlemont that he does not want his boxes opened: 'There are Trumpery among them that I would not have exposed.'[17]

' There were others, too, who acted as agent in matters of this nature: the Abbé Peter Grant, a Scottish Catholic, the favourite of the Pope, and a professional go-between for English-speaking travellers. There was John Parker, an English painter more or less permanently resident in Rome, in much the same line of business. Of Parker and Grant we shall hear much presently.

One architect, the Dutch-Italian Vanvitelli, a late-comer in the long line of architects associated with St Peter's, better and more worthily known as designer of the Palace of Caserta, had some dealings with Charlemont, and was invited to produce a design for a garden temple. But he pitched his prices too high, and on the advice of his agents (who seem to have had the casting vote in the matter) Charlemont refused the bait.[18] Then there was Maini, a sculptor commissioned by Charlemont to make 'bustos', who inconveniently died, and left Charlemont's agents at great trouble to recover money owing by his representatives. But in spite of these and other difficulties, the unceasing flow of packing-cases from Rome to Jervis-Street continued long after Charlemont had gone home. Occasionally, in the correspondence between him and his agents, we get a glimpse of the moral squalor underlying the process; the whole of Rome seems to be seething with defaulting statuaries, touts, confidence-men and sycophants of every type connected with the fine arts. But Charlemont trusted his agents, and it seems that they were worthy of his trust. The relations between them were now to be tested very severely indeed.

Across the chattersome small-talk of bustos, snuff-boxes and the like, there now sounds a note of something much bigger and much less closely tied to the period. Charlemont, in a word, had the misfortune to fall foul of Piranesi, a man of genius whose work transcends the limits of his time as certainly as his personal character exhibits that touchiness and undependability which so many people are so very ready to impute to any artist. We, at this distance of time, can pardon the imagination which produced the famous 'Carceri', for succumbing too readily to ideas of persecution. Piranesi's neurotic power as an artist stands in such curious contrast to Roman society in the seventeen-fifties, that the very contrast is, with him as with Blake, almost half an explanation. It is at least an excuse; and happily there are grounds for supposing that Charlemont accepted it as a valid excuse.

Giambattista Piranesi was born in Venice in 1720, the son of a mason and nephew of an architect. He settled in Rome in 1738, and from 1741 onwards devoted his energies to the engraving of architectural subjects, graduating from existing buildings to imaginary ones, and thence to the structurally impossible Prisons, and the rank gardens seething with serpents, writhing figures, bones and obscene simulacra, known as the 'Grotesche'. In his own department he has never since been equalled. His supreme achievements date from 1750–1, when he was barely thirty. He died in 1778.

Probably in 1752, he was introduced to Charlemont by Parker. At first all went well: that is to say we have no evidence to the contrary. Piranesi, having published his finest collection, the *Opere Varie*, in 1750, was at this time resting on his laurels, issuing single prints for which his reputation guaranteed a ready sale. But in 1753 he began a work which he intended as his masterpiece. By no means alone among artists in a mistaken idea of where his true strength lay, he thought himself a serious archaeologist. While his *Antichità Romane* was still in embryo, he approached Parker and asked permission to dedicate the book to Charlemont.[19] He claimed later that he waited more than a year before Parker replied, but this, like all Piranesi's statements, is to be received with caution.

At all events, he managed to secure an interview with Charlemont, satisfactory to both parties. Charlemont appointed a day on which Piranesi was to bring the dedication-plates for his approval. When the day arrived, Piranesi was refused admittance by Parker to Charlemont's house. He continued to call daily at all hours, without more success. We have only Piranesi's word for these allegations; and here, as always, he is careful to absolve Charlemont from all responsibility for the actions of his agents. His tone is similar to that of a political pamphleteer, who protests loyalty to a king while regretting that he is hoodwinked by his ministers.

Charlemont, it appears, paid at least one visit to Piranesi's house. The latter would have us believe that his patron had been kept in complete ignorance of Piranesi's own visits. Since Charlemont came accompanied, he was unable, he says, to unfold his grievances before other people. But he had been induced by Parker to hand over the dedication-plate designs, ostensibly to show to Charlemont. At this point matters stood when Charlemont left Rome in March 1754.

PLATE IV

See page 92

TITLE-PAGE OF PIRANESI'S 'LETTERE DI GIUSTIFICAZIONE . . .'
1757

He spent the best part of a year travelling in Northern Italy, Spain and France, before his arrival in England. It is hardly surprising that a certain amount of misunderstanding should have arisen from the irregular forwarding of letters, particularly as for part of the time Parker was ill at Naples.

Piranesi appears to claim in one place that he brought two copies of the work to Parker two months after Charlemont's departure, and that when he asked Parker to tell him what Charlemont wanted him to do with them, Parker would not reply. In view of the fact that all copies of the work bear the date 1756, two *years*, not two months, after Charlemont had gone, there seems to be something wrong here. It is certain that Charlemont returned the inscriptions to Piranesi, after moderating the grandiloquent terms in which they were at first couched.

Piranesi spends a great many words explaining the admitted delay in the book's appearance, from which we may infer that the grievance on the side of Charlemont or his agents, was this delay. On the other side there was a grievance which, if well-founded, may be allowed to be more serious. According to Piranesi, Parker told him that he had 200 scudi to give him from Charlemont, for which he wanted a receipt, though, on the ground that Piranesi was an Italian and therefore unreliable, he would be paid only half that sum until the work was finished.

He protests frequently that he is not interested in money, that the dedication was not made from pecuniary motives. This protestation is invariably followed by the observation that if money is to change hands at all, it had better be on a respectable scale, to accord with the magnificence of the work. His other primary

G

grievance is that for two whole years, while the book
was in preparation, he received no inquiry either from
Parker or from Charlemont concerning the progress of
the work. The grievances which came to the surface
later, when the tormented etcher had worked himself
up into an ecstasy of fury, are in another class. The
primary grievances may be in some degree real. It is
quite likely that Charlemont saw the vision of this
sumptuous publication receding into limbo, and lost
interest. Piranesi's implied demand for big money may
have found Charlemont embarrassed (if indeed it
found him at all). Parker, bereft of instructions from
his employer, may have extemporised. The ingredients
of a first-class explosion were certainly present.

Early in 1756 the four volumes of the *Antichità
Romane* appeared, each prefixed with a plate embodying a dedication to Charlemont. Simultaneously, it
would appear, Piranesi despatched to Charlemont an
enormously long letter,[20] reciting the allegations already mentioned, and a great deal more to the same
purpose, together with much matter to very little purpose at all. Among other things he said that a 'great
lord' had offered him a large sum of money to alter the
dedications in his favour; that Lord Stanhope had
taken the trouble to come and look at Piranesi's work,
whereas Parker had not deigned to open it when sent;
that Parker had refused to honour debts owing by
Charlemont to various artists in Rome; that he had cut
the agreed prices to be paid to others, withheld a pension which Charlemont was paying to a French master;
and generally had been responsible for the break-up of
the 'academy' of artists which Charlemont had maintained when in Rome, and which Parker was supposed
to be keeping in being as a permanent institution. In

one breath Piranesi declares his readiness to cancel the dedications; in the next he is trying to blackmail Charlemont with the threat of a higher bid from another quarter; and more than once he threatens to print and circulate the letter unless he receives a satisfactory reply. In the whole of this prolix and repetitive catena of complaint, there is perhaps one sentence only which strikes home. Regretfully he protests that if he has to choose between saving his own reputation or that of Milord, he will save his own, for 'A great lord is, for the time being, the last of his name, while a professional man is the first of his; and both must have the same delicacy'.

This letter certainly reached Charlemont, for the original remains among the Charlemont papers. Whether the latter replied or not, Piranesi chose to make a point of his not having done so. On January 20th (says Piranesi) Parker summoned Piranesi's bookseller and ordered two copies against the money paid to Piranesi. Piranesi, by now determined to erase the dedications, told the bookseller to recall the copies and sent his solicitor to Parker to try to return the money and recover the receipts. He was met by Parker with offers of paltry tips, only a little larger than those which Piranesi was accustomed to give Parker himself as commission for sales. In May Parker writes to Charlemont that the book is at last published, that it is 'a very fine work', that Piranesi insists on having two copies heraldically and magnificently bound for the dedicatee, and that he (Parker) has refused to accept the money which Piranesi wants to return. In the meantime he awaits Charlemont's instructions.[21]

In the absence of any statement on Charlemont's side at this stage of the affair, we may comment on some of the charges made by Piranesi above. We are told much later by Parker that the 'great lord' was a runaway valet who masqueraded as the 'Baron d'Hanau', imposed upon the English in Rome, and in 1759, having made that city too hot for him, fled therefrom on foot, leaving a trail of debts behind him.[22] As for the disruption of Charlemont's 'academy', this, Parker avers, was partly due to Piranesi's calumnies, but mostly to the exploits of a painter named Patché, who was banished from Rome for sundry offences, whereupon Charlemont himself gave orders for the Academy to be dismissed till further orders, since, during Parker's absence and illness at Naples, it was becoming an asylum for artistic scamps. Regarding the debts which Parker is alleged to have repudiated, and the prices he is said to have cut, Parker caused the persons concerned to make affidavits certifying that the charges were untrue.

Some forty or so copies of the work with the full Charlemont dedications had got into circulation when the final breach came, marked by Piranesi's erasure of the inscriptions. A point which seems to have escaped the notice of English writers on Piranesi is that this manoeuvre was carried out piecemeal. In one copy at least Charlemont's name in the Preface has been erased by scrabbling out with a more or less blunt instrument. The compliments which accompany it remain intact, and only three out of the four frontispieces have been altered. Possibly he was unwilling to burn his boats in haste.[23]

If so, he soon gathered confidence and went from strength to strength. In the first and fourth volumes he chiselled away the inscriptions and substituted new dedications to the public, which start out from the page

and appear as if clamped on over the originals. The enquiring eye can discover in the first the mutilated remains of the Charlemont arms scattered on the ground.
The alterations in the second and third volumes, in
which there were no large inscriptions to begin with,
are only to be found by those who seek them, and then
hardly without the aid of a magnifying-glass. Scurrilous observations in Latin, in minute characters, seem
designed to escape rather than to court notice; and
only those who look very hard indeed can detect the
restrained use of indecent pictorial symbolism.

Prefixed to every set which he sold from now on, was
a printed version of the long letter already sent to
Charlemont together with a later and shorter one which
seems never to have been sent, but to have been con-
ceived from the outset as an 'open letter' for publication. It purports to have been written six months after
the first, and to enclose a letter from the 'great lord'
whom we have already met. It consists largely of
threats, most of which had already been put into practice by the time it appeared.

Parker and the Abbé Grant took immediate counter-
measures. On the 13th of June, 1757, the Governor of
Rome, Mgr Caprara, summoned Piranesi and formally
enjoined him under severe penalties not to publish anything, whether in writing or in print, concerning in any
way the person or the honour or the convenience of the
most excellent milord Charlemont, being absent; as also
concerning not offending or molesting, either in deeds
or words, the abbé Peter Grant, and much less pub-
lishing ... anything respecting his person etc. etc.[24]

The effect of this solemn experience on Piranesi was
that he promptly reprinted the two letters to Charlemont, together with a third to Grant, in a pamphlet

embellished with scurrilous engraved headpieces depicting Parker, Grant and poor Murphy in ignominious attitudes, together with reduced reproductions of the altered dedication-plates.[25]

Parker and Grant, it appears, were not expecting this turn of events. But before describing its consequences we must turn back to trace Grant's part in the affair. Grant is not mentioned in either of Piranesi's first two letters. We know, from a letter of March 1754 on other matters, that Charlemont had employed Grant before. Nevertheless, in view of the complications already owing to the employment of agents with sketchy instructions, and of agents of those agents, it was hardly prudent of Charlemont to hand over the conduct of the negotiations to Grant at this stage. The Governor's injunction of June 1757 specifically mentions Grant, and the letter to Grant bears the date May 31st of that year. The interview between Grant and Piranesi therefore took place before then. On Grant's side we know only that 'I communicated to him, with all the smoothness and coolness of temper imaginable, your sentiments with regard to his dedication to your lordship'.[26] What these sentiments were we are left to guess.

Piranesi's account of the matter is much more colourful.[27] Grant, he says, began by showing him a letter with Lord Charlemont's seal. He then, somewhat inexplicably, confessed that he or Parker had forged the letter, that Piranesi's correspondence with Charlemont had been intercepted, and other matters unspecified which (says Piranesi) so burdened the Abbé that he sought the interview for the purpose of getting them off his chest. Still more surprisingly, Grant went on to tell Piranesi that unless Milord's wishes were carried out, Milord would see to it that Piranesi was assassinated. To lend colour to the charge of forgery, Piranesi accuses Grant of having spun him a tale of Milord's having lost the use of his writing hand. If Grant said so, it was probably true, for Charlemont was at this time suffering acutely from rheumatism. But we may forgive Piranesi for not having believed it, and for allowing it to inflame his injuries' still further.[28] After the interview Piranesi consulted with a cleric, who, he would have us believe, confirmed his suspicions and advised firm action. To clinch the point, Piranesi informs Grant that during the entire conversation a hidden witness who knew Grant, was present and heard every word. If we are to trust a later statement by Parker, this witness was—who but the 'great prince', the *soi-disant* Baron d'Hanau!

The climax of the affair now approached; and the plot, already thick with conjectural imaginings, was complicated by a singular circumstance: the age and feebleness of the reigning pontiff. 'We are not at a great distance from a change of a padrone sopremo' writes Grant to Charlemont, 'and as nobody knows who may in some months hence be his master, every body is immensely loath to disoblige any one cardinal'. Piranesi's case, in brief, had become a part of the general jockeying for position in the Sacred College, of which he had three members on his side.

A politico-legal tussle followed, of which we have more or less parallel accounts in letters from Grant to Charlemont, and from Parker to Murphy.[29] The absence of recriminations between Grant and Parker, whom Piranesi had done his best to divide, is very strong evidence in their favour. It is all the more impressive because there did exist differences of opinion between them: Parker, for example, mildly reproaches

Grant for not having taken care to have his name included in the Governor's injunction. He considers Grant too soft and easily imposed upon; in particular, Parker believes the governor's *luogotenente* Cherubini to be playing a double game, angling for bribes from both sides, whereas Grant says he is 'entirely on your lordship's side of the question'. But these divergences crop up only in passing: like the discrepancies in the Gospels, they improve the case as a whole. The contrast between Piranesi's incoherent and febrile protestations and the unflurried tone of his adversaries, is very damaging indeed to the former. It is not simply a matter of Saxon and Latin temperaments.

Charlemont received an accession of strength from an unexpected quarter, the Irish Friars in Rome, who presented a memorial to Cardinal Corsini of the Piranesi party, and succeeded in convincing him that he had been imposed upon. We need not dwell on the moves in the game. It will suffice that the luogotenente seized the plates of Piranesi's pamphlet, confiscated the outstanding copies of the letters, and cornered Piranesi morally if not physically. He was not imprisoned, but he was bound to write and print a recantation. The unfortunate man wrote fifty separate sketches of this document, one after the other, and all were returned by the Governor as unsatisfactory. But Piranesi had the final word. The last draft of the recantation was accompanied by a notice that if this were not acceptable no more drafts would be forthcoming. The governor, understandably weary of perusing Piranesi's prose, capitulated.

The final version, quite a short document, was printed in French and Italian, and bore the date March 15, 1758. A copy was sent to Charlemont. It concludes:

In my writing, then, which is full of the praises due to mylord, and of the profound veneration in which I hold and will always hold him, if there should have crept in any phrase, or any word, which could be interpreted as prejudicial and offensive to mylord and to those who belong to him, I protest and will protest before all the world, that my intention has had no hand in it, my veneration for him having been constant, as also has been my esteem for monsieur l'abbé Grant, for monsieur Parker, and for monsieur Murphy, of whom, over and above their personal qualities, the honour of having been esteemed and loved by mylord, who is a most enlightened nobleman, and apt at discerning merit in others, may be sufficient eulogy. I protest then again that I am very grieved to find myself under the harsh necessity of bringing forward my justification, and for all the gold in the world I would not have found myself under that necessity ...[30]

Hardy states that Charlemont intervened and protected Piranesi from more serious punishment, and that 'the belligerent parties were again on amicable terms'. It is to be hoped that this statement was made on the strength of something more substantial than the printed apology. But one of the salient features of the affair is the complete absence of any documentary evidence, direct or indirect, of what Charlemont's opinion was. Every shred of evidence on the Charlemont side has been made the most of in this narrative, while only the main points of Piranesi's case have been mentioned. This treatment, if it errs on the side of over-simplicity, has probably made a better case for Piranesi than he made himself. It has seemed worth while to deal with it at some length, not only because no previous account in English has drawn fully on the evidence in the Charlemont manuscripts, but also because the dealings of an outstanding man of genius with the social norm of his time, have in themselves an interest which never dies.

One final shred of negative evidence may be added. At the sale of the Charlemont library in 1865, the only Piranesi item listed was the *Opere Varie* of 1750.[31] The mystery—for it remains a mystery—is slightly, but only slightly, less obscure by the measure of this fact. If Charlemont thought this volume worth keeping in spite of all, he knew well enough what he was at.

NOTES

1. H, I, 35 sqq., from RIA MSS., VII, 535 sqq.

2. The word 'damn'd' has been restored from the MS.

3. The wedding implemented a secret clause in the Treaty of Aix-la-Chapelle, but Charlemont was apparently not aware of this.

4. HMC, I, 183–4 and also April 12th, 1751, in RIA MSS., IX.

5. Ibid.

6. Compare Plate in Chambers's *Civil Architecture*, 1759, with the plan of Marino House given in *Georgian Society*, V, plate CXXI. As Marino House no longer exists it is impossible to determine how close the resemblance was, but the connexion is attested in Chambers' text.

7. In National Gallery of Ireland. The painting, a parody of Raphael's *School of Athens* in the Vatican, unfortunately lacks a key, though all the names are given. But the Gallery possesses three studies for the completed picture (with names also given), from which it is possible to identify some of the figures more certainly.

8. Mr la Touche, of the famous firm of Dublin bankers, was also in Rome now or soon afterwards, but he is not included in Reynolds's painting: HMC, I, 247.

9. HMC, II, 269.

10. In HMC, II, 403, is an undated letter from Marlay to Charlemont, clearly written to Italy, in which he says: 'I am told Mr St Leger is a great favourite with the Pope.'

11. *Public Characters of* 1798, Dublin ed., p. 180. The tale is repeated by the *Gentleman's Magazine*, and thereafter by other retailers of gossip.

12. HMC, I, 325 sqq.

13. For the differences between the 1759 plans and the building as erected, see Appendix.

14. Allan Cunningham: *Lives of the Painters*, etc.

15. Strickland: *Dictionary of Irish Artists*. Vierpyl's sons carried on their business after the father's death. Among his pupils was Edward Smyth.

16. HMC, I, 222 and 322–4.

17. RIA MSS., IX, 44.

18. Ibid., 35, is an almost illegible letter from Vanvitelli. See also HMC, I, 221 and 227.

19. The facts and inferences given in this account are drawn from Piranesi's *Lettere di Giustificazione*, etc., 1757, his printed 'recantation' of 1758 (French text) and the letters and statements of Parker and Grant, for which see Index to HMC, I. Number 1 of the *Lettere* exists in MS. in the RIA MSS., IX, in Italian. The pages are arranged in the wrong order, and it is so printed (in Italian) in HMC, I, 231 sqq. There is a misprint at the bottom of page 235 (chiamarir for chiamarvi), and another (perfido for porfido) on page 233. But I do not think that a careful examination of all the evidence will lead to any other order of events than that which I have adopted in the text.

20. This is No. 1 in the *Lettere*.

21. HMC, I, 227.

22. HMC, I, 254, RIA MSS., IX, 76 supplies omissions.

23. Copies in which the volte-face is complete are the commonest. I have also seen a set with the dedications untouched.

24. Latin text in HMC, I, 243.

25. Ibid., 241.

26. Ibid.

27. It occupies Letter III of the *Lettere*.

28. It is not easy to be sure from Piranesi's words whether he is referring to a single interview or to several.

29. HMC, I, 240 sqq. and 245 sqq.

30. Ibid., 244–5 (in French).

31. Lot 1803 in *Catalogue of Sale*, 1865 (Vol. VIII, RIA MSS.)

CHAPTER V

POLITICS 1753–62

During 1753, while he was still based on Italy, he made a flying visit to London and Dublin. The evidence is fragmentary, and the purpose of his journey is by no means clear. In August he is in London 'excessively busied with ten thousand troublesom affairs' and 'obliged to set out for Ireland tomorrow'.[1] He expects to return in January or February of 1754. But a letter from Lord Bruce to Charlemont, of August 1753, seems to suggest that Charlemont had already written from Ireland. 'I am sorry', Bruce writes, 'to find that the corruption of England has infested a neighbouring island. Four thousand pounds for a seat in the house of commons of Ireland when his majesty is seventy years old!' And he compliments Charlemont's letter thus: 'Never were portraits better drawn, higher coloured, or more like. You observe justly that in drawing characters one is not to fall into satire . . .' It appears that Bruce had particularly asked Charlemont to write the letter in question, somewhat of a set piece.[2] But we can hardly believe that a rogues' gallery of the Irish political scene was sufficient inducement to so long and wearisome a journey. At all events, we find him again in Rome[3] in December 1754, having evidently either cancelled or curtailed his second visit to Dublin.

His final departure from Italy was delayed till the late summer of 1754. In company with Murphy, he made a detour to Barcelona, of which no account has survived. Thence to Bordeaux, where he became 'intimate' with Montesquieu.[4] 'Intimate'—the word is continually cropping up in the Charlemont records, and must not be accepted at its present enhanced value. His account of his conversations with the great thinker is given in full by Hardy, and may be passed over here. They were shown into his library, where the first object that presented itself was a table, 'at which he had apparently been reading the night before, a book lying upon it open, turned down, and a lamp extinguished. Eager to know the nocturnal studies of this great philosopher, we immediately flew to the book; it was a volume of Ovid's works, containing his elegies, and open at one of the most gallant poems of that master of love. Before we could overcome our surprise, it was greatly increased by the entrance of the president [Montesquieu] . . .'

They discussed Irish politics together, and Montesquieu expressed himself in favour of a legislative Union with Gt Britain. His interest in the matter may have been stimulated by the fact that his secretary was an Irishman. In turn, it may well have stimulated the young nobleman to reflect that here was a foreign savant who held reasoned opinions on matters domestic to which he himself had as yet given hardly a thought.

In the spring of 1754 he was in Paris. His younger brother Francis Caulfeild writes in May that he would like to join him in France.[5] Brother Francis had already, though not entirely by his own fault, given James a certain amount of cause for anxiety. In Adderley's letters to Italy, Francis is usually referred to as 'the Governor', a family joke which alludes to the Charlemont Fort. Oddly enough, the jocular title was mooted as a reality some years later, when the real Governor, a Captain Johnston, offered Francis the reversion of the post as part of a tortuous scheme of military jobbery.[6] The long series of attempts to find brother Francis a congenial billet in the scheme of things ended only with his untimely death in 1775. He had already figured in Charlemont's first political venture, the Armagh election of 1753, of which the immediate issue had not been altogether happy. Three years earlier Adderley had written 'I believe before I leave this for the North I shall enter him in the College'.[7] Immediately after the election fiasco he was to sit for his degree 'and will I believe take it with credit'.[8] Adderley suggests putting him to the study of the law. Four months later, as Charlemont has made no comment on this suggestion, he begs leave to remind his Lordship, 'for really I know not what to do. This town swarms more than ever with profligate young men, & tho' the Governor is extremely well inclined, yet I fear they will laugh him into folly'.[9]

. Brother Francis seems to have seen his own case in much the same light. 'At present', he writes to James, 'I am endeavouring to apply to a little reading . . . and . . . also to gain some knowledge of French, but I am unavoidably interrupted by many engagements which I know it is my interest to fly from.'[10] It sounds very like the elder brother's own predicament a few years earlier. But there was no Murphy to suggest a similar cure. Adderley did not consider their cases parallel, or perhaps he merely felt that, financially speaking, the Grand Tour was wasted on a younger son. When Charlemont had arrived in London, he wrote 'The Governor is very desirous to wait on your Lordship in London; how agreeable that may be to you I do not know; . . .' He adds that in his opinion Francis has not resolution sufficient to resist the inevitable temptations. In any case 'the Pest of Party has laid fast hold upon him' and Adderley, like the trimmer and temporiser he was, was finding his hand of cards difficult to play.[11] He continues to harry his stepson on the matter: will he please get Murphy to write to Francis, 'that I may be at some certainty about him' regarding the visit to London. It finally took place, and no very terrible consequences seem to have flowed from it.

Of Charlemont's sojourn in Paris Hardy gives few particulars. Evidently it made little impression on him. Montesquieu had travelled from Bordeaux a little before him, and with him and other savants Charlemont improved the occasion. As regards Montesquieu, he was only just in time to do so, for he left the philosopher in the first stages of an illness of which he shortly died. For Paris itself he seems never to have had any feeling: by January 1755 he was in London.

All through January and February Adderley bombarded him with weekly and even more frequent letters,[12] a strenuous correspondence-course to cram him for the ordeal of the Irish political arena. It is not altogether surprising that Charlemont was in no great hurry to return home. He loitered in and around London.[13] He spent a good deal of money, though exactly what he did with it is unknown. But he settled one hundred pounds a year on Murphy 'till such time as, by preferment or otherwise, he shall be in possession of five hundred pounds a year'. After putting his hand to the home-made indenture, he scribbled 'I'll settle this affair in a more proper manner as soon as I can inform myself of the legal method'. And Murphy endorsed it: 'Received this high compliment and great mark of tender friendship and goodness from my dearest friend, Lord Charlemont, this 17th of May, 1755, in

London, soon after our return from our tour of nine years travels.' Though it was a pension, he had not been pensioned off.[14]

On the 7th of October, 1755, Charlemont took his seat in the Irish House of Lords.[15] The newly-appointed Viceroy, the Marquis of Hartington, was a personal friend; and accordingly, as Charlemont observes in his political autobiography, 'the outset of my politics gave room to suppose that my life would have been much more courtly than it afterward proved'. He is not using the word 'courtly' in reference to personal, but rather to political demeanour. 'The debate lasted from two in the evening till past 12 that night when the court lost the question by 4; the numbers on the country-side being 122 to 118.'—Thus Adderley to Charlemont in 1753. The opposition of 'court' to 'country',[16] and the large numbers involved in this particular division, make it clear that not only were the issues thought to be definite, but they were also felt to be important. The terminology is not that of thirty years later, but it seems to represent something similar. How similar, and how real the conflict was, is a matter of some interest.

Until the Viceroyalty of Townshend in 1767, the Viceroy was not normally resident in Ireland. He arrived to open Parliament and, having seen the session through, returned home as speedily as possible. In his absence he committed the government of the country to a number of Lords Justices. In their hands most of the real power rested. The Archbishop of Armagh was normally *ex officio* one of this commission. The necessary votes in the House of Commons were provided by a small body of men known as the 'Undertakers', a handful of large borough owners who between them commanded a majority. This support was not given for nothing: it was exchanged for patronage, and the more important undertakers at least, sat with the Primate as Lords Justices.

'These men,' says Charlemont, 'were, as everyone knows, styled "Undertakers"; and justly were they so, as from education, and from habit, they certainly were well fitted to preside at the funeral of the common weal'.[17] We may expand his witticism a little further, and observe that the body politic was at this time racked with two contending afflictions, the Stone and the Boyle. George Stone, the Primate, was an energetic politician and head of the English or court interest. Henry Boyle, a descendant of the great Earl of Cork, had been Speaker of the House of Commons since 1733, and owing partly to personal jealousy of Stone, was leading the patriotic party.

Though personal in its origins, this conflict assumed a much wider importance. It came to a head in 1753, when there was open conflict between the Irish Parliament and the English Cabinet over the right of disposal of surplus Irish revenue. The English interest was defeated in Parliament, and the Dublin populace carried flaming torches before the Speaker's carriage. But a defeat of the Government in the Irish Parliament meant only that the Government could not do what it wished to do; it did not mean that anybody else could take office and carry out another programme. The relation between executive and legislature was in England itself sufficiently nebulous at this period. In Ireland it was virtually non-existent. The most that Boyle and his friends could do was to make the financial side of government unworkable for those in power: when that point was reached, those in power would have to come to terms.

H

This state of affairs is partly responsible for the Irish tradition of obstruction in politics. It explains why Irishmen venerate Grattan, who spent his whole life in opposition with hardly the prospect or the desire of office,[18] not as a politician, but as a *statesman*, and justly so. All through the eighteenth century the British Government was attempting to rule Ireland through a group of men whose economic interests, and whose national self-respect, it was continually injuring by the enactments of the British Parliament, devoted to British prestige and the imperatives of mercantile economics. It was not surprising that the result was a series of fissiparous growths of opposition. Boyle's parliamentary rebellion was the first serious manifestation since the old Irish had been crushed for ever at the Boyne. No matter that it was ignorant of things Gaelic and hostile to things Catholic: it stood for control by Irishmen, and that is sufficient. Nor did it lack theoretical preparation: the Drapier's letters, Berkeley's *Querist* and the pamphlets of Lucas ensured that Boyle stood for something bigger than he knew or intended.

Charlemont was first drawn into the conflict in his absence, when Adderley entered young Francis for Armagh in Boyle's interest, under the very nose of the Primate, whose nominee was William Brownlow. The experience was expensive for Charlemont, heart-rending (no less) for Adderley, and certainly vexatious for poor brother Francis, who was defeated. Adderley's pen splutters with fury;[19] Stone is likened to Wolsey, the pot draws attention to the 'corruption' of the kettle, bewails the wind which carried one of Stone's voters from England in the nick of time, and devotes to perdition a certain Mr John Preston, who repeatedly assured

Francis of his support, and finally turned the scale by
his single vote for Brownlow. One unfortunate, Mr
Thomas Butler, was dragged from his sick-bed at
Stone's orders to vote, and died a day or two later of
his exertions, while three of Adderley's voters were ill
and stayed in bed or in England. But Adderley's most
fervent prayer was answered, for later in the same
letter, after recording the treachery of Mr Preston, he
hears the news of his sudden death. The mortality in
this epic contest was high, yet one feels that it might
have been higher, had Adderley commanded Stone's
resources for total war.

The subsequent history of some of the protagonists
is so illuminating that it should not be passed over.
Brownlow, who had entered Parliament as the tool of
Stone, had no sooner taken his seat than he pursued an
independent and apparently incorruptible line of his
own. He was rapidly forgiven by Charlemont, and
they remained for forty years on the best of terms.
Charlemont supported Brownlow's re-election in 1776,
and Brownlow played a conspicuous part in the Volunteer movement and attained the distinction of having
his name coupled with Grattan's and Charlemont's in
patriotic songs and toasts. The Primate's most important allies among the undertakers were the Ponsonby
family. The elder of them, Speaker Ponsonby, seems to
have died unregenerate in 1787, but his son and others
of the clan took patriotic parts. In 1794 Charlemont
commends them for 'honour, spirit, and integrity', and
in 1795 his opinion is that they have 'acted a manly,
consistent, and truly disinterested part'. Four of the
family voted against the Union, and none for it. The
implications of this typical progression may be passed
over for the present.

On his return from abroad, Charlemont was drawn into this embroilment in the character of mediator. Adderley had hinted before his arrival that in his opinion 'there is no one better qualified for so good a work than your lordship'.[20] 'My alliance with the Ponsonby family on one side, and on the other . . . an old family friendship for Mr Boyle'[21] alike impelled him to fill the role. Peace was restored in 1756, but, as Charlemont sourly observes in his memoirs, the most important provisions of the treaty were agreed upon behind his back. They included the Earldom of Shannon and three thousand pounds for thirty-one years for Mr Boyle, and 'various other emoluments to his followers'.[22] Brother Francis came in for a cornetcy without pay, which Charlemont had not asked for and which in the event caused more trouble than it was worth. In 1757 Francis was peacefully returned for Armagh.

Charlemont regards this episode, unsatisfactory as its upshot had been, and in spite of the undignified dignity of his own part in it, as a turning-point in the country's politics.[23] The lesson 'that government might be opposed with success' had been learnt. Even if Boyle were enjoying his well-earned repose in the Lords, there were others in the offing who had learnt his tactics without adopting his principles. For such people, whatever their social origins, Charlemont kept a vigilant look-out.

His political influence, apart from the imponderable quantity owing to his personal character and his record, was limited by his own seat in the Lords, and the two seats in the Commons which were filled by the Borough of Charlemont. At this date, these latter were occupied by Adderley and by Charlemont's uncle, the Honourable John Caulfeild, and so they remained till the death of George II. On his own account, Charlemont embarked on a maiden parliamentary venture, a 'bill for the better regulating of juries'. The preparations were evidently a penance to him, and on the very point of speaking to his own bill, he was struck down again by rheumatism, and remained incapable of business for two years. There may indeed be some causal connexion between the attempt and the attack, for he never again succeeded in speaking in public.[24] In spite of an 'eager desire' to become a public speaker, his nervous disposition defeated every effort to conquer the weakness. He might get his speech by heart, he might study every point in the debate till he was perfectly accomplished, but all was in vain. 'The aggregate of those very men, whom singly and individually I despised, was sufficient to terrify me from my purpose.' Only when anger or indignation had brought him impromptu to his feet, was he able to jerk out a few words 'which my friends have assured me were not inadequate'.[25] He is puzzled to account for this infirmity. Vanity, he concludes, rather than modesty, is probably at the root of it. If vanity it was, there was later to be some vicarious satisfaction in the thought that under his aegis the voice of Grattan was first heard in College Green.

The extent to which he had already become the admired of all beholders is not easy to account for on any basis of solid achievement. But it is reflected in the award of an honorary Doctorate of Laws in Dublin University in July 1755. We may guess that Thomas Leland the historian had a hand in this honour, for he had been tutor to brother Francis and in 1756 dedicated his translation of Demosthenes to Charlemont, a compliment which may have caused the would-be-orator a twinge of mental pain. Ten years later, in 1765, it was Leland who was apparently most concerned in giving Samuel Johnson for the first time the title by which he is best known.[26] It is more than possible that Charlemont, in his turn, was an agent in this manoeuvre, which reflects, perhaps, even more honour on the University than it does on Johnson.

In 1761 a performance of the *Beggars' Opera* took place at Carton, in which Charlemont played Peachum. Lady Louisa Conolly was Lucy, and other participants were Marlay (by now a Dean), Lord Powerscourt, Mr Conolly and the Countess of Kildare. No doubt there were other similar occasions, for theatricals and opera were a feature of Irish society. In 1764 Charlemont was asked by his fellow-Governors of the Rotunda to engage a female singer in London[27] for the assembly rooms in Dublin. And in 1756 he had subscribed fourteen guineas to Bishop Pococke's fund for the restoration of St Canice's Cathedral, Kilkenny. We regret to record that only five peers contributed, and that Charlemont's subscription was not the lowest of the five.

The remaining years of the reign of George II were comparatively stagnant in Irish politics. Charlemont's illness prevented him, in any case, from playing an active part. But the illness was not without its political effect. The only doctor who was able to give him relief was Charles Lucas, who was at least as interested in patriotic politics as in medicine. In spite of a chronic weakness ('for he was always carried into, and out of the House, being so enfeebled by the gout, that he could hardly stand for a moment') he was evidently able to heal others. The wry and tortured statue by the great sculptor Smyth, which stands in the Dublin City Hall, suggests his power over an audience. When Charlemont met him first, he had withdrawn to

England to escape the subservient Irish Parliament whose wrath he had aroused by his patriotic pamphlets. Later he returned, sat for the City of Dublin, and lived near Charlemont at Clontarf. We may be sure that a good deal of political infusion was mixed with his ministrations to his patient.

Charlemont had not yet formed the most important resolution of his life, 'that it was my indispensable duty to live in Ireland'. Until he makes it, we may defer any description of his domestic arrangements in Dublin. He had a house in Hertford Street, London; he was frequently at Harwich; he is heard of in Aix-les-Bains[28]. In December 1756 Mrs Delany meets in Spring Gardens, London, '. . . Dr Barber, who is going to quit his charge, Lord Charlemont, and return to Ireland next week; Lord C continues in a very weak way.' Mrs Delany, at Delville, Glasnevin, was also a neighbour of Charlemont at Clontarf, and a little later we hear of pineapples from the Clontarf gardens being sent to her as far away as Mount Panther in County Down, by Charlemont's orders. By the autumn of 1759 she is writing from Delville: 'Thursday, Lord Charlemont, his brother and sisters, dined here. He is perfectly recovered, and a very agreeable (ugly) man—sensible, lively, and polite. I wish he would fall in love with Miss Mary Hamilton, as she would make him a very proper wife.'[29]

His wanderings at this time may probably have been largely due to a genuine need for changes of air and water. But they seem to show a natural disinclination to settle down on one side or the other of the Irish Sea. Recovery brought the first signs of decision. Soon after the date of Mrs Delany's letter, he allowed himself to be elected a Governor of the Rotunda Hospital.[30] He was

not the man to take on such a position without the
intention of living up to it, and the minutes of the
Hospital's Board bear this out. In the same year
Chambers had published the plans of the Casino. No
building had yet taken place, and it was still doubtful
where, if anywhere, the dream was to take tangible
shape. From now on it became increasingly certain that
it would be in Ireland.

With the return of health came renewed activity.
He returned to opposition in the Lords in 1759. The
Duke of Bedford was Viceroy, and Stone was again in
the ascendant. In February 1760 a French squadron
appeared in Belfast Lough and captured Carrickfergus
Castle. 'The wretched castle of Carrickfergus', Charlemont calls it, 'whose whole defence consisted in a half-
ruined wall'.[31] One of the largest and most impressive
Norman castles in Ireland fell an unprepared and easy
victim. But the time occupied in taking it enabled the
citizens of Belfast to put their town in a state of defence.
There was an acute shortage of British troops, and the
army that faced the French was essentially a people's
army, and very much *ad hoc*.

'As I was lieutenant of the county of Armagh [he had
been appointed in 1748, when barely twenty] I thought
it my duty to repair to the invaded country . . .' 'The
appearance of the peasantry, who had thronged to its
defence, many of whom were of my own tenantry, was
singular and formidable.' By the time he arrived the
French had evacuated the Castle, and Charlemont's
role was to look after the wounded General Flobert and
twenty of his men. It was a gentlemanly business.
There were parties in Belfast; parties in Dublin. The
Viceroy's permission for Flobert to go to France on
parole. Lord Charlemont, too, happened to be going to

London, and so they went together. Flobert gave
Charlemont his money to keep safe from highwaymen
'who would not, he imagined, attack me'. More parties
in London. The naval commander, Thurot, who escaped
at Carrickfergus only to fall in an engagement with
Hawke, was, it seems, an Irishman whose real name
was Farrell.[32] One wonders whether his treatment
would have been as gentlemanly as Flobert's. Be that
as it may, the Irish Catholics gave no sign on this occasion of sympathy with France. Already the first signs
of alleviation of the penal laws had appeared; and for
this it is only fair to give some credit to the detested
Primate Stone. But more than that: 'singular and
formidable' as the armed peasantry of Ulster had
appeared, 'from such men' in Charlemont's opinion
'the renown of the Irish Volunteers might even then
have been foreseen'.

On his arrival in Carrickfergus he had been assured
by 'a few ancient matrons of the place . . . in terms at
least as positive as querulous, that the violation of
their property was not the only species of violation
which they had to lament. He condoled with them; but
to remedy their complaints was, of course, beyond his
power.'[33] But almost immediately he was presented
with an occasion on which it was possible to redress
the wrongs of the ladies. George the Second died on
October 25th. His son, on his accession, found himself
a bachelor, an omission which he speedily resolved to
repair. A number of Irish peeresses made haste to
London to attend the marriage of their sovereign to the
Princess of Mecklenburgh-Strelitz. Judge, therefore, of
their dismay when they were informed by the Duchess
of Bedford that there was no place for them in the
ceremonial arrangements.

Now the Duchess had for the past four years been consort to the Viceroy of Ireland, in which capacity she had not met with Charlemont's approval. Charlemont had consistently opposed the Duke, 'a man of excellent parts, though deficient in common sense'. 'By thwarting his temper, her wily grace was wont to provoke him, which was not difficult, to hasty, rude, and even savage expressions of anger . . . Of this lady', he concludes, '(the most artful and dangerous of women) I am almost afraid to speak.'[34]

But he was not afraid to fight. The Irish Peeresses appealed to him in their dire extremity (he was then in London). 'At my age the commands of ladies were not to be disputed . . .' Charlemont was in his element. He tried to whip up the Irish lords then in London, but 'the honour of their country was an idea totally foreign to their thoughts'. He applied to the new Viceroy, Halifax, who promised to lay the matter before the King. The King referred it to the Council, and would Lord Charlemont find some precedents in the matter? For a moment it looked as though all were lost, for 'the rights of Ireland, in this respect, were not better known by me than those of China'. Luckily he remembered in time that an acquaintance had written a pamphlet on the subject. 'After an uneasy night, at seven in the morning I waited upon him.' Armed with his precedents, he hastened back to have them laid before the Council. The Council failed to reach agreement, but the King in Council settled the matter out of hand in favour of Ireland. The Irish peeresses, who had laid out large sums in finery, were assured of their reward.[35]

Charlemont saw to it that at least one of each grade of the Irish nobility should take her place immediately after her counterpart in the British peerage. Some days

later, having thus consolidated his advantage, he was
approached by Lady Hervey with a proposal from
Bute that in the approaching Coronation the entire
Irish peerage should walk as a separate body. He saw,
or fancied he saw, a catch in this proposal: nevertheless
'I thought that walking at the Coronation upon those
terms, as a distinct peerage, was by no means un-
favourable to Ireland, since a distinct and separate
legislature was thereby strongly marked'. And so it
was: 'we walked as an independent body representing
a separate kingdom.'

Unreal and trivial as the business may appear to us,
it was real enough and serious enough to him. A meticu-
lous and ceremonial legalism remained, we shall find, a
mark of the Irish patriotic movement. This courtly
contest was an example of the prevailing punctilio, an
extreme example no doubt, but quite in character.

With these military and courtly laurels fresh upon
his brow, he returned to Dublin and to the new Parliament. The politics of the next few years are more than
ordinarily dull,[36] and concern us only as they impinge
upon his altered family circumstances. The new members for Charlemont were brother Francis and a Mr
Moore, the latter also a relative. The causes of Adderley's disappearance seem to go back some little distance
in time. In August of 1760 Charlemont wrote to Adderley a carefully-composed letter of which he kept a fair
copy.[37] 'I have had some Reasons', he wrote 'not to
think quite so highly of you as I formerly have done . . .'
What these reasons were he is far from stating clearly:
indeed in this letter, 'the most disagreeable I ever
wrote' he is so ill at ease that the more words he uses
the less trenchant do his charges become. But he does
mention more or less openly 'the Transaction with

Miss Ward', 'your manner of behaving in Parliament last Winter' and 'the Affair of my Brother's marriage'. Clearly he suspects Adderley of disingenuousness, and though he protests that he could not wish for a better business manager than his step-father, it is precisely his business affairs which he is taking out of Adderley's hands.

One well-informed authority[38] suspects that both Adderley and Charlemont wanted to marry Miss Ward in 1758 or so. Neither of them did, but this may have exacerbated the aftertaste. Whether the marriage of brother Francis was haunted by the same spectre is unknown. As for Adderley's conduct in Parliament, any suspicions of his political rectitude were immeasurably strengthened when, in November, Adderley wrote to Charlemont offering 'seven or eight hundred pounds' for his seat. 'You ought to know me well enough to be very certain that I never should make a pecuniary bargain for any favour in my power to bestow, and least of all for a borough.'[39] Adderley, on this occasion at least, had thoroughly mistaken his man. Yet the edge of this high principle is by modern standards somewhat blunted by his admission that 'with regard to the borough . . . I thought myself indispensably obliged to favour my own nearest relations.' He had indeed intended Uncle John and Mr Moore for Charlemont. But the day before, a letter in the large and childish handwriting of Sir Capel Molyneux of Castledillon, had explained that, for a mysterious reason tellable only by word of mouth, Sir Capel regretted his inability to use his county interest in favour of brother Francis at Armagh.[40] Two such disappointments was too much, and so 'I now find myself obliged to reserve a seat for my brother'. But he wishes

Adderley luck in another direction, and sure enough in
1761 we find him sitting for his home town of Bandon.
The whole episode is an object-lesson in Charlemont's
slow but steady advance from the position quite happily held by his relatives, that boroughs, political and
social position and influence, were private property to
be used as their 'owners' thought fit. They, in their own
eyes, found themselves by God's grace in a position to
make the country comfortable for themselves. In Charlemont's mind the conception of a sacred trust was
gradually growing. It was an idea which never quite
lost a certain pompousness, but within its limits it was
perfectly genuine.

In 1760 brother Francis sought Charlemont's approval of his intended marriage. Charlemont, without
knowing the lady, replied[41] that he had already made
it clear that he considered the union improvident, that
he supposed that Francis wanted rather endorsement
of an already determined course of action, than advice.
And if by endorsement he could be understood to mean
merely his best wishes for all happiness, then he freely
gave it from the bottom of his heart. It may be conjec-
tured that Francis would have liked the endorsement
to take the form of a financial settlement. If so, Charlemont ignored the hint, which he was probably in no
position to act upon. In what way Adderley trans-
gressed remains unknown, and speculation is idle.

Francis was by this time a Captain, and in 1762 was
stationed in Clonmel. Some disturbance taking place
at Cashel, Francis was discovered absent without leave,
and on his return was put under arrest. His superior
officer was a relative, Lord Drogheda, and the difficulty
of the situation was aggravated by their mutual animosity. He seems, too, to have been troubled by the

problem of keeping his wife in barracks, which he did not wish to do though she, it seems, insisted upon it. He implores Charlemont to do something to help, at least to have him transferred to another command. James did his best to patch things up, but Francis as a military man was never altogether a success. No doubt he ultimately borrowed enough money to buy himself out.[42]

What with Mrs Delany's pious hope that he might fall in love with Miss Hamilton, and Adderley's manoeuvres in the matter of Miss Ward, Charlemont's way was set about with snares. We may be sure that the drawing-rooms of Dublin speculated along similar lines. His old friend Marlay, from his County Down rectory, rallies him repeatedly on the point, coupling his name, perhaps merely in fun, with that of a Miss Otto. 'I find', he writes, 'many people believe that you are now determinded to bind yourself with the marriage chain . . .'[43] Charlemont seems to have been nettled by this, but perhaps that, too, was an attitude assumed in fun. He sent Marlay an 'essay or rather rhapsody on love and tenderness . . . very pretty and ingenious'. Such is Marlay's verdict, but he goes on to observe that 'reason requires a long long time before it can form a true judgment of a mistress or a friend'.[44] Evidently Charlemont had been in the habit of inveighing against the married state, for Lord Bruce, writing to tell him of his own approaching nuptials, says 'I know your thoughts too well on the marriage state in general: I only beg to have your good wishes . . .'[45]

This would be well enough if it were all. But an anonymous correspondent, who had written to Charlemont before on political matters, who is evidently his social equal and well-known to him, has an interesting tale to unfold. Writing from London on June 12th,[46] he begins: 'I was formerly chosen by you as a Confidant between you and a most worthy Lovely Friend; now, a very amiable one of yours chooses me between you and her . . .' The lady, it seems, is uneasy at not having heard from Charlemont for three months. And, still more interesting, the 'little friend' is 'intirely exposed to the accidents and uncertainty of both your lives . . .' 'I have seen *it*', the writer continues 'and I really admire your manufacture prodigiously; nothing can exceed it; vous n'avez pas épargné l'étoffe . . .' It is further emphasised that the lady has no ambition to control the 'little friend's' fortune: she desires only the security of knowing that 'it' will be provided for. The correspondent, having promised to write to Charlemont, concludes by enquiring when he may be expected to come over again to London.

As no further complaints from this quarter have come down to us, we may be allowed to presume the best, and perhaps in passing to regret that we know so little of the episode. That we know of it at all is probably owing to an oversight. The second Earl went through his father's papers, and admitted having destroyed several[47] which had already been bound and indexed as dealing with financial matters. They may perhaps have had to do with the endowment of this distant slip of mortality. It certainly seems probable that the letter quoted must have escaped the son's enquiring eye. It will be best to judge both father and son with a like indulgence.

NOTES

1. HMC, I, 383, quoted from BM Add. MSS. 22, 394. ff. 33, 35. I have been unable to inspect this in person, and cannot therefore be sure whether the date has been correctly transcribed.

2. Ibid., 186.

3. Ibid., 187.

4. H, I, 60 sqq.

5. HMC, I, 194.

6. RIA MSS., IX, Nos. 94, 98, 99.

7. Ibid., IX, 10.

8. HMC, I, 190.

9. RIA MSS., IX, 14.

10. HMC, I, 194.

11. His own words in RIA MSS., IX, 26.

12. Mostly given in HMC, I, 198 sqq.

13. He seems to have spent some time, on and off, at Harwich, to judge by letter-headings of this period. See also HMC, I, 10 n.

14. HMC, I, 217.

15. The date is given as 1754 in many authorities. It is here corrected from the *House of Lords Journals*.

16. Compare HMC, I, 198: 'all the court and country pamphlets'.

17. H, I, 217.

18. With, perhaps, the rather doubtful exception noticed later, on p. 169.

19. HMC, I, 188 sqq.

20. Ibid., 198.

21. Ibid., 6.

22. Ibid.

23. A letter to Lord Powerscourt, which must be of this time, declares that 'I am sick of Ireland and of almost everything in it', but that he has been happily able to plague the primate. This is an interesting sidelight on what he thought at the time of this first essay in politics. There is here no trace of the grand manner. HMC, II, 382.

24. The only recorded exception is at the end of the National Convention of 1783. Verbatim reports of the Lords' Debates are lacking.

25. Ibid., 9.

26. See the letter given in Boswell's *Johnson*.

27. Rotunda Minutes. In 1789 he was a member of the Musical Committee: ibid.

28. HMC, I, 228.

29. Mrs Delany, *Life and Correspondence*: III, 455, 511, 566. There is no other trace of the plural 'sisters'.

30. 2nd November, 1759. For this and other information from the Rotunda Minute-books I am indebted to Mr C. P. Curran.

31. HMC, I, 10 sqq. and notes.

32. So, at least, says the anonymous author of the official guide to Carrickfergus Castle, Belfast, 1936. The fact was unknown to Charlemont and apparently to Lecky.

33. So Hardy, I, 114. The original is omitted from HMC, I, 13, and the MS. (RIA, VII) reads 'and some old women *told me* they had been ravished'.

34. HMC, I, 10 n.

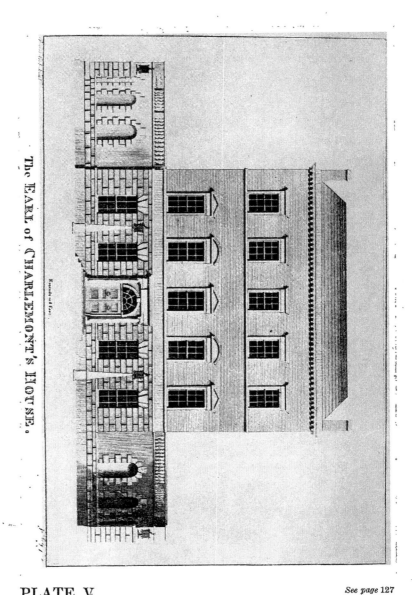

PLATE V

See page 127

CHARLEMONT HOUSE: ELEVATION

From Pool and Cash: *Views . . . in the City of Dublin*, 1780

35. Ibid., 15 sqq.

36. We may, however, note from RIA MSS. XII, 37, that 'I dined yesterday, by way of Amusement, at my Lord Mayor's, and was seated between the Law and the Gospel . . . drank the English History quite through'. It would seem that Stone was sitting at the head of the table. This, a draft of a letter to Marlay, gives a refreshing angle on his life. Would that more of his letters to close friends at this period had survived.

37. RIA MSS., IX, 81.

38. R. Elrington Ball: article on Adderley already cited. He does not mention Miss Ward by name.

39. RIA MSS., IX, 86.

40. Ibid., 85.

41. HMC, I, 256.

42. RIA, MSS., XII, 31.

43. HMC, I, 271: RIA MSS., XII, 32, etc. etc.

44. HMC, I, 272, top of page. Miss Otto is said to have been an Italian singer.

45. Ibid., 268.

46. RIA MSS., XII, 26.

47. e.g. RIA MSS., X, Nos. 70, 72, 78, 83. It is still evident that appended to the last of these was a large seal.

I

CHAPTER VI

MARINO AND CHARLEMONT HOUSE

A chance phrase taken from its context, may, it is well known, give rise to the most diverting misconceptions. When we read an allusion by Parker to 'the Venus, that Virepoyl was to bed',[1] our attention is sharply arrested, only to be released again when we notice that the next line continues: 'in a frame'. But these aberrant readings are sometimes surprisingly apt. 'I have purchased', says Parker a few months later, 'the Seven Liberal Arts; they are now putting in order[2] . . .' The vast implications of this remark are quickly modified, no doubt, as soon as we realise that a picture or a group of statuary is all that is intended.

Yet, in a sense, Charlemont was indeed employing Parker and his colleagues to purchase the seven liberal arts, so far as that might be possible. He knew as well as any that something more than mere cash was called for; and the imponderable part of the price he was equally ready to pay.

The authors of the earliest valuable picture-book of Dublin,[3] allude to 'an edifice' as 'the most lasting monument of human greatness'. On reflection, we may decide that in practice there is no art-form more perishable than a building. Certainly we must insert a caveat lest it should be thought that Charlemont's motive was the commemoration of his own greatness. But, 'When, in the revolution of States and Empires, the power and riches of ancient nations have been annihilated, and even the remembrance of them lost, buildings although in ruins, remain faithful monuments of their former splendour.' In this quotation from the same source we are on surer ground. Part of Charlemont's motive was to commemorate the society of which he was a member. King William, that legendary figure who has played so many roles in Irish thought, was now appearing as an apostle of classic order. If Charles II was a baroque figure, William of Orange was almost palladian. Grinling Gibbons's equestrian statue of the victor of the Boyne, standing in front of the Palladian colonnades of the Parliament House, was, if the verbal play may be forgiven, the palladium of the Anglo-Irish state. Secularism and stability were, it was hoped, the keynotes of the *status quo*.

Only the sense of some such purpose as this could have enabled such a man as Charlemont, with his background of travel in long-settled lands, to settle and build in Ireland. Had it merely been a question of purchasing the liberal arts for cash, the obvious course was to build palaces and garden temples in England or even in Italy, on Irish rents. There was something heroic in the plan of imposing classic order on this rainy and boggy little island on the farthest fringe of Europe. The cynical obverse of the medal is that it was easier for an Irish nobleman to make a figure of consequence in Ireland than anywhere else. Lest the ideal interpretation seems to the reader too far-fetched, we may observe that the unimaginative Francis Hardy, Charlemont's biographer, called Marino 'the child of patriot, civil wisdom, as well as the graces'.[4]

There is no evidence that Charlemont occupied the house in Jervis Street after his return from Italy. Just before his return (January 1755) we find Adderley suggesting that he should occupy Mr Bernard's house, as

suitable to his rank in Dublin.[5] This would have been a
family arrangement, but it came to nothing. In the
previous June, however, Adderley had written to offer
him 'a house at Donnycarney' which he had just built
and now wished his stepson to accept as a present.
There were drawbacks, to be sure: the land was not
rent-free, and there was no furniture save a telescope
and a concave mirror. But it was a handsome offer and
Charlemont accepted it. He seems to have renamed it
'Marino' almost immediately.[6]

Marino House was and remained an unpretentious
dwelling giving an impression of comfort and hospitality from outside. It is alleged that Adderley's building
embodied some part of a house built by Basil, Cromwell's Attorney-General for Ireland. Marino House was
completely demolished in the early nineteen-twenties,
and this can no longer be verified. But from the plan
it seems more than possible.[7] When Charlemont first
accepted it, it was a small house. It grew under his
hand: Chambers, for example, furnished designs for
additions which were carried out, forming wings to
north and south.[8] But it never became large, and any
additions served to confirm its rambling and hap-
hazard character. It was evidently a most attractive
habitation, but not being a show-piece it unfortunately
came in for less documentation than the Casino or
Charlemont House.

The estate was modest in size[9] but very varied in its
attractions. From the shores of Dublin Bay—at its
nearest point less than two miles from College Green—
it rose in a gentle wooded slope, on which the main
house stood, to higher ground on which there was and
still is a walled garden of nine acres. From the garden
southwards towards the house stretched a chain of

miniature lakes, and a little to the east of these the Casino was in due course built. When Charlemont first occupied it, the house was surrounded by farms for which he paid rent, and only gradually were they re-moulded and planted to form the demesne.[10]

In April 1755 Charlemont was, as we have already seen, in treaty with Vanvitelli for designs for garden-houses. The first such building to be erected at Marino was by an unknown designer, and came to be known, why, is not clear, as 'Rosamund's Bower'. An account of 1835[11] describes it as 'an erection in the enriched gothic style; the front representing a highly ornamental screen, adorned with tracery and niches: a noble pointed doorway with receding columns, and fretted mouldings, opens in the centre, and a crocketed pin-nacle a little retired conveys the idea of a spire; the interior has been fitted up to imitate the nave, and side aisles of a cathedral, with clustered columns, deeply moulded arches, and groined ceiling; the hearth at the upper end, has been, when perfect, a beautiful compo-sition of elaborate tracery; the light is admitted by four quaterfoil windows of stained glass, and the floor is constructed of marble in Mosaic; in its original perfect state, this edifice was supposed to present as pure a model of a Gothic, as the other did of a Grecian temple.' We may doubt it, in view of the date of erection and the fact that the Casino is, of course, not Greek in inspiration, but Roman.

Murphy viewed these improvements with misgiving and perhaps some jealousy. He writes[12] from London when Charlemont had barely arrived, 'It has been hinted to me that you are going to lay out Mony at Marino'. Evidently he had heard of the negotiations with Vanvitelli. The 'mony', he observes, would be

'much better laid out upon some other places'. When
he sees that Charlemont's heart is set upon building
there, he tries to dissuade him from spending more than
£200 or £250 at most on the place.[13] Possibly Rosa-
mond's Bower might have been built for that sum, but
even this is very doubtful.

The Bower stood at the head of the principal lake.
Among the other adornments mentioned in early accounts are 'moss-houses', 'rustic hermitages' ('the hermitage is nature itself'), 'rural alcoves' and 'a cane-
house constructed after the Eastern model'.[14] This last
we may surmise to have been the product of Chambers'
lighter moments.[15] Nor must we omit to record that
'There are sheep here with four, six and eight horns',
a startling feature reported by a trustworthy eye-
witness. After that it is a little easier to swallow the
marvels which Giraldus Cambrensis saw in Ireland.

It is clear from this description, and even from the
remnants of the layout which are still visible, that
Marino was designed from the first on the 'English' or
'natural' principle of gardening, after the school of
Pope, Shenstone and Capability Brown. This was, at
so early a date, somewhat exceptional in Ireland. Such
houses as Castletown and Saunders Grove had a large-
scale formal setting to match their architecture. Rosamund's Bower, too, is more to be regarded as a parallel
impulse to Strawberry Hill, than as an imitation of it.[16]
Not that Charlemont, even at this stage, was in any
sense a Goth. There is no evidence that he lavished on
the Bower anything like the time or the money or the
attention which he devoted to the Casino.[17] In England
at least, there are probably more classical country
houses in landscape settings than there are houses of
the same formal type with geometrical parterres and

ponds and rectilinear vistas. The landscape school was
not fundamentally opposed to the classical ideal. True
classicism recognises the existence of nature, and draws
a clear distinction between nature's works and works of
art. The contrast between the ordered building and its
picturesque background is deliberate, even if the
latter's artlessness is artfully contrived. Beyond the
laying-out of two regular terraces in front of the Casino,
no attempt was made to extend its formal element to
include the setting. Even now the wisdom of such
moderation is evident; even in its mutilated state the
park-land round the building makes a poignant contrast.[18]

There was another reason for this. Marino was never
really a *country* house. 'My health', says Charlemont,
'to which sea bathing and the social neighbourhood of
a metropolis were absolutely necessary, would not
allow me to settle on my estate in the north, and, without some pleasant and attractive employment, I
doubted whether I should have resolution enough to
become a resident . . .'[19] Marino satisfied all these needs.
It was, in fact, a suburban villa, exceptionally close to
Dublin. There was therefore every inducement to make
the miniature demesne as much like the country as possible. If one wished for perspective vistas, one could go
into Town. Dr Delany's house at Delville was equally
suburban, and there the classical temple with Swift's
inscription: 'Fastigia Despicit Urbis', looked down upon a meandering stream.[20] Grandeur was not the object
in either case.

During the early 1760s Charlemont divided his time
between Marino and London. But 'being thoroughly
sensible that it was my indispensable duty to live in
Ireland, [I] determined by some means or other to

attach myself to my native country'. Residence in Ireland he calls in the same passage 'the first of political
duties, since without it all others are impracticable.
Let it not be said that Ireland can be served in England.
It never was: and, even though we were to hope, a vain
hope, for the power of serving her there, we are but too
apt to lose the desire.' He would soon be tempted, he
adds, 'to affect to deride his native manners and
partialities. The Irishman in London, long before he
has lost his brogue, loses or casts away all Irish ideas,
and, from a natural wish to obtain the goodwill of those
with whom he associates, becomes, in effect, a partial
Englishman. Perhaps more partial than the English
themselves.' 'The resident Irishman may be of consequence even in England. The English Irishman never
can.' '. . . Ireland must be served in Ireland. The man
who lives out of his country is guilty of a perpetual
crime[21] . . .'

The logical consequence of all this was a town house
in Dublin. By 1762 he had chosen the site. Whether the
house was begun before or after the Casino, it was certainly finished first.[22] By 1763 Chambers had outlined
the design,[23] and by 1776, when Arthur Young visited
it, it was virtually complete.

Rutland Square, like Mecklenburgh or Brunswick in
London, is three-sided. The south-east corner opens
into Gardiner's Mall (Upper Sackville Street), and the
east side of the square is a main traffic artery. The
south side is occupied by the Rotunda Hospital, facing
away from the square, which rises behind it to its highest level on the north side. The site which Charlemont
chose occupied the centre of this north side, so that it
faced south down the hill over the Rotunda Gardens.
Such a situation lent itself to special treatment.

Almost all Dublin houses are faced in brick, though
a rusticated granite ground-storey is not unusual. Five
stories including basement is the rule. The total frontage of Charlemont House is 100 feet, roughly twice
that of most of its neighbours. It is faced in smooth-
jointed Arklow limestone, and presents three visible
stories to the street, the dormers of the top storey being concealed by the parapet. The gound-floor is rusticated, with a shallow columniated doorway and fan-
light, formerly flanked by a pair of obelisks for lamps.
This central block is set twenty feet behind the street
frontage, and connected to the adjoining houses by
sweep walls with niches,[24] terminating in piers which
carry wrought-iron lamps. These curtain-walls are each
a little more than the quarter-circle, so that they seem
almost to embrace the open space in front. The five
windows of the first floor are crowned with alternate
triangular and segmental pediments, and the building
is so scaled that its three storeys are equivalent to the
four of its next-door neighbours. The roof is concealed
from all near viewpoints. An interesting feature is that
each of the flanking houses has, in addition to a rusticated ground-floor which carries through the motif of
the curtain-walls, an extra cornice or string-course
carrying through the line of the Charlemont second-
storey lintels. In practice, the perspective effect is
rather to reinforce the Charlemont cornice, a good deal
bolder than is usual in Dublin houses.

Chambers originally suggested that the space in
front of the house should be enclosed by a grille with
gates at either end, but this never seems to have been
carried out. At the same early stage, it was still un-
decided whether the front should be mainly of brick or
entirely of stone. Charlemont's replies to Chambers's

letters have not survived, but from the latter we can
infer the amount of care which Charlemont took in
answering. When Chambers has alternative suggestions
to make, he gives them just so much explanation as
would stimulate a man well conversant with the art to
weigh the advantages. On more than one occasion he
gives alternative specifications for cheaper substitute-
materials,[25] but in every instance now traceable, his
patron declared for the real thing, cost what it might.

There is every reason to endorse a contemporary
description of the house as 'a well-designed mean, between the vast piles raised for magnificence, and those
smaller ones wherein convenience alone is considered'.[26]
The doyen of Dublin houses, Leinster House, stood
emphatically in its own grounds, as did also Moira
House on the southern Quays and Tyrone House.
Powerscourt House, an extremely impressive and lofty
pile, was always difficult to see in its narrow street.
Others such as Clonmell House, Northland House and
Antrim House were flush with their neighbours and
built of the same brick, distinguished only by being a
little larger, not always even by that. The nearest ana-
logue to Charlemont House was Belvedere House close
by, flanked by arches and commanding the vista of
North Great George's Street.

Designed by an architect who may never even have
been in Ireland, Charlemont House is not typical of
Dublin street architecture. But its influence can be
seen in subsequent work by native architects. Chambers, or more probably the trustees of the Rotunda
Estate, decided to treat the North side of Rutland
Square as a freely unified composition with Charlemont
House as centre. The congruity already observed on
the adjoining houses, diminishes with the distance from

PLATE VI See page 130

CHARLEMONT HOUSE

the Great Corridor, looking North; showing the bronze Mercury by
Giovanni di Bologna. From a photograph taken in 1865

the centre. A similar policy was adopted by Francis Johnston, or by the local builders, with regard to the Dobbin house in Armagh.[27] In design it owes much to Charlemont House, and the whole street block is treated as a roughly balancing composition. Again, there is the same decrease in uniformity away from the centre.

Symmetrical street and square-schemes like those of the Woods or Nash in England are almost unknown in Ireland, and quite unknown in Georgian times. Whatever may have been intended,[28] nothing of the kind happened in the period. Instead of the exact correspondence of Fitzroy Square, we have Rutland Square North or Merrion Square East. There are no geometrical circles or ellipses as in Bath or London or Edinburgh; instead we have the organic curves of Harcourt Street, the gradual angles of Pembroke Street-Hatch Street, or the bold sweep of the Liffey Quays and the two canals. Almost the only exceptions to this rule are Beresford Place, behind the Custom House, and Hardwicke Place, in front of St. George's Church.[29] Yet even here, none of the perspective approaches, though straight, are ever axial, nor do they approach their subject from any precise geometric angle.

There was something in the air of Ireland which prevented Irish Georgian, even when the buildings were erected from English drawings, from toeing an English or continental line. The latitude for idiosyncrasy in the ordinary street vernacular always remained greater, and when the moment arrived for a salient feature, the architect was free to make it more emphatic than it could have been in London. One has only to contrast Gandon's river-fronts with that of Chambers, even as it once was, to see that this is so.[30]

The plan of Charlemont House was rather more imposing than the exterior. A modest enough entrance hall was bounded on the left by an open colonnade leading into a large and well-lit waiting-room. To the left again of the small back-hall, the main staircase, the curved return of which projected beyond the main block, gave access to the drawing- and other rooms on the first floor. This staircase, with its delicate wrought-iron balustrades and half-dome ceiling, lit by lunettes, must always have been one of the principal beauties of the interior. It is now the only surviving one, though one or two mantels and ceilings remain *in situ*.[31]

The lot on which the house is built is nearly three times as deep as it is wide, and the use made of this space is perhaps the most remarkable feature. From the first the use of the whole site was planned. Behind the main staircase a long vaulted corridor ran northwards, ornamented on the left (west) side with niches, and on the right looking onto the garden. Half-way along, it widened into a square vestibule, and here there stood a bronze Mercury, superbly lit. Beyond, a short flight of stone steps led to the continuation of the corridor, which finally debouched into the famous 'Venus Library'. This, a smallish room, was nearly square in plan, with a small and very beautiful central dome, pierced by ten windows.[32] To the left on entering, another half-dome crowned the alcove in which stood the Venus. The inscription, misquoted from Dryden's Lucretius, ran

> Auspicious Queen of Love!
> Since then the race of every living thing
> Obeys thy power; since nothing new can spring
> Without thy warmth, without thy influence bear,
> Or beautiful, or graceful can appear,
> Be thou my aid!

CHARLEMONT HOUSE

the principal library with Volunteer relics. From a photograph taken in 1865

PLATE VII (*a*)

See page 130

CHARLEMONT HOUSE
the Venus Library. From a photograph taken in 1865

PLATE VII (*b*)

See page 130

Sketch-plan of Charlemont House: ground floor

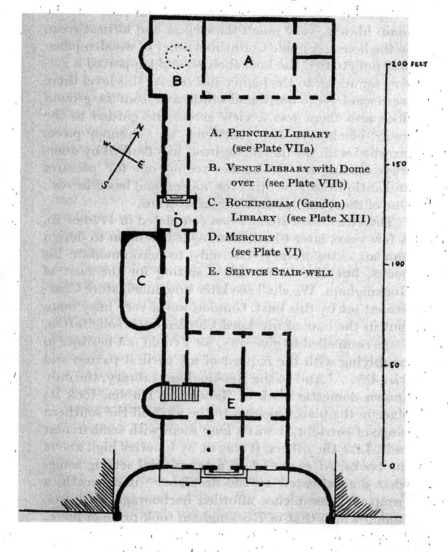

A. PRINCIPAL LIBRARY
   (see Plate VIIa)

B. VENUS LIBRARY with Dome
   over   (see Plate VIIb)

C. ROCKINGHAM (Gandon)
   LIBRARY   (see Plate XIII)

D. MERCURY
   (see Plate VI)

E. SERVICE STAIR-WELL

We are reminded of the parentheses in the journal of his Greek travels.

Opening to the right (eastwards) from this, was the main library, very much the largest and loftiest room in the house. A noble Corinthian order of wooden pilasters punctuated the bookshelves, and supported a gallery for access to the higher shelves. At this level there were windows to north and south, and from the ground floor also there was a view across the garden to the main block. At the east end the chimney-piece, crowned with the inevitable bust, was flanked by doorways leading to two smaller rooms, one for 'pictures and antiquities', the other for 'medals and bas-relievos'. One of these was his sanctum sanctorum.

Thus the house stood when completed in 1776 or so. A few years later Charlemont asked Gandon to design him an extra library, not only to accommodate his books, but also to furnish a setting for the bust of Rockingham. We shall see later how much store Charlemont set by this bust. Gandon was a very busy man, 'but in the case of my Lord Charlemont's solicitation, I was compelled to give way, for I could not hesitate in complying with the request of my earliest patron and friend[33] . . .' And so the Rockingham Library, the only known domestic work of Gandon in Dublin, took its place in the plan. Opening to the west off the southern range of corridor, it was a long room with semicircular ends. Like the others, it was lit by lunettes high above the books. At each end, in a ceremonial setting somewhat domesticated by the fireplaces[34] underneath, a group of three niches afforded harbourage for busts, among which that of Rockingham took pride of place. Murphy's heads of the Roman Emperors stood rank on rank round the cornice, and above their heads in

plasterwork, trophies, eagles and the letters S.P.Q.R.
completed the apotheosis. On the full implications of
all this we shall have more to say later.

His collection of books was the finest private library
that Ireland is ever likely to see, and one of the finest
ever brought together on this side of the Atlantic. It
will readily be seen that Charlemont House was designed not merely as a dwelling-house—for Marino was,
after all, not more than a mile and a half distant—but
as a repository for his books and pictures. Among the
latter were two by Hogarth; 'Judas returning the
Thirty Pieces of Silver', a more than doubtful Rem-
brandt; a portrait of Cesare Borgia, allegedly by Titian;
and a 'Dead Christ' by Annibale Caracci which may
perhaps have been authentic. A 'Tintoret', a 'Borgog-
none' and a 'Vandyke' are also mentioned. Whether
genuine or not, his pictures were commonly reckoned
the best collection in Dublin, and their attributions
afford evidence of his tastes.[35]

When Charlemont House, after serving from 1869
till the Treaty as the General Registrar's Office, was
handed over in 1929 encumbered with extra buildings
but still more or less intact, to the Dublin Corporation
for conversion as the Municipal Gallery of Modern Art,
it seems more than a pity that those responsible did
not remember that the house had originally been virtually a gallery of art. Though a scheme was put forward
for re-adapting it for that purpose, everything north of
the main block was finally destroyed.[36] The hall and
front rooms were knocked into one, and on the site of
the libraries and gardens the new gallery was built.
The original work rubs shoulders with some very thin
pastiche. Worse still, an unnecessary and uncomely
portico was erected in front, and the obelisks gratui-

tously abolished. Other irritating works of supereroga-
tion slightly affected the exterior. It is only just, however, to add that as a gallery the new buildings are a
model of their kind. Many worse fates have overtaken
Dublin houses; and there is something singularly apt
in the mere fact that Charlemont House has found its
final role as a gallery of modern art.

Some time in the year 1761 or 1762, Charlemont laid,
with what ceremony we know not, the first stone of the
Casino. A brass plate carried the date and an 'Inscription, importing that "this Building was erected as a
Testimony of Gratitude to Public and Private Virtue,
during the Administration of *William Pitt*; when the
Glory of the British Empire arrived at its highest
Pitch".'[37] Charlemont was then 33 or 34. We may wonder whether he knew that he had embarked on a virtual
life-work, destined to last till the time of a second
William Pitt, whose name Charlemont would come to
hold in detestation.

The wording of the inscription may sound misleading
to our unaccustomed ears. There was in fact nothing in
it which a patriotic Irishman might not, at that time,
have endorsed. The use by Anglo-Irishmen of such
terms as 'British', 'Irish' and 'English' is confusing,
and sometimes confused. But one or two broad lines
may be drawn. 'The British Parliament' meant what it
said, often in opposition to the Irish. The word 'Briton'
is sometimes used in distinction to 'Irishman'. A resolution of the Irish Lords and Commons of 1782, worded
by Grattan, speaks of a 'high sense and veneration
for the British character' and disclaims any intention of 'wounding the pride of the British nation'.[38]
In 1788 or so Charlemont's Belfast friend, Haliday,

CHARLEMONT HOUSE DUBLIN

See page 128

PLATE VIII

CHARLEMONT HOUSE

showing the corner of Rutland Square. Etching by James Malton, 1791

writes to him 'what a shabby race the British are at present'.[39]

But in general the use of the word 'British' is reserved for institutions rather than for people. The struggles of 1782–3 were concerned with extorting from the British a 'British' constitution for Ireland. And the 'Empire' was in 1762 a 'British' institution of which Irish Whigs might, even as Irishmen, feel themselves proud. We may perhaps compare the term 'republic' applied to the monarchical state, a usage which moderate Whigs dropped after 1791.

The Casino, begun under these auspices, remains essentially a private building, untainted by imperialist rhetoric of style. Indeed, so subtly is it proportioned that most visitors have no suspicion that it is nearly seventy feet square overall, and fifty feet in total height. The effect is miniature in spite of facts, in spite even of the generous dimensions of the Saloon. The building stands on a square podium surrounded by a deep area. To north and south the area is arched over to form flights of steps. On plinths stretching diagonally at each corner the four lions couchant[39a] keep guard. Beneath their front paws the terminations are carved into panels on which pairs of fauns support wide and shallow urns, carved with unexampled delicacy which weathering has rendered if anything more exquisite. Between them on east and west a balustrade screens the area.

The building is a greek cross on plan, and from outside appears to be of one storey only.[40] This trick of scaling, so deftly managed, is the principal element in creating the illusion of smallness. The entablature is basically square on plan, broken out beyond the arms of the cross, and carried by twelve columns. The order

K

is an italianised Roman Doric, unfluted but enriched on neck, echinus and abacus with rosettes and slender mouldings. The frieze, with triglyphs alternating with shields and boukrania, is crowned by a bold mutulated cornice. As in the Custom House, a relatively severe attic tops it to north and south, while east and west there are small pediments. The circuit is completed by balustrading round the corners. The attic, relieved only by double swags and a smaller echoing cornice, is crowned by an urn at each end, supported by naiads and tritons, and serving as a chimney. These urns, being of a tall outline, contrast with that in the centre of the steps to the south. The steps are here cut away, and the oval urn which masks the area opening is perhaps the most beautiful piece of readily visible carving in the whole building.

The door, to the north, leads into the semicircular hall, in which there formerly hung a chiaroscuro by Cipriani. The operative part of the door is, for reasons already explained, only a small part of the door as apparent from outside. There was formerly a window sliding in the thickness of the wall, which could be pulled down to close the aperture in suitable weather.[41] There is a great deal of such 'false-work' about the Casino: of its five visible windows all but two are to a greater or less degree dummy. Such devices were inseparable from this kind of building: one must either accept them or transfer one's admiration to other quarters, where the subterfuges may seem to some more honest.

The white plaster of the frieze, carrying musical instruments and other trophies in fragile relief, contrasts with the pastel colours of the half-domical part of the ceiling. Three curved doors lead from the hall;

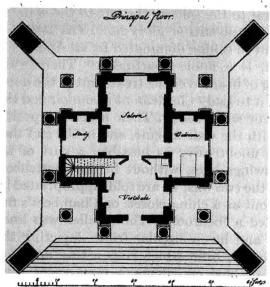

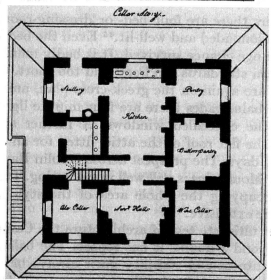

Plans of the Lord Viscount Charlemont's Casine at Marino

the central to the saloon, the left to the staircase, the right to a cupboard or glory-hole. The saloon, with a deeply-coved ceiling dominated by an Apollo's head in gilt rays, is a noble apartment.[42] There was much searching of heart over the treatment of the doors leading from it to Lady Charlemont's boudoir and the Zodiac room or small study. Their necessary position did not fit with the wall-scheme, and in the end they were made as unobtrusive as possible; a part of the wall simply swings back without further pretence.[43] The larger of the two was, we are told, appropriated by Lady Charlemont as a china-closet: on Chambers's first plan it is called a 'bedroom'. The smaller was lined with books,[44] and has a circular frieze depicting the signs of the zodiac, from which rises a tiny dome, painted a shade of blue conveying a remarkable illusion of space.

Upstairs there are four bed- or dressing-rooms, the largest colonnaded and well-lit.[45] Even the bed has by some strange chance survived. It is badly mauled and by modern standards too bony and too short. On this level we are again on the greek-cross plan, and so behind the balustrades there are four minute light-wells serving the concealed windows. A further stairway leads to the flat roof of the attic, fitted for an awning on sunny days. The prospect across Dublin Bay to the Wicklow Mountains is still well worth seeing. The basement, occupying the whole area of the stylobate, is even more extensive.

By the ultimate test of architecture the Casino succeeds beyond a doubt: it has repose. The balance between lightness and stability must always be struck, though the precise blend will vary enormously. Outside, solidity and delicacy are perfectly married. Within, the

fresh inventiveness of the decoration is untiring. There
is a particularly happy use of shell and love-knot motifs,
blossoming with lyrical felicity in the most unexpected
corners. Common hay-rakes are coaxed into an appearance in moulded plaster, and survive triumphantly.
There are hundreds of square feet of blank wall
altogether, and yet a pretty reed-moulding carries
downstairs into the servants' hall.

It is little wonder that by those authorities who have
penetrated as far as the Dublin suburbs, the Casino is
ranked high among European examples of the kind.[46]
The best that may be said of Wren's Orangery or
Gabriel's Trianon, may be said of it. This being so, we
need expatiate no further on particular beauties. But
a few observations, of interest mainly to specialists,
remain to be made; and one or two footnotes may stimulate the common man.

The workmanship of the Portland stone masonry
leaves nothing to be desired. And, as is not uncommon
in the period, some of the unseen brickwork is very hap-
hazard. But how thoughtful the essential structure is,
may appear from the following. There are, as has been
told, four small roof-yards at the angles. These, with
the neighbouring slopes of pediment, drain into the out-
ward corners. From there the water falls vertically
through the angle columns to the basement floor level,
whence it is treated as internal drainage. These angle
columns appear to rest on the stylobate, but in fact
carry down to lower ground level. Where they are exposed to the weather, they are formed of solid drums
drilled through the centre: underneath and indoors
they are composed of (presumably less costly) seg-
ments. On wet days one may stand there and listen to
the drops falling their forty-odd feet. As there is an

opening like the bottom of an organ-pipe, one may watch them as well.

The 'Boudoir' and the Zodiac Room use each only part of their respective windows. But instead of the surround - meeting the adjacent glazing-bar, it is brought to the same distance as that which bounds the full aperture, where there is of course a sash some half-an-inch wider. That is to say, it is treated as though the glazing-bar were a sash, and a narrow slit of daylight is the result. At the expense of verisimilitude, symmetry is preserved even on this minute scale.

The flutings of the urns collect in the Irish climate a good deal of moisture. To release this a series of very small holes have been bored at the foot. The effect is decorative, certainly no disfigurement. Similarly, to prevent water flowing down the steps and soaking the grass at their foot, the bottom step is channelled and at each end there is a little colander. Touches of this kind could be multiplied indefinitely. Never on a building so small can more care have been expended.

The same, perhaps, may be said of money. A local tradition tells of the workmen telling each other to be careful when handling the carved stones, for each one harmed would be another townland gone. (A townland in Ireland is the unit next below the parish.) The Casino cost its builder some sixty thousand pounds.[47] His income was probably something less than eight thousand per annum: he was never in the richest class of Irish landlord, nor indeed near it. His rents for the very land on which it was built fell sadly into arrear. His landlord dunned him: even his architect was reduced to reminding him in 1777 of a mere thirty-seven pounds owing since 1773.[48] In 1779 he complained at not receiving Charlemont's pleasant letters for some time past. The reason, alas, is not far to seek, for at the end of the letter the miserable thirty-seven pounds crops up again, six years old this time. The joke about the townlands was no joke in truth, for in 1776 we find him disposing of ancestral estates in County Tyrone.[49] He complains to a creditor that he never has any ready money, nobleman or no nobleman—for that was the drift of the creditor's argument.[50] There is no reason to doubt his word.

It was a mad undertaking by these standards. And yet not mad in the final count. He had twenty years' use of it when built, and all the delight of building. Whatever it stands monument to for us, madness is not the word.

But one feature is mad by any standards. From the basement area there radiate a number of tunnels. Most of them are mere cellars. But two of them go an enormous distance—how far nobody knows, for one is now waterlogged and the other is blocked up after some sixty feet. The latter has an arm terminating in a servants' latrine; some distance away it also serves a well. There are no detectable sanitary facilities for the dwellers above-stairs. In these underground galleries the perennial local legend of the secret passage has come to life at last. During the War of Independence Michael Collins used them for machine-gun practice. On any reading they assort very oddly with the Casino itself.

Four statues once graced the platforms in front of the attic-ends. They have been left to the last, for in their fates they figure forth a melancholy symbolism. There were two to north and two to south, and until twenty years ago three of them were still in place. They are now reduced to two on the north front. Those which

have fallen were Venus and Apollo. Those which still
stand are Bacchus and Ceres. That the Casino is a
sensitive building none can deny, but who could have
foretold that it would have proved so sensitive to the
phases of Irish history?

Once before in Ireland a perfect miniature building
had arisen at the bidding of one man. Cormac of Cashel,
king and bishop, called into being the chapel on the
rock of Cashel which now remains the unique substan-
tive masterpiece of Irish Romanesque. Charlemont,
nobleman and scholar, probably knew little[51] of his
predecessor of six hundred years before. But he crystal-
lised the ruling Ireland of his day with equal sureness.
The divergence of motive is not the least poignant part
of the contrast.

Happily, the twentieth-century Irish government
was persuaded to accord recognition to the Casino as
the moral property of the Irish people. The late Professor
R. M. Butler spent a lifetime urging, in a desperate
race against the dilapidations of time, the claims of the
Casino for preservation. The Ancient Monuments Act
of 1930 was framed with an eye to eighteenth-century
buildings in general, and to the Casino in particular. In
the very nick of time the building was taken over.
Once again, by devious and difficult routes, official recognition in its most valuable form came to Charlemont as promoter of the arts in Ireland. At the moment
of writing, it is the only eighteenth century monument
in the country so scheduled. Though hardly matter for
congratulation, this calls for thankfulness at least.[52]

NOTES

1. HMC, I, 218.

2. Ibid., 225.

3. *Views . . . in Dublin*, by Robert Pool and John Cash, Dublin, 1780. Its value lies not only in the beauty of the plates, but also in that it appeared at the earliest date at which there was a sufficiency of fine buildings to illustrate. The quotations are from the Preface.

4. H, I, 322.

5. RIA MSS., IX, 26.

6. See note 12.

7. See Ball: *History of County Dublin*, Vol. IV, and *Georgian Society*, Vol. V. In the latter is given the plan of Marino House. The hall, we are told, was low and badly lit, and the walls adjoining it show on the plan as very thick.

8. Compare the plan cited with Chambers's plan of Lord Bruce's Casino in *Civil Architecture*, 1759. And see also Chambers's note to his Plates XXXIX and LII in the same work.

9. Milton: *Views in Ireland*, 1783, says 200 acres.

10. At some period, the course of the main Malahide road was altered to run farther eastwards.

11. Which I have been lent by the kindness of Brother Roche, of the Christian Brothers, Marino. But even the staff of the National Library have been unable to identify the work from which the pages were taken. A MS. note on the first page gives the date as 1835, which cannot be far wrong.

12. RIA MSS., IX, 46. He enquires 'Are you getting the cooll (sic) £5,000 per an.?' This is the first traceable instance of the name 'Marino'.

13. *Irish Times*, Sept 16, 1886 [Prendergast]. The original letter (1756) has apparently disappeared.

14. Charles Topham Bowden: *A Tour through Ireland*, 1791, 78 sqq. He it was who saw the many-horned sheep.

15. In the geometrically fretted balustrades which adorn the hidden portion of the stair which leads from the upper floor of the Casino on to the roof, we may detect a trace of Chambers's Chinese manner. I owe this subtle observation to Mr T. A. Greeves.

16. Strawberry Hill is approximately 1754 onwards, so that Rosamund's Bower is nearly contemporary.

17. The Bower is now barely discernible. The walls have been built up and the apertures filled in. There is no longer a roof, and the site is, and has for half a century been, the burying-place of the Christian Brothers. The pond immediately below has almost ceased to exist, only a small pool is left serving as the present school bathing-place. But the old trees still remain to a large extent, in particular a remarkable old yew.

18. In HMC, II, 241 and 263 may be found Charlemont's views on Payne Knight, Capability Brown and the Picturesque in general.

19. Ibid., I, 14.

20. Delville is of course somewhat earlier, as it was complete well before Swift's death in 1745.

21. HMC, I, 14–15.

22. When Arthur Young visited Charlemont House in 1776 (*Tour in Ireland*, Dublin, 1780, I, 3) it was evidently complete. The latest mention of the Casino as 'not quite finished' is Milton: op. cit., 1783.

23. Letter from Chambers, HMC, I, 273. Hardy (I, 320) places the building later, in 1772–3, erroneously as I think.

24. Round the niches the masonry is rustic and vermiculated. See the letter of Chambers in HMC, I, 273, suggesting treatment in alternative materials.

25. As, in connexion with the Casino, HMC, I, 284–5, 304.

26. Pool and Cash, op. cit., p. 116.

27. Now the Bank of Ireland, in Scotch Street. It occupies the site of St Patrick's first church in the Primatial City.

28. Mr C. P. Curran informs me that some such scheme was intended in Mountjoy Square, but frustrated by the death in 1798 of Lord Mountjoy. Both sides of Leinster Square, Rathmines, have symmetrical treatment, but this is much later. Organic forms such as Mount Pleasant Square, Ranelagh, are much more characteristic. Marino Crescent, with a suggested dominating block near the centre, is also typical.

29. It is true that an elliptical 'Royal Crescent' at the west end of Eccles Street was intended (as many maps bear optimistic witness) in about 1820; but it was never carried out.

30. Especially the ludicrous dome of the otherwise superb Somerset House.

31. For this information I am indebted to a perusal of the plans of Charlemont House before its conversion, in the Office of Public Works, Dublin.

32. A drawing, hardly adequate, of this feature can be seen in D. A. Chart's *The Story of Dublin*.

33. Gandon: *Life*, 1846, 79 sqq.

34. That at the Rockingham end was blocked by the inscription, for which see pages 173-175 below.

35. Lewis's *Topographical Dictionary* and the many Dublin Guide books of the early nineteenth century, as well as the accounts of Arthur Young and other visitors, give many details of the pictures. The library is the only private library in Dublin separately treated by Lewis, and the Catalogue of 1865 is still a stand-by to the bibliographer. It includes, for example, a first folio Shakespeare (sold for £455) and a MS. *Roman de la Rose*, possibly used by Chaucer (£244).

36. It seems, however, that the south-westernmost of the small galleries which open off the main series, preserves the walls, though nothing else, of the Rockingham Library.

37. Milton: op. cit., 1783. Mr H. G. Leask, who was in charge of the restoration of 1930, reports that no trace of it was then visible. It is probably buried in the foundations.

38. Grattan: *Speeches,* ed. Madden, 1847, p. 89.

39. HMC, II, 393 (letter undated).

39a. The lions are the work of Joseph Wilton, Chambers's-father-in-law. They are male but almost maneless.

40. See Appendix.

41. Mr Leask kindly tells me that it was found *in situ* in 1930.

42. 20′ × 15′.

43. See the letters in HMC, I, 286 and II, 372. The latter, from Charlemont to Chambers, is of particular interest. It mentions also 'Munt's Gothic design'.

44. The bookcases, very deftly devised, are still *in situ.*

45. The present columns are mostly conscientious and scholarly restoration, as this part of the building suffered severely from neglect. .

46. I may mention Messrs A. E. Richardson, Sacheverell Sitwell and Osbert Lancaster. The last-mentioned, in *The Cornhill* for May 1944, likens it also to Giulio Romano's *Palazzo del Te* at Mantua. I do not see the force of this, but then I have never been to Mantua.

47. I have been unable to trace this statement back further than Blomfield's *History of Renaissance Architecture,* where it is given without a source. But there is little reason to question its likelihood.

48. HMC, I, 338 and 349.

49. Information of Major Burges of Parkanaur, Castlecaulfeild. Major Burges kindly tells me that the negotiations started in 1771. On Sept 6, 1775, Francis Caulfeild writes 'I am exceedingly glad to hear my Brother intends to borrow Money instead of selling so much of his Estate'. Later in the same letter he mentions 'this affair of the £50,000'. It appears from the same source that Charlemont stood to gain £450 per annum by his brother's death: RIA MSS., X, 60. Understandably, Francis is anxious for the future of his wife and four children. He provided for them by selling his annuity to Sir Annesley Stewart. This is not much more than a month before his death in shipwreck took place: ibid., No. 62.

50. HMC, I, 342 and RIA MSS., X, 73–76, 84–86. Matters came to worse lengths than this, as in 1790 we find a correspondent writing from Calcutta that he thinks he can find someone to lend Charlemont £50,000 at five per cent, and suggesting further mortgage of Irish estates: RIA MSS., XV, No. 44.

51. Knowledge of the Irish past was growing, however. He had a nephew called Cormic: RIA MSS., XIII, No. 102.

52. In many details concerning the Casino I have profited by the kindness of Mr H. G. Leask, Inspector of Ancient Monuments, who has put his great knowledge unstintingly at my disposal.

CHAPTER VII

EARLDOM AND MARRIAGE

He was not a model landlord. Such lands as he held in Dublin were recent acquisitions for personal use, and the bulk of his estates remained in Armagh and Tyrone. Though he never lived on them, they were not entirely neglected. As early as January 1755 Adderley reports the discovery of limestone quarries at the Moy, across the river from Charlemont 'and should you think of giving encouragement to build a town there, it will be a treasure'.[1] It is. The centre of Ulster abounds in well-laid out landlords' villages, and among them the Moy is one of the most attractive. It consists of a square regularly planted with trees, and from the centres of the sides radiate roads, of which one descends steeply to the bridge below the Fort. Charlemont is credited with the design of the town, which is said to be modelled on Marengo in Lombardy. But I can find no evidence for either of these traditions.[2]

The work was hardly begun until 1763, as appears from his agent's letters on the subject. 'I again recommend it', the writer continues, 'not to part with any of the Manor of Castle Caulfeild, more than what is now fix'd on . . .' But the northern estates were rapidly assuming a second place in his interests. The turning-point is marked by an entry in the Vestry Minutes of Castlecaulfeild Church, of 2 Feb 1762. 'The Rt. Hon. Lord Viscount Charlemont gives to the . . . Rector of the Parish, the situation of the family seat in the church, to accommodate it.' Whatever 'it' may be, it is clear that Charlemont was abandoning any ideas of resident proprietorship. But a room in Castlecaulfeild House still shows traces of stucco, and local tradition names this corner of the deserted mansion as the spot in which he used from time to time to transact business with his tenants. It may be so. In any case, brother Francis was established about this time[3] in a house near the Moy, so that one member of the family fulfilled a token occupation.

But it was as a local landlord that he held the office of Lord-Lieutenant of Armagh. In 1763 that county was the scene of serious disturbances. The Oak-Boys, one of many similarly-styled associations of this and later times, were for the most part Protestants, and their grievances were the tithes of the Established Church, and the road-tax. Charlemont considered that the clergy and the assessors of the tax were respectively to blame. The people, in his view, 'never do wrong but with just cause'. In his district the disturbances, though alarming, were not attended with loss of life. In more Catholic areas this was not so, 'a difference which however I do not so much ascribe to the diversity of religion, as to the horrid oppression under which these latter wretches had long laboured. A rebellion of slaves is always more bloody than an insurrection of free men'.[4]

Charlemont wrote to Stone announcing his intention of going to Armagh. Stone replied that he would be grateful for first-hand information as to how many additional troops would be needed. On arrival at Newry, Charlemont was dissuaded from making the journey to Armagh: at least, urged the burghers, let him go under strong military escort. 'To this I replied that I could by no means bring myself to think of travelling through my own country with a military guard.' He consented, however, to scouts being sent out to sound the rioters' intentions. With his friend William Stewart of Killymoon and another gentleman, he set out. He had two armed servants but no other guard. A well-appointed gallows, hung with 'an excellent new cord' straddled the road, and with a good grace he rode under it. From Armagh he wrote to Stone. Though it is not quite clear that, as he claimed, he deprecated the sending of many troops, there is no doubt that 'the principal difficulty I had to encounter was the unnecessary filling of the jails'. The disturbances were peacefully quelled, and characteristically he observes that 'if I was less than others affected with fear, it was probably because I had not been in the way of seeing these violences, and of being for a long time hourly liable to them'.

It was for these services that in December 1763 he was offered the earldom. He accepted on two conditions: that he should remain free to oppose the government, and that his patent should rehearse not his own services, but those of 'the first peer of my family, and the remarkable circumstance of an earldom having been intended for my ancestor so early as in the reign of James the First.'[5] The first, at least, of these conditions was very necessary, in view of the normal meaning attaching to honours offered by the Viceroy.

He was pressed by the Viceroy, Northumberland, to accept some additional honour. He at first refused, but finally asked for a seat on the Linen-Board, a position which carried no emolument. This was promised 'whenever a vacancy takes place'. But Charlemont protested in the House against the Address on the Treaty of Paris, and no more was heard of the seat. The Lord

Chancellor struck out the word 'unsolicited' in his patent, as being contrary to precedent. Ultimately Charlemont added a testimonial to that effect, on his own account, when a new avalanche of 'honours' reminded him of the different circumstances attending his own.

The mention of the Linen-Board reminds us that, whatever his shortcomings as a landlord, he made some effort to interest himself in local industries. He was a governor of the Tyrone Collieries, and of the Lagan Canal Company. Such positions were achieved by subscription, and they did not profit their holders. He was approached in 1772 on the subject of establishing a porcelain factory in Dublin, and in 1797 he had evidently given some countenance to a gentleman who had perfected a rapid method of tanning hides.[6] But it cannot be claimed that these topics absorbed very much of his attention.

With the deaths of Stone and Boyle in 1764, a change comes over the personalities of Irish politics. We are almost on the threshold of the great period, but Charlemont, still spending as much time in London as in Dublin, seems hardly aware of anything stirring. The first of the great names, Henry Flood, is already in Parliament. He is at this time a close associate of Charlemont's, but the only extant letters are full of trivial personalities and cryptic gossip.[7]

His heart was more in the affairs of the London Society of Dilettanti, to which he had been elected in 1756. In 1764 he was one of the committee which petitioned the King for ground on which to build premises for the Society. He was also of the committee which sent Chandler, Revett and Pars to Asia Minor. When the results were published, he had the mortification of hearing from Chambers 'The dilettanti book is published, and a cursed book it is, between friends, being composed of some of the worst architecture I ever saw; there is a degree of madness in sending people abroad to fetch home such stuff'.[8] It was not the first time Charlemont had been so embarrassed: his draughtsman Dalton had projected an attack on the authenticity of Wood's *Palmyra*, and intended to call on Charlemont to support his charge.[9] He must have weathered this contretemps, for Wood was with him on the committee of 1764, and remained one of his friends. Evidently Dalton had been entirely dropped as the price of peace. As for Chambers's faux-pas, it must have been delicately ignored. In 1766 it was Charlemont who proposed Reynolds as official painter to the Dilettanti, and the proposal was carried.[10]

But in spite of the claims of these London interests, it was in Dublin that he presently found himself a wife. The story is told[11] that the initial motive for marriage was born of his love of Marino. Brother Francis, it seems, had paid him a visit there, and Charlemont, taking him for a walk round the demesne, had pointed out a particular tree and remarked with regret that it would have to come down. 'Never fear', said Francis, 'when I come into the property I shall sweep away all your improvements.' Charlemont said nothing at the time, but at the first opportunity he flew in great distress to consult his friend Doctor Lucas, who very sensibly pointed out that, as a doctor, he could recommend a simple method of keeping the property out of such sacrilegious hands—a method which stood a good chance of succeeding.

Very suitably, it was at Clontarf that he found the lady of his choice. It is said that Lucas recommended

PLATE IX

THE CASINO, FROM THE NORTH-EAST

From an engraving by T. Milton after Wheatley, 1781

See page 136

'the daughter of a decayed gentleman of his acquaintance'. Mary Hickman was of Fenloe or Brickhill, Co. Clare, and was doubly connected by marriage with the O'Brien family of Thomond. Various apocryphal stories are told of the circumstances whereby he became aware that his love was reciprocated.[12] It seems at least probable that their acquaintance was the result of his close political association with Sir Lucius O'Brien.

Mary Hickman left Clontarf for Clare late in May 1768. Thinking things over after she had gone, Charlemont decided to send a letter after her by the hand of a Miss Jephson. It is evident that already there is some understanding between them. He explains that he cannot follow her into the country because 'my health will not permit me in its present state to venture an intermission of sea-bathing' and also because he wishes to avoid public remark. He is suffering from 'a violent nervous palpitation', and he begs her to return as soon as possible: 'Come then, my Love—quickly come to your longing James!'[13]

In his next letter, written two days later, he is remarkably frank. He explains what first caused him to fall in love with her: among the usual causes appears this: 'Your situation too which I could not avoid being sensible of, so different from what your superior merit might have challenged, induced a tender pity.' Perhaps more surprisingly he observes later: 'Experienced as I am in the business of making love, I found that this pursuit was totally different from any I had ever yet entered into, and now, for the first time, to my shame be it spoken, I felt a passion whose purpose and designs were perfectly virtuous.' There are, he points out, three drawbacks. In the first place, he has got into 'a long and inveterate habit of living principally for myself...'

L

and this may not be easy to alter. Secondly, 'my fortune is not at present what it might have been, partly from misfortune' but mostly, of course, from his expenditure of capital on buildings. And finally he observes that he is already a chronic valetudinarian, 'and there is nothing more possible than that you might begin your marriage state by becoming a nurse'. In a postscript he again implores her to give no answer in haste, impatient as he is of the event.

On the 25th of June he drafted, though perhaps he did not send, an impassioned plea for her return. He has been reduced to hunting for her in the Dublin theatres, but without avail. This unexplained delay in her appearance was the last hitch: on July the 2nd they were married. He was almost on the eve of his fortieth birthday. Leland wrote a charming letter of congratulation to Lady Charlemont, with a postscript in verse, an epithalamion in the manner of Percy's *Reliques*. The Earl's father-in-law, Thomas Hickman, wrote from his county Clare home a touching epistle, attesting his 'knowledge of the sweetness of Temper and Goodness of her Mind', and his delight in 'an event so far exceeding what . . . her Ambition could suggest'.[14] Apparently she brought not a penny piece by way of dowry; but the Earl was well content.

Their marriage was ideally happy. Lady Charlemont, it is true, does not leave a strong impress on her husband's life. But no news is in this case good news. Early in their courtship he is said to have unwittingly melted her heart by relating how he used to breakfast alone at Charlemont House on a cup of cocoa with no other companion than a tame mouse which ate out of his hand and even crept into his bosom. After his marriage he continued to breakfast alone: but in other respects

Lady Charlemont took the mouse's place. She took, indeed, the place of a long line of predecessors besides.
At some period the Earl compiled a catalogue of his
loves. It begins in verse:

> Betty, a maid of low degree
> Was first assigned by Fate
> To curb my heart by Nature free
> And rule the infant state . . .

but it ends up in prose: 'Jacypitha, Then an Interreg-
num, Thirty Tyrants, Divine Ninetta, Leonora, Mar-
uchi, Fanny, Urania, Mary the 1st, Cecilia, Two Consuls, Betty the 2nd (Plebeian) Julia (Patrician) A Republic always ends in the reign of one—"Queen Mary
the Great".'[15] The latest of these who can be dated—
perhaps the Patrician Julia—was the recipient of a
letter in 1764, signed with an embarrassingly infantile
pet-name.[16]

By 1769 the works at Marino and Charlemont House
were occupying so much of his time that Chambers
writes to him: 'As your lordship so seldom visits London, would it not be better to give up your house in
Hertford-street. It must stand you one way or another
in at least £200 a year . . .'[17] The Hertford Street house
was still in use at least as an accommodation-address
as late as February 1773. But though visits to London
are frequent till the events of the late seventies and
eighties left little time for them, he must have given up
the house soon after this. He extended such hospitality
at Charlemont House to his Hickman-O'Brien relatives, at the expense of the Caulfeilds, that the latter
named it in derision the 'County Clare Hotel'.

There were other reasons for a more steadfast residence in Dublin. In 1767 the English Government
made a determined effort to find a Viceroy who would

reside permanently in Ireland. The object in view was
to break the power of the undertakers, who for most of
the time ruled the country as Lords Justices. The
undertakers, with all their faults, were mostly resident
Irishmen; and if any trial of strength between them
and the English administration were in prospect, Charlemont and his friends had need to keep a close watch
on developments. In 1768 was passed the Octennial
Bill, limiting the life of Parliament to eight years. The
factors which conspired to ensure its passage both in
Ireland and England make an extremely complicated
relation not without its touches of ironic comedy.[18] It
may suffice that of those who had voted for it, Charlemont was among the few who welcomed its unexpected
passage into law. Its effect was to lower the price of
boroughs but to increase the opportunities for selling
them. It will be seen that this combined with the residence of the Viceroy to increase the pace of Irish political life.

The English Government had some difficulty in finding a nobleman prepared to comply with the new conditions attaching to the viceregal dignity. In George,
fourth Viscount Townshend, they found such an one,
but not before three others had proved unequal to the
task. Two at least of these peers accepted the usual
£3,000 for expenses, without setting foot in Ireland.[19]

Townshend's administration opened auspiciously,
but in the five years of his term he managed to forfeit
the regard of all parties. While still Viceroy, he became
involved in an affair of honour with Charles Coote, Earl
of Bellamont. This transaction, in the opinion of an
expert,[20] 'takes rank among the highest on record' for
scrupulous regard to the finer points. Lord Bellamont
was refused access to the Viceroy by an aide at the

Castle, whereat he took offence. It was impossible in
Ireland for a private individual to fight a duel with the
Viceroy. Accordingly, Lord Bellamont waited till his
opponent was divested of his special status. The better
to free himself for the business in hand, he also resigned
his commission in the service.

On Christmas Eve, 1772, Lord Charlemont waited
upon Lord Townshend in London. He 'commenced
matters by requesting permission to read a statement
on the part of his noble friend, which was at once accorded'. Townshend asked him what form of apology
was required. Still reading from his paper, Charlemont
replied 'that of asking Lord Bellamont's pardon'. This
Lord Townshend refused, on the ground that 'it would
be an acknowledgment of an offence I never intended'.
But Charlemont politely persisted, saying that he was
not authorised to receive any message or any other
form of apology. Seeing that Townshend remained
adamant, he urged him to comply, for, he said, he had
in his pocket another paper which he would be obliged
to read should his Lordship remain obdurate. On meeting with a final refusal, he drew the paper from his
pocket, and in all solemnity read: 'I am enjoined by
Lord Bellamont to state to your Lordship that he considers you divested of *every principle* that constitutes
the character of a man of honour.' Townshend asked
permission to call in a friend, and in his presence Charlemont again rehearsed his rigmarole. He was again
obliged to decline carrying any message, and so took
his leave. Christmas Day was observed as a truce.

On St Stephen's Day Charlemont was called in by
Lord Bellamont to witness the delivery of a message
from Townshend's emissary, Lord Ligonier. Further
negotiations took place, and on December 30th Charle-

mont reported to Flood that the affair was happily concluded, and though it had occasioned him much anxiety 'yet I have been amply repaid by the opportunity it has afforded me of intimately knowing Lord Bellamont, whose character can only be sufficiently admired by being intimately known'. Little did he know how near he was to losing a friend; for the two men met and fought unknown to him. Bellamont was badly wounded, but managed to recover. For reasons easily understood, Charlemont was not considered suitable to preside over a scene of bloodshed. 'Duelling,' in his opinion, 'though, thanks to the increasing polish of our manners, less practised than formerly, is still too fashionable . . . offence can seldom, if ever, be given among men of good breeding, and the gentleman's maxim ought to be neither to offer nor to bear any real affront.' The justice of his view is evident when it is considered that, though by no means a coward, he was never involved in such an affair himself. It was, in general, the 'duelling set' who brought upon themselves such ordeals, though any man who spoke his mind honestly in Parliament might find himself measuring paces in the Phoenix Park.

In December 1773 his daughter, the Lady Elizabeth Caulfeild, was born. She died unmarried in 1830. Another child had been born to them some time earlier, for we hear of the loss of one in January 1774. Topham Beauclerk, the friend of Johnson and of Charlemont, writes in great distress at the realisation that a joking letter of his must have reached Charlemont just after his bereavement.[21] But on January 3rd, 1775, he was blest by a son and heir, Francis William, who lived to succeed to the Earldom. Two more sons followed in 1776 and 1779.

Brother Francis was no longer a menace to Charlemont's arcadian ambitions. He had a family of his own, and he still sat for the borough of Charlemont. In 1773 he is described in a confidential Castle notebook[22] as follows:

> Hon. Francis Caulfeild Brother to Ld Charlemont whose (sic) has this borough he will follow my Ld's directions.

He is marked 'C', signifying that he will vote against the Government. But a similar entry two years later[23] carries new overtones of implication:

> ... Towards the middle of last Session, Mr Caulfeild shewed some Disposition to support Government—He is very poor and greatly embarrass'd in his Circumstances.

In the index he is now classed as 'for'. Charlemont himself is the subject of a pretty paragraph:[24]

> ... has been always in Opposition both to Lord Townshend and Lord Harcourt, and always will to Government—In private Life amiable and respectable—In Publick violent, petulant, and waspish.

The development of the brothers' divergences was abruptly cut short. In November 1775 Francis and his wife were lost at sea on their way from England. He left two children;[25] but more important still, he left a vacant seat. The filling of that seat was, if not the cause, at least the occasion of a most momentous association.

NOTES

1. HMC, I, 200. More to the same purpose may be found in RIA MSS., XII, 38 and 40. The two last are from the men on the spot in 1763.
2. On the subject of Cartesian town-planning and Montesquieu, see an amusing passage in H, I, 67 sq.

3. RIA MSS., X, 24. Francis to Lord C: 'I have seen a farm of yours near Moy which tho' small I think will do tolerably well for me to build on.' See also Marshall, *Charlemont and Mountjoy Forts*, already cited, p. 64.

4. HMC, I, 21 sqq., 137 sqq.

5. Ibid., 22, 136.

6. HMC, I, 305 and 307, and 312. Other information from minutes of Lagan Navigation Company, High Street, Belfast.

7. A very large number of letters from Charlemont are given in *Letters to Henry Flood*, 1820, but they are less interesting than might have been expected.

8. HMC, I, 298. See Cust: *Hist. Notices of the Dilettanti Soc.*, 60, 61, 74, 76, 78, 83, 90, 108.

9. HMC, I, 201.

10. Cust: loc. cit.

11. The story is told in *Irish Political Characters*, 1799, pp. 34 sqq.

12. In *Irish Times*, Sept 9th, 16th and 17th, 1886. The author was J. P. Prendergast, whose close connexion with the third Earl gave him special advantages. But the stories he tells fly in the face of documentary facts.

13. RIA MSS., XII, 57 and 58. See also HMC, I, 286 sqq.

14. RIA MSS., X, 23.

15. *Irish Times*, loc. cit.

16. RIA MSS., X, 3.

17. HMC, I, 297. See ibid., 314 (1773).

18. See HMC, I, 24 sqq.; and Lecky, IV, 367–381.

19. Ibid., 371–2.

20. Steinmetz: *History of Duelling*. From this source are taken such of the facts (a small minority) in the following narration as do not derive from HMC, I, 313–4, and from the *Gentleman's Magazine* of 1772 and 1773.

21. HMC, I, 317 and H, I, 349.

22. Bodkin: *The Irish Parliament*, 1773, in Procs. of RIA, XLVIII, C, IV.

23. *The Irish Parliament*, ed. W. Hunt, 1907, p. 12.

24. Ibid., p. 68.

25. Two, it would seem, were lost with him, as well as his wife.

CHAPTER VIII

PARLIAMENT AND VOLUNTEERS

This is not a political history of the period, and the enumeration of the events which led to the rise of the Volunteers must therefore be brief. In 1769 a Money Bill, originating from the English Privy Council, was rejected by Parliament. There was nothing unusual in this, but the rejection was accompanied with a protest couched in terms which asserted the rights of Ireland. In subsequent formal recriminations Charlemont played some part, in alliance with Flood.[1]

In the following year a bill for the augmentation of the Irish army establishment received his support, not, as he explains, because he approved of it, but because it involved, in form at least, some subjection of the Crown's prerogative to the Irish Parliament. Shortly before the recall of Townshend, Charlemont introduced a mild Catholic Relief Bill, whereby Catholics might be allowed to hold leases for 99 years. It was twice read, but on the third occasion 'the House was crowded with zealous supporters of orthodoxy and oppression, and I was voted out of the chair, not wholly unsuspected of being little better than a Papist'.[2]

The administration which followed, that of Harcourt, introduced a Bill to tax the revenues of absentee Irish landlords. It was, of course, popular in Ireland, though it was a Tory measure and Irish patriots were, if they were anything, Whigs. The English Whigs, whose voice was Burke, were responsible for its defeat. Its chief sponsor in the Irish Parliament was Flood,

who, Burke observed, 'will have the merit of coming
over to Government entirely in an Irish interest'. The
comment is cynical, and Burke in the whole transaction shows a cynical freedom from any attachment to
the interests of his native land. Charlemont himself supported the Bill, but in later life came to believe that
he had been mistaken.[3] By then, he felt, Ireland had
become of such consequence that all men of good will
would naturally practise the duty of residence: as for
the rest, Ireland could well spare them. Though he dis-
liked the mere idea of any kind of land tax, his change
of opinion was not selfishly motivated. Class-interest
was no doubt behind the idea that this might be the
thin end of the wedge. But his view of the class position
was the very reverse of ours: he will speak quite innocently of the 'dependance' of his tenants on himself,
where to us it seems that he was dependent on them.[4]
We cannot expect him to have held ideas which had
not yet come into currency.

A calm amounting almost to stagnation now en-
folded Irish politics. The opposition dwindled, and in
1775 'Flood, my friend Flood,—the dear partner of my
heart and of all its councils,—anchor of my hope, and
pillar of my trust,—Flood gave way, and deserted the
glorious cause in which he had been for fourteen years
triumphantly engaged'.[5] Flood, with whom Charlemont
had exchanged sheafs of cryptic gossip and even
verses,[6] deserted to the enemy and accepted the position of vice-treasurer. But, badly as Charlemont was
hit by this defection, it seems to have made little stir
in the world at large. As if by instinct, he turned to his
friend Marlay's brilliant young nephew, Henry Grattan.
As the treachery of Flood left a gap in Charlemont's
heart, so the simultaneous death of Francis Caulfeild

left a vacancy in his borough; and Grattan filled them both.

Grattan had hitherto led a life of preparation. As a young Templar in London he had apostrophised the trees of Windsor Forest by moonlight, had been overheard by his landlady addressing empty space as 'Mr Speaker!' In Kilkenny and Rathfarnham amateur theatricals and poetry had claimed him: he had been called to the Irish Bar, but spent much of his time in London, attending the debates of the British Parliament, or the Italian opera. In Ireland he had fallen under the influence of Flood, with whom he had collaborated in political journalism.

He was now in his thirtieth year. Like his patron, he was of an uncertain constitution, and suffered recurrent bouts of ill-health. But he had a determination which Charlemont lacked, and though his voice was weak and his delivery bad, he was perhaps the greatest orator in English. Above all, he brought a creative mind to bear on the common traffic of politics.

The outbreak of the American war brought into prominence the similarity between America's position and that of Ireland. The British Government laid an embargo on the Irish provision trade, but the opposition in the Irish Parliament was powerless to interfere. Trade with France was at a standstill owing to the war, and a general economic depression settled over Ireland. It was, perhaps, the darkest hour before the dawn. The first sign of awakening was the success of Luke Gardiner's Catholic Relief Bill in 1778. It was a very mild measure, and closely resembled Charlemont's own attempt of six years earlier,[7] but this time it got through. Charlemont's heart was for emancipation, but his head against it. His humanity detested the Penal Laws, while he justified their political prudence. As a lover of toleration he welcomed any relief short of the two essential points 'the free and uncontrolled use of arms, and a share in the legislature'. But, he points out, in a society afflicted with so deep a cleavage as that in Ireland, the reservation of the essential points only makes their attainment all the more an object of desire to the dispossessed.[8] He did not, in short, believe at this time that the discordant elements in Irish life were capable of a synthesis. Grattan did; and his first principle was that 'the Irish Protestant could never be free till the Irish Catholic had ceased to be a slave'.[9] The Union prevented the endorsement by events of either view.

As for the English measures against Irish trade, the Irish opposition, strong in the country but weak as yet in Parliament, retaliated as best it could. Charlemont and his friends took part in a voluntary boycott of English goods. In this they had the support of the Irish manufacturers, but it is not clear how widespread or how effective the movement was. Some slight abatement of the restrictions was ventured on by Lord North's government, but English vested interests prevented any important changes. And already the economic and political struggle was on the verge of taking another form.

In 1778 there was, as there had been in 1760, a threat of a French invasion, and an acute shortage of troops in Ireland. The Irish Government lacked even the means to pay such troops, had they been there. Belfast was, as before, the danger-spot. In spite of the close sympathy of Belfast Protestants with the American cause, they had no stomach for French occupation. The Mayor appealed to the Government for troops, and was told that no effective help could be sent. In an incredi-

bly short space of time, the whole of Ulster had put itself under arms, and under the command of the local
nobility and gentry. Charlemont found himself at the
head of the first Company of Armagh Volunteers.

It is necessary to emphasise that, whatever the role
which France later came to occupy in the Irish mind,
a very complete unanimity subsisted at this time between Protestant and Catholic. The Catholics were still
disqualified from bearing arms, but they subscribed
liberally to the Volunteer funds, and numbers of them
were later enrolled in the ranks of that force.[10] The
national movement was in its first and perhaps its
happiest phase, setbacks and disappointments were
still to come, and no internal strain had yet exposed
the cracks in the solid front. To such a man as Charlemont the movement was the incredible fulfilment of a
dream. To us, the history of the next three years seems
more dreamlike still. No wonder he threw himself into
it with passionate idealism.

The infection of volunteering spread rapidly over the
rest of the country. Wexford, indeed, must divide the
honours with Belfast, for there a parallel inspiration
had taken root perhaps a little earlier. Lord Altamont
pranced at the head of the Mayo men, and the remote
aborigines of the Dingle Peninsula echoed the national
rallying-cry. Grattan was Colonel of the Independent
Dublin Corps, commanded by the Duke of Leinster. In
July 1780 Charlemont was elected Commander-in-chief
of the whole force.

The Government observed these evolutions with
mixed feelings, the most prominent of which was, says
Lecky, 'an impotent dismay'. They could not carry on
government without them—the very judges were es-
corted by Volunteers in default of the regular military

—but almost from the beginning they were aware that this mushroom organisation held the real power in the country. Their only safeguard was the eminence of the leaders. They naturally tried to retain a remote control over the movement by polite diplomacy towards such men as Charlemont and Leinster. But some time was to elapse before the effects of this policy were evident. Charlemont, though a moderate and a naturally timorous politician, was not a fool. He would not allow himself to be used as a ministerial damper upon the enthusiasm of the hour. There were several immediate aims on which the Volunteers and the country at large were unanimous: until these were achieved there was no hope of driving wedges into their ranks.

In Parliament itself, the system of corruption erected by Townshend and the Viceroys who followed him, Harcourt and Buckinghamshire, had achieved a temporary stability. At the beginning of the American War the Government had a comfortable majority, and was able to commit Parliament to supporting the war. But before the opening of the session of October 1779, the Opposition members held an advance conference at Bray in Wicklow. In reply to the Speech from the Throne, Grattan moved an amendment to the Address, demanding free trade. It was carried without a division. Both Houses passed votes of thanks to the Volunteers for their exertions in the defence of the country. On November 4th, the Volunteers celebrated King William's birthday by parading round his statue, in front of which they had placed two cannon bearing the labels 'Free Trade or else—'. These cannon were in theory trained on the French invader; it was hoped that England would not overlook their existence; and should the honourable members forget themselves, they could

easily be moved round a few degrees towards the colonnades of the Parliament House.

Dublin's blood was up. Fired by the spirit of the
Volunteers, the inhabitants of the Liberties burst forth
into demonstrations which the tact of the Volunteers
barely sufficed to moderate. 'Talk not to me of peace,'
said Hussey de Burgh in the House, 'Ireland is not in a
state of peace; it is smothered war. England has sown
her laws like dragons' teeth, and they have sprung up
in armed men.' Submissively, Lord North's government
in England repealed the commercial restrictions.

On April 19th, 1780, Grattan rose to move a Declara-
tion of Irish Rights. The question at issue was the
thorniest yet touched upon. In 1494 a statute of a subservient parliament of the Pale (known as Poyning's
Law) had enacted that all Irish bills, before being laid
before Parliament, must previously be approved by the
English Privy Council. A similar tendency had been
shown by the Declaratory Act, a British Statute of
1720. Grattan's motion was an attack on these, and as
yet it was an indirect attack. Charlemont was approached beforehand to prevent him from bringing it,
but refused to interfere.[11] The debate lasted for fifteen
hours, and at half-past six on the morning of the 20th
it was indefinitely adjourned, and left unrecorded in
the journal of the House. In July Charlemont and
Grattan set out together to review the Northern Volunteers. On the 12th they celebrated the Battle of the
Boyne by a review in Belfast. By the 31st Charlemont
was staying with his cousin and banker, Sir Annesley
Stewart, in Donegal, preparing for another review.
Significantly, he notes that the Donegal gentlemen are
less forward in pressing their country's claims than
those of Belfast.[12]

The next year was spent by the Government in rebuilding their organisation in Parliament, so badly shaken by these events. They proceeded on the assumption that affairs would duly resume their normal complexion, and that 'the epidemic madness' as the Viceroy Buckinghamshire described it, 'so assiduously circulated by Lord Charlemont, Mr Grattan' and others, would die a natural death.[13] But in this they were mistaken. Another invasion scare in the spring of 1781 kept the avowed purpose of the Volunteers alive, and conspired to foster the growth of other purposes.

Perhaps the most fascinating aspect of the period, to the political historian, is the study of the interplay of Volunteers and Parliament. Parliament showed signs of grace only when some such external stimulus as that of the Volunteers became too insistent to be ignored with safety. During the calmer intervals, the Castle engineers were busy as ever, tunnelling away to undermine the lines of communication between Parliament and country. The former was, as a talking-shop, second to none, but it had a constant tendency to become a closed system functioning in a vacuum. Statistically speaking, the Volunteers were a much more representative body. It was therefore not surprising that when they were not urgently engaged in polishing their firelocks, they should fall to discussing the state of the country and questions of political tactics. The most important Volunteer leaders, Grattan and Flood and Charlemont, were also in Parliament. As patriots, they soon realised that only some kind of pressure from the Volunteers could induce Parliament to act on Grattan's speeches, which, though much admired in the House, were still being outvoted. But as Whigs, Grattan and his friends could not welcome the idea of a Parliament

PLATE X

THE CASINO TODAY
from the West

See page 142

dominated by any outside force. But here again, the hidden conflict did not come to the surface until after the first glowing fruits of victory had been plucked.

In the last days of 1781 the South Armagh Volunteers decided to hold a provincial Volunteer Convention at Dungannon. 242 delegates from all parts of Ulster assembled in February. Charlemont was not in the chair, and apparently was not even present, possibly from motives of delicacy.[14] But before the Convention met, he, Grattan and Flood met together at Charlemont House, to draft a series of resolutions for the Volunteers to pass.[15] A few months earlier, Flood had been stimulated by Grattan's oratory to desert the ministerial benches. The Convention passed the Charlemont House resolutions in their entirety, calling for the modification of Poyning's Law and a limitation of the Mutiny Bill, the main point then outstanding between Opposition and Government in the House. They also welcomed the relaxations of the Penal Laws against the Catholics. There was hardly a dissentient voice.

The Ministry of Lord North, then tottering to its long-awaited fall, can hardly have noticed this one among the many disastrous dispatches under which it sank to ruin.[16] But the accession to power of Rockingham in March was the cue for the complete concession of the Irish demands. Rockingham was an old personal friend of Charlemont's; Fox had been intimate with him during his visit to Dublin in 1777 and earlier;[17] the English and the Irish Whigs were apparently in complete accord. It was understood between gentlemen that this was the moment when all might be granted without humiliation. Lord North, who had played the camel to the Volunteer straw, might serve as scapegoat as well. And so it was.

M

Not that relations between English and Irish Whigs were without their hitches, even at the very outset. Lord Buckinghamshire's successor, Lord Carlisle, was recalled by Rockingham, and the Duke of Portland sent in his room. His secretary, Colonel Richard Fitz-patrick, was an Irishman and a poet. To quote a con-temporary Irish account, 'As if the legendary tale of St Patrick banishing all venom from the land, was true,—a Fitzpatrick was to be the secretary to this glorious embassy'.[18] His first action was to call at Charlemont House with a letter from Rockingham, personally requesting Charlemont to consent to an adjournment of the sitting. The Government, he said, would be grateful for a few weeks in which to consult with their Irish allies.

In consultation with Grattan, Charlemont decided against granting the adjournment. He was sorry to have to refuse a request 'coming from the man in the world whom I wished most to oblige'.[19] But in conver-sation with the Viceroy he was adamant, and Portland gave in with a good grace. Charlemont wrote kindly but firmly to Rockingham: 'We ask but our rights, our uncontrovertible rights . . . Bind us to you by the only chains that can connect us, the only chains we will ever consent to wear, the dear ties of mutual love and mutu-al freedom. So shall you gain a kingdom in the place of those provinces which your predecessors have lost . . .'[20] Fox, too, had written to Charlemont, also asking for the adjournment, and enlarging on the theme of Whig-gery as an international association of men of good-will, rather than a mere collection of national parties called by the same name. It was a tactful letter, but it was clear to Charlemont that 'the motive of the wish of ad-ministration was to give his Grace leisure, not for travelling, but for consideration and dangerous consultation'.[21] He met Fox with the same friendly refusal, 'For, my dear sir, with every degree of affection for our sister kingdom, with every regard for the interests of the empire at large, I am an Irishman. I pride myself in the appellation, and will, in every particular, act as such . . .'[22]

Both Grattan and Charlemont refused office from the new Government, and Grattan would not even receive Fitzpatrick before the decision in Parliament was taken. On the 16th of April Grattan passed through streets solidly lined with Volunteers, to move his amendment to the Address, demanding the legislative independence of Ireland. It was carried without a single dissentient voice.

It was the happiest moment in Irish history. Other moments have had more lasting effects, and have signalised a triumph over obstacles incomparably greater. But they have been tainted with the memories of bloodshed and destruction, of past treachery, and present recriminations. Not a shot on this occasion had been fired save in fun, not a drop of blood had been spilt; the triumph was more whole-heartedly and more universally shared than any before or since. It was a happy ending, and like all happy endings, it was much too good to be true. When Parliament reassembled on May 27th, Portland announced that unconditional assent had been given.

We know now that May 1782 was the turning-point. We know that the Whig Viceroy came very soon to feel more an Englishman than a Whig, and that his successors reorganised the Castle system to nullify the constitutional gains of the Irish party. We know so much that Charlemont in that month of May did not know, that Grattan himself hardly suspected. We know, for example, that John Fitzgibbon, later Lord Clare, was a member of that unanimous House of April 16th.[23] There is a strong temptation to dismiss Grattan's Revolution as unreal, to suggest that the whole country was so elated by rhetoric that it left the ground entirely and soared through the empyrean till it returned to reality with a bump. It is easy to conclude that the fuss was all about words, that the revolution was a revolution primarily of terminology. The members of this unanimous parliament were men who had previously taken their orders from the Castle, and would do so again. In a few months they would be bitterly embroiled in a struggle over the merest form of words. The question of Simple Repeal or Renunciation would set Grattan and Flood at each other's throats. Some of the Volunteers would be in the United Irish ranks, but most of the men of property would support Lord Camden's yeomanry. Grattan's Parliament would vanish almost as though it had never been, leaving behind it as memorial only the rhetoric of words and the rhetoric of stone.

In reversing this judgment we shall no doubt be accused of judging by superficial appearances. Let it then be so in good earnest. We judge the past by its surface. The Athens of Pericles, the Rome of Augustus, stand by their cultural products, however discreditable the scholars' revelations of day-to-day political traffic may be. The contemporaries of Grattan said that he spoke 'like a man inspired', and even in cold print the inspiration is very evident. Can we, therefore, believe that that which inspired him was of no real moment? Even the most gorgeous fictions must have a solid basis to retain their value for so long. Grattan's Independence was short-lived and in many ways illusory, but Dublin looks and feels like a capital city still. Public buildings are acts of faith, and Dublin, as we know it, remains the expression of the confidence of the Anglo-Irish nation in its destiny.

Charlemont is the very embodiment of this spirit. We have already seen that as a private builder his motives were as much social and political as they were artistic. As a politician he was the most single-minded of the patriots in this sense: that he saw the events of his time as a pageant of patrician and republican virtue. He was aware, indeed, of the squalid trafficking which went on behind the scenes. But he and Grattan and a handful of others were so utterly untainted with corruption that the colonnaded scenery was for them the reality, and the wire-pulling behind a mere sordid accident. The practical result of their judgment was of course disastrous: but we should be rash metaphysicians if we decided that they were absolutely wrong.

We may say that, as he saw architecture from the political angle, so his view of politics took architectural form. As a member of the Architectural Committee of the House of Lords, which entrusted Gandon with the works made necessary by the new constitutional status of that body, he was in his element. But nothing brings out his attitude more clearly than the affair of the Rockingham Library.

Rockingham died on the 1st of July 1782. 'Few English statesmen of the highest rank', in the opinion of the great historian, 'have been more destitute of all superiority of intellect or knowledge.'[24] And yet his death was a matter of the first consequence. The Whig ministry fell asunder, and the Viceroy Portland, the mouthpiece of England's magnanimity, hurried home

as a candidate for the vacant leadership of the party.
Though Charlemont welcomed his successor[25] as an
ideal appointment, he was 'too well acquainted with
English parties to place, after the death of my dear and
honest friend, much confidence in any of them'.[26] In
retrospect, he came to regard his personal loss as a symbol of Ireland's also.

We have no precise information as to when he first
called upon Gandon to design a shrine to Rockingham's
memory. Our first intimation is a letter from Burke in
July 1787,[27] evidently in reply to one from Charlemont
expressing his desire for a bust of his dead friend. It
appeared that none of the likenesses made during his
lifetime could be relied upon; and so Lady Rockingham's help was enlisted. She was tireless in the performance of her pious office. Nollekens was called in, and
made cast after cast, which were attentively scrutinised
by the widow, and found wanting, 'for there was a
poverty in the character of those, and a tame, but
agonized look, which expressed nothing of *him*, either
in life or death[28] . . .' At last, however, the sculptor
achieved a happiness that satisfied remembrance.
Burke was called in, and agreed with her judgment.[29]
This was in December. In October of the following year
she writes again to Charlemont, explaining that she
could not think of letting the finished bust be despatched without herself giving it a final inspection. Her
health had at last permitted her to go to London for
this purpose, and

I must now speak a word upon its merit. The marble is as
beautifully perfect as anything can be; and I really am as much
contented with the resemblance as it is possible to be with that
sort of thing. I hope you will think it has greatly profited by
the pains I took, and the patience that the artist exerted in

following my directions. Be so good as to place it so as for the
right side of the bust to strike the eye first. The front and the
left side have not to my eye so strong a resemblance; but, upon
the whole, I hope it is worthy of the place your lordship has
kindly destined for it; and your accepting it as a mark of my
gratitude . . . will be the highest satisfaction you can confer
upon me. [30]

Charlemont had not, of course, meditated accepting
the bust as a gift. He writes with touching gratitude,
assures her that the setting satisfies all her stipulations,
and promises to send her a copy of the inscription 'with
the first opportunity'. Why it was not sent immediately
will appear from a transcript:

The most noble, Charles Watson Wentworth,
Marquis of Rockingham,
On whose Character,
A consciousness of partiality would prevent my expatiating,
If I were not confident,
That the utmost ardour of friendship may be necessary
To give warmth to a delineation,
Which, even thus inspired, must fall far short of his merits.
Genuine patriotism, unshaken fortitude,
And immaculate honour,
Dignified his public conduct.
While his private life
Was marked, adorned, and sweetened
By every elegance of taste,
By all the tender endearments of friendship,
And by the constant practice of every social duty.
A Patron of all the Arts, useful and ornamental,
His Perspicuity discovered,
His Influence protected, his Liberality encouraged,
His Courtesy distinguished and animated
Innumerable votaries to true Genius,
Whose modest Merit might otherwise have been concealed,
And lost to their Country.
As a Minister,

History will best speak his Praise.

. . .

[nine lines are here omitted]

. . .

Public Necessity,
And the Voice of the People,
Again called him to the helm of the sinking State,
Which, though now reduced to the last extremity,
By weak and evil governance,
Was saved from impending destruction,
By his persevering skill and courage.
The most jarring and discordant spirits
Were harmonized and kept together,
By the love of his Person, the reverence for his Character,
And the universal confidence in his honesty.
Upon him, as the great centre of attraction,
The confidence, and consequent safety of the whole depended.
He found the Empire involved in the fatal consequences
Of short-sighted, arbitrary, and tyrannic Policy,
When, following the dictates of wisdom,
And of justice,
He gave Peace and Security to his Native Land,
Liberty to America,
And coinciding with the unparalleled efforts
Of her virtuous Sons,
Restored her rights to Ireland.
As his Life was the support,
His death had nearly been the ruin
Of the British Empire,
As if his lamenting Country
Had been loth to survive her darling Son,
Her friend, her benefactor, her preserver.
M.S.P.
CHARLEMONT

In its platitude, this inscription[31] is not unsuitable to
Rockingham's political character, while in its length it
is a fitting tribute to the owner of one of the longest
houses in England. One might have thought it suffi-

cient, but no. Directly under the bust was the following:

> This striking resemblance of her departed Lord,
>   Perpetual source of her grief, and pride!
>   Was the precious gift
>   Of Mary, Marchioness of Rockingham,
>   Under whose painful inspection,
>   And pious care,
>   Exerted in behalf of his ever-lamenting friend,
>   And by the help of whose faithful memory,
>   The model was made
>   1788

In June 1790 Lady Rockingham thanks him for a drawing of the bust in its setting, pronounces the inscription 'every thing that a friend could wish from a friend . . . in words that flow from the heart'.[32] In conclusion she thanks him for two canisters of snuff. 'Your supplies of Irish snuff are always so excellent, that my taste becomes too nice.' 'The memorial of Lord Rockingham ought', wrote Burke, 'to be in the house of the man whom he resembled the most, and loved the best; it is a place fit for a temple to his memory.'

The 'dear, though melancholy present' was in fact a copy by Nollekens of another bust, which found its way to the Duke of Richmond's. Later in 1790 Bishop O'Beirne transcribes for Charlemont's benefit an epigram by Burke's son Richard,

> ON THE BUST OF LORD ROCKINGHAM
> Placed by the
> DUKE OF RICHMOND
> in his Grace's Cabinet

> Hail, marble, happy in a double end,
> Rais'd to departed principles and friend!
> The friend once gone, no principles would stay;

For very grief they wept themselves away.
Therefore from Death they feel one common sting,
And heav'n receives the one, and one the king.[33]

No contrast within· the· same convention could well·
be greater. We may smile at Charlemont's solemn
liturgy, even as we relish the flavour of a mode of feeling so utterly remote from ours. But it is, I think, important to recognise it for what it was, an attempt to
enshrine in an architectural expression a moment of
history which had irrevocably passed.

NOTES

1. HMC, I, 28 sqq.

2. Ibid., 44.

3. Ibid., 36 sqq.

4. H, II, 299. See also in HMC, I, 42, his scornful mention of 'needy adventurers, who crowded and disgraced the house of commons, and whose only rents were the salaries of their offices'. Hardy, we note, calls Charlemont 'a child of the people' (H, II, 303). But on the other hand, in 1795 (HMC, II, 263) Charlemont observes that wages have not risen, though other forms of remuneration, including rents, have: and this he considers an injustice. See also RIA MSS., VI, 479, where he calls the people 'the real and effectual Riches of the State'. These views are not really contradictory, but they should put us on our guard against a too glib interpretation.

5. HMC, I, 38.

6. See particularly the poem on the birth of Charlemont's heir in RIA MSS., XIII, No. II.

7. Save that on this occasion the leases were to be for 999 years. See Lecky, IV, 477 sqq.

8. HMC, I, 47–48.

9. Lecky, IV, 474.

10. C. L. Falkiner: *Studies in Irish History*, 27. Stuart: *History of Armagh*, 1819, 560, etc., etc., etc., Lecky, IV, 494 sqq.

11. Dunlop: *Grattan*, 1889, p. 34.

12. HMC, I, 376.

13. Lecky, IV, 508.

14. H, II, 2. See also, for this and other details, Dobbs: *History of Irish Affairs*, 1779–1782, Dublin, 1783, passim.

15. Dobbs and James Stewart were also present, Dobbs, p. 52.

16. We may note here how little Irish affairs bulk in such a contemporary English account as Wraxall's *Memoirs*.

17. H, I, 163 n., 368; II, 11, 12; HMC, I, 370; II, 85, etc., etc., etc. See also Falkiner, op. cit., p. 16. Barrington, *Rise and Fall of the Irish Nation*, Duffy edition, p. 79, where he considers Fox, rightly I think, quite indifferent to Ireland. See Charlemont on Fox, H, II, 386.

18. Dobbs: op. cit., 69.

19. HMC, I, 55.

20. Ibid., 56. There is a certain malice in the mention of America.

21. Ibid., 59 n.

22. Ibid., 58.

23. He sat for Dublin University, and it is only fair to his memory to add that he voted with the majority only under pressure from his constituents. Falkiner: op. cit., 111.

24. Lecky, III, 93.

25. Nugent Temple Grenville, Earl Temple and subsequently Marquis of Buckingham. He held office under the former title from Sept 1782 till June 1783, and under the latter from Nov 1787 till Jan 1790. He is not to be confused with the Earl of Buckingham*shire*, who was Viceroy 1777–1780, and whom Lecky unaccountably alludes to as 'Lord Buckingham' (IV, 485, and elsewhere).

26. HMC, I, 81.

27. HMC, II, 57.

28. RIA MSS., XIV, 106. This letter and the next (from Malone) have become confused in the binding, and the confusion has infected the text in HMC, II, 60–61. The date (Dec 7th, 1787) is wrongly given as November.

29. HMC, II, 383.

30. This, with Charlemont's reply, in HMC, II, 77.

31. This inscription, as well as others to the memory of Reynolds, Sir Joseph Banks and Earl Camden, are in Appendices to *Hardy*, Vol. II. In Gandon's *Life*, p. 166, may be found a similar tribute from the Earl to Sir William Chambers, who predeceased him also, dying in 1796.

32. RIA MSS., XVI, 40 H, II, 232.

33. HMC, II, 130.

CHAPTER IX

VOLUNTEERS AND PARLIAMENT

In following up the political aspect of the revolution of 1782, we have necessarily lost the thread of Charlemont's personal life. The private and the public man are one on the subject of the Rockingham bust; but from now on we can follow one only at the expense of neglecting the other. 'From the camp, to the peaceful shades of Marino, and his excellent library, was Lord Charlemont's usual transition in those days.'[1] To follow these transitions dutifully to and fro would be merely confusing. The day-to-day political narrative becomes ever more complex, and—what is more to the purpose —it is increasingly a tale of degeneration. Charlemont has moments of optimism right to the end, but they serve only to emphasise his gradual loss of touch with the ascendant political realities. For several years to come the Volunteers take a heavy toll of his energies. But in spite of this, he soon ceases to be an adequate embodiment of their aspirations, and they themselves in time cease to represent a political force of importance.

At the second Dungannon Convention in June, 1782, he was elected in his absence Commander-in-Chief of all the Northern Volunteers.[2] They also presented him with an emblazoned copy of their resolutions on that occasion, which he had framed and hung in the great library of Charlemont House as a 'perpetual monument'.[3] He also commanded a Dublin corps of Volunteers, and was frequently chosen as reviewing general by the local Volunteer bodies all over the country. Their numbers have been estimated at sixty or seventy thousand all told: we hear of him reviewing ten thousand men at Ballincollig, Co Cork, in 1782. Other Cork reviews took place at Bandon (his mother's territory) and Inishannon (his step-father's), and in Cork City itself, where they were held on the Mall. The Armagh reviews took place on the Mall there (at that time the racecourse), a peculiarly suitable setting for such an occasion. On one occasion the rain prevented this, and he reviewed the troops from the window of what is now the Beresford Arms Hotel. In 1781 a mock attack and defence of Belfast, which he witnessed, involved some five thousand men. Another five thousand were reviewed at Downpatrick in 1783. We find him as far afield as Loughmore, Co Limerick, and of course at Fort Stewart, Co Donegal, where he commonly stayed with his cousin and banker, Sir Annesley Stewart, reviewing the Derry Volunteers en route.[4]

His function was to observe and applaud the manoeuvres, to present medals for swordsmanship and marksmanship, and to give political advice when he was asked for it, which was not seldom. But the drums and the tramplings, the glint of sunlight on swords and cockades, were in practice mere brief interruptions in the weary business of travelling the rough roads of Ireland. It was doubtless gratifying to his vanity, but mostly it was devotion to the public service which sustained him. Though he was not yet sixty, his constitution was increasingly undermined by nervous ailments. He grudged every minute spent away from his books, but there is some ground for supposing that the external action of volunteering was in itself a medicine.

Irish provincial towns were at that time even more isolated than they are now. In proportion they had, it is true, a much more vigorous life of their own. Yet they could hardly afford to miss the colour and the excitement, the sense of great events on their doorsteps, attendant upon a volunteer function. Hardy considers that the volunteer movement contributed powerfully to the civilisation of the minor country gentry:

> The different ranks of society became more mingled. Those who were uninformed, frequently, often daily met those who were not so. Liberal intercourse took place, and many were ashamed of continuing ignorant. Reading became, though slowly, a fashion, and what was originally fashion, gradually changed into a favoured, and pleasing habit . . . unquestionably more books were bought, and continued to be so, after the voluntary institution was formed, than ever before in Ireland.[5]

Although elsewhere Hardy comments on the baneful effect of political preoccupation in smothering literature and the arts, there is something in his earlier observations. It is possible even that he has unwittingly suggested an explanation of the strange barrenness of classical Anglo-Ireland in all cultural fields except architecture. It is possible that for a short time there was just enough political activity, and that sufficiently optimistic and unanimous, to stimulate an interest in literature. Previously there had been too little, later there would be too much and of too desperate a character.

It was only to be expected that relations between the Volunteers and the regular military should be somewhat equivocal. Lord Clanricarde reports to Charlemont that there have been some passages between the Galway Volunteers and the 66th Regiment, which was stationed there.[6] But the Government transferred the regiment elsewhere, and the problem solved itself without injury to Volunteer prestige. Such incidents would have been more frequent and much more serious, had the government been in a position to send troops to Ireland in any quantity. No one would have been more distressed than Charlemont if any incidents had occurred to inflame the less fruitful kinds of national animosity.

But there were, of course, Royal troops in Dublin itself. It was usual for them to fire three volleys from their barracks, on a signal given from Dublin Castle at the close of the Ode annually sung there on the King's birthday. In June 1782 the official Commander-in-Chief discussed with Charlemont the project of a combined performance by Volunteers and Regulars, firing alternate volleys. Were they to parade at opposite ends of the Quays, or on either side of Stephen's Green, or the Regulars in College Green and the Volunteers in Stephen's Green? 'The distance is not too great for the vollies being heard and the alternate firing being kept up distinctly.'[7] The officer in question was none other than General Burgoyne, whose name is inseparably linked with the surrender at Saratoga. He was an Irishman and a dramatist of some distinction, and he had now been placed by the Whigs in a situation where he was unlikely to lose another army, for want of an army to lose. He and Charlemont, with whom he remained on the very best of terms, made a pretty pair.

Charlemont, on his way to review the Limerick Volunteers, passed through Nenagh where there were none but regular troops. These latter accordingly mounted a guard of honour for him.[8] Conversely, the Viceroy deigned to attend a Volunteer review in the Phoenix Park, murmuring soft words to their Commander-in-Chief.[9] When Earl Temple departed the Volunteers attended on him; but this honour was not at first accorded to his successor, on the ground that he had not yet had the opportunity of doing anything to deserve it.[10] Such a combination of high mettle and scrupulosity, of jealousy, courtesy and magnanimity, distinguished the movement at the height of its influence.

This influence was lost almost overnight by their most dramatic manoeuvre. A third Dungannon Convention, representing 269 military corps, was held in September 1783. It was there decided to hold a National Convention in Dublin in November, in order to discuss ways and means of Parliamentary Reform. Charlemont, with some misgiving, gave his assent to this proposal.

To understand the reasons for his uneasiness, we must briefly advert to parliamentary matters. The settlement of 1782 still stood, but one or two ill-judged pronouncements from English sources had given rise to the idea that it was in danger.[11] The notion grew that England had not done enough in repealing Poyning's Law, that she should also pass a law declaring that Poyning's Law had always been unconstitutional. This view entirely lost sight of the fact that what the British Parliament had unsaid it could always say again. It involved the old fallacy of the future limitation of sovereignty. But in spite of its fallacy, it gained currency, and Flood, who had played a subordinate part in recent happenings, saw in it a means of regaining the limelight. He espoused the cause of Renunciation against Simple Repeal. Grattan pointed out that an additional form of words was no safeguard. Years later, in his last speech against the Union, he was to say 'What security has Ireland? [The minister] answers with great candour—Honour—English Honour. Now, when the

PLATE XI (a)

See page 136

THE CASINO

Urn masking the area between the steps to South

PLATE XI (b)

See page 135

THE CASINO

One of the corner-panels

liberty and security of one country depend on the honour of another, the latter may have much honour, but the former no liberty.'[12] In 1782 his argument was that no form of words did anything to secure the position. In effect he appealed to the existence of the Volunteers as the best security.[13] Ironically it was Flood who carried the country with him for Renunciation, and it was Flood who gained control of the Volunteer movement.

The Volunteers were by no means unanimous over Renunciation: but they were almost all in favour of Reform. Charlemont was with them here, Grattan was with them, Flood was with them. On the subject of Catholic Emancipation many of the Volunteers, especially those from Ulster, were enthusiastic.[14] Charlemont was opposed to the discussion of this question, and so was Flood, who writes to Charlemont in January 1782, 'I am frightened about the Popery business. It ought to be touched only by a master-hand. It is a chord of such wondrous potency that I dread the sound of it . . .'[15] But Grattan was already sympathetic to the Catholic claims. More decisive for the moment was the emancipating zeal of the Earl-Bishop of Derry.

Frederick Augustus Hervey, Earl of Bristol and Bishop of Derry, is by common consent the strangest figure of his time, almost of any time. In particular the analysis of his motives has continued to baffle the historian. It even eluded Charlemont, who had every reason to adopt a purely partisan tone about him. After retailing a number of anecdotes which, if true, are gravely to the discredit of the Earl-Bishop, he observes that 'he sometimes deviated into actions of a nature perfectly contrary, which puzzle our judgment, and tend to show the astonishing contradictions that meet in the composition of this singular man[16] . . .'

N

This 'eccentric and baleful comet, whose short peri-helium of unnatural heat is contrasted by ages of torpid frigidity' saw in the Convention an opportunity of gratifying his political ambition. His interest in the approaching function was shared by the Castle authori-ties. On September 23rd Charlemont was on the point of setting out for the South to review his Volunteers when he received a note from the Viceroy asking him to dine at the Lodge, and to hold 'some confidential conversation upon the present state of affairs'.[17] Grat-tan also was present (it was in fact an informal meeting of the Privy Council), but nothing of importance took place. We can only conclude that Charlemont, inten-tionally or otherwise, made his independent position so plain that it was not thought worth while to attempt any arrangement with him. Between the opening of Parliament and that of the Convention, he was accosted in the House of Commons by Mr Secretary Pelham who begged for a few words in private. 'Pray, my lord,' said Pelham when they were alone, 'what can the Volunteers mean by this convention in Dublin?' 'Sir,' replied Charlemont, 'I apprehend they mean to meet on the tenth of November.' Mr Pelham was a young man, and these tactics found him at a loss. But he per-sisted in his attempt to extract information on behalf of his employers. He was roundly rebuked in his char-acter of secretary, but as Mr Pelham he was cordially invited to wait upon the Earl at Charlemont House.[18] But in truth Charlemont was himself quite as uneasy as the Castle authorities.

The Earl-Bishop, as a Volunteer delegate from Derry, made his state entry into the capital with every circum-stance of magnificence. His coach was drawn by six horses, and he was accompanied by a troop of Volunteer dragoons, commanded by his nephew, George Robert Fitzgerald, whose end was murky.[19] His way took him past Charlemont House, and here he dismounted to pay his respects. Charlemont had prepared for his advent with considerable forethought.

'It was fitting that the Derry troop should be received in a military manner, and accordingly a guard of infantry and a squadron of horse were drawn up at my door, who saluted them at their arrival. But lest the bishop should suppose that any particular honours were paid by the Volunteers to his person, I took care, by my orders, that his coach should be prevented from coming close to the door, that so, under the appearance of respect, I might receive him at some distance from the house, and that, returning with him from his coach, the subsequent salute should appear to be made to me as general, and not to him. This manoeuvre he clearly understood, and appeared with difficulty to refrain from showing some symptoms of displeasure.'[20]

In due course the Earl-Bishop proceeded southwards towards the Royal Exchange. At the House of Lords portico he halted, and his entourage sounded their trumpets, 'the sudden and unexpected clangour of which echoed throughout the long corridors.' A strange amen, indeed, to the prayers with which the day's business was even then opening. When a number of members had stumbled into the daylight, the Earl-Bishop gave the signal for another fanfare and for the bands to strike up the Volunteers' March. The astonished Lords and Commons retreated into their privileged fastnesses, and, as Barrington says, 'with great solicitude awaited the result'.

But the first honours of the contest went to Charlemont. He was elected President of the Convention.

There was insufficient room in the Exchange, and the Convention adjourned to the Rotunda, very much further alike from Castle and from Parliament House, and almost on the doorstep of Charlemont House. The omens, it seemed, were good. The Convention resolved into several Committees, and went to business.

'The Bishop', says Sir Jonah Barrington in a sentence of inimitable felicity, 'disappointed of the chair, lost no time in rendering it a seat of thorns.' He delighted to dangle the spectre of violence before the President's fastidious nose. Matters, he observed, were taking a promising turn: 'We must have blood, my lord, we must have blood!' On another occasion he taxed Charlemont, *sotto voce*, with lukewarmness on the Reform issue, and insinuated that opinion was turning against him. Charlemont was nettled, and retorted that some people seemed to view with equanimity the prospect of civil war. The Bishop, we may suspect, was waiting for this; for he innocently enquired whether his lordship did not think the reform 'worth the risk of a little confusion'. But now Charlemont was roused, and if his own account is to be trusted, he turned on his tormentor and trounced him energetically and effectively. 'When Ireland was in effect subject to a foreign legislature, there were no lengths I would not have gone to rescue her[20] . . .' But, strongly as he felt about the desirability of reform, he was not prepared to endanger the public peace. The values underlying this speech are significant, and there is every reason to suppose that he meant what he said. The Bishop, we are told, retired in confusion.

Charlemont was able to prevent the adoption of the Catholic franchise by the Convention as a whole. But he was not strong enough to stand against the alliance

of the Earl-Bishop and Flood. He could not prevent
Flood from hastily drafting a reform bill and carrying
it from the Convention to the House of Commons. He
could oppose such tactics only on the score of diplomacy; for he was himself in favour of the bill and his
influence rested largely on this fact. Late in the proceedings he had broken his long silence to express his
readiness to give the borough of Charlemont back to
the people in trust for whom he held it. Flood had his
way, and he entered the House in an evil hour.

The Bill was rejected so completely that the very
leave to introduce it was refused. Barry Yelverton, one
of the finest intellects in the patriotic party, spoke
against it, and even Grattan's speech in favour was a
mere feint. As Charlemont had foreseen, the essence of
Whiggery was affronted by the manner of its introduction. It was unnecessary for the Castle to meddle in the
business: an armed assembly had attempted to over-
awe Parliament. The Whig fiction of legalism had been
assailed, and that was enough.

It was now November 29th. The 30th was a Sunday,
and a large private meeting at Charlemont House
decided that the Convention must be brought to an end
before it did any more damage. On the Monday a delegate arose and began a tirade against Parliament's re-
ception of the Bill. Charlemont adroitly silenced him
by pointing out that it was a rule in parliamentary
assemblies never to take notice of the proceedings in
another house. On the Tuesday a Volunteer Address to
the King protesting loyalty and calling for a reform
was agreed to, and the Convention adjourned *sine die*.[21]
Flood carried the address to England, and the Earl-
Bishop retired to his diocese where, as Charlemont
vindictively remarks, he felt more secure from the long

arm of the Castle.[22] For three weeks Sackville Street
had been pregnant with electrical tension; the positive
pole at the Rotunda and the negative pole at College
Green. The flash had come as the current leapt the gap;
and now there was nothing but an echo, a wisp or two
of smoke, and perhaps a blindness in the eyes from the
too sudden brilliance.

Though we may deplore Charlemont's part in the
Convention, it would be a mistake to underestimate his
abilities. To have retained sufficient control of that assembly to be able to procure its dissolution, was a considerable feat. But it is the kind of action which seldom
appeals to the imagination of posterity. Sir Jonah Barrington, who speaks of Charlemont's 'courteous feebleness', his 'indecision' and his 'imbecility', has succeeded, by simple mis-statement of fact, in establishing
the idea that Charlemont stabbed the Convention in
the back. He states that Charlemont and his friends
resumed sitting at an earlier hour than usual on the
Monday, and adjourned it before most members had
arrived. The adjournment was in fact procured by
means entirely above-board. We need not waste time
on Sir Jonah's belief that Charlemont was in any sense
a 'tool of Government'.[23]

More serious is Sir Jonah's charge that the Earl had
'an odious tinge of bigotry'. The phrase does credit to
its author's heart, but not to the sources of his information. His position with regard to the Catholic claims
was a simple one: he did not think it safe to grant liberty
to those who did not believe in liberty themselves. This
view may be true or false; but the important point is
that he held it in a form unmixed with rancour against
Catholics as people. We shall examine it more closely
when we come to tell of his later change of outlook.

Whatever his attitude had been, he would still have opposed the intrusion of the question into the debates of 1783. The saddest thing about the Convention is the spectacle of three able and well-intentioned men, all sharing some aims in common, and all pulling against each other.

Flood went to the English Parliament, where he failed to live up to his great reputation as an orator. He disappears almost completely from Charlemont's life,[24] and dies in 1791. After the Convention Charlemont abstained for four years from going to the Castle levees, so completely had he lost the confidence of government. His political and personal isolation was intensified by the breach with Grattan in February 1784.

In June 1783 the Viceroy Northington had invited Charlemont to become a member of the Irish Privy Council. He finally agreed on condition that Grattan also should be made a member. During the Convention period Grattan was frequently summoned to Councils, while Charlemont was passed over. Charlemont happened to comment upon this to Grattan, and the latter refused to attend councils to which Charlemont was not also bidden. Oddly enough, it was this stipulation, apparently the counterpart of his own a little earlier, which gave offence to the Earl. 'The being called to a council at the solicitation of any man was not very flattering to my vanity[25] . . .', and so, though invited, he abstained from attending. Grattan wrote to him, hinting at a plan whereby 'we might become the government ourselves, having that confidence in each other which it can not be expected any minister will have in us'.[26] Charlemont thought this a wild scheme, and wrote a friendly note asking Grattan to come and see him.[27] But Grattan never came, and Charlemont, who had already fancied some coolness on Grattan's side, gave him up for lost. Grattan still sat for Charlemont borough, but he seems to have set about resigning the seat, negotiating through Sir Annesley Stewart, his co-member for the borough. In this he was unsuccessful, and so, as he was now acting on his own in Parliament, he purchased the borough of Longford for Sir Annesley's son. Charlemont made it clear that though he approved of young Stewart being brought into Parliament, he would not consider him a political connexion. As for obligation, 'The Friendship of an honest Man is inestimable—*That* you have possessed in the highest Degree—For *That* alone you are obliged to me, an Obligation which nothing can cancel, and which cou'd only have been repaid by an equal Return'. It was a touchy and pompous letter,[28] and it makes sad reading. Grattan's reply[29] was dignified. Charlemont, he said, could not lose a friend so easily; but as to putting an end to intercourse, '. . . it is what you certainly can do—but you can do no more—you cannot diminish the opinion regard and love which I retain for your [Lord] ship in the highest degree . . .'

With the loss of such powerful allies, and the cessation of relations with the Government, Charlemont leaves the centre of the political stage, to our relief and perhaps also to his own. Until the Regency Crisis of 1789, we shall not find him playing a leading part.

But we may glance back at an episode in which political and family affairs were alike involved. His stepfather, Thomas Adderley, it will be remembered, had parted company from him in 1761. Though they lived on adjacent sides of the same square, they seem to have held no communication. The Viceroy Temple, who held office from September 1782 till March 1783, employed much of his time in cleansing the Augean stables of the higher Civil Service. Among the casualties was Adderley, who, as treasurer to the Barrack Board, 'was found deficient in a very large sum'.[30] Temple had written to Charlemont before even his vice-regal appointment was made public, and now he consulted him before taking any action against Adderley. Charlemont replied that if Adderley were dear to him as a brother, he should still applaud his excellency's conduct. Adderley was accordingly dismissed, and though he defended himself in Parliament, the Attorney-General sued him for recovery of the money. Even the powerful protection of Lord Shannon was of no avail. Times, it seemed, had changed since the day in 1739 when the relatives of Lord Santry could save him from punishment for murder by threatening to cut off the Dublin water supply.

By 1783, the peak of his political career, Charlemont was fifty-five. His daughter Elizabeth was ten, his son Francis William was eight, James Thomas was seven, and Henry was four. The unusual sequence of his life, in which the years of vigour were spent in cultivating his garden, while those of middle and old age were the season of external activity, must have prevented him from seeing very much of his children at the age when most fathers play lions with their sons. The Volunteer reviews kept him on the move, and Marino, Lady Charlemont and the children were left much to themselves. One letter[31] of hers has survived, and gives a charming picture of the deserted family.

July the 18th [1783]

I had your welcome letter, my dearest, this day, & it has made it a happy one for me, I was one Post without hearing from you & I did *not like it*, tho I was reasonable enough to

consider the matter & to allow that you cou'd not help it—
Sir John & your Sister are arrived with their son, Cormic, &
many &cs—Sir J has brought Mrs Walcott's treasures & I
think she will be perfectly satisfied . . . He has brought a Dog
for himself from France I believe to keep his tongue in practice,
for he speaks vile bad French to it incessantly—Poor Mr Bernard will be in great trouble, he has lost the poor *Hare*, he
died last Week of a fit, I cannot help being sorry for him, or
rather for what his Father will feel on the occasion, Sir John B
tells me that Mr Bernard had left him near three thousand pds
a year & a large sum of money in his Will—do not forget a bit
of crape for him—it will do for Mrs Purse [?] also who departed last Week—I am very sorry for Sir John O'Neill's behind, but a wiser one might have been singed when fire was
abroad. Mr J Stewart's illness was a serious matter, I am glad
he did not know it 'till it was over, I love him for his own sake
as well as for being your friend, & the last motive is sufficient
for a great deal of anxiety on such an occasion—Frank came
home this day in very good health, & as noisy as a *school* Boy—
We have had our Hay rain'd on all the Morning, but the Lawn
before the Building is safe in Tramp Cocks—I am content to
bear rain when it does not fall on Review days—Good night
my dearest, you are this moment at supper at Fort Stewart, &
I am retiring to *solitary* rest—

the 19th.

My Eyes still a little weak, I have abstain'd from Mrs Sid-
dons out of prudence, more rain upon our Hay—The Children
send you a thousand loves, Henry says he will keep six Kisses
for you—Nancy desires her Love—remember us to our friends
at Fort Stewart—the Pea and Guinea chickens send their
duty—

My Paper is magnificent, but it is like writing on butter.

To turn from this to the gossip-columns of the *Town
& Country Magazine*[32] is like stepping from a solid pave-
ment onto a quicksand. That journal carried in its issue
of December 1785 two engraved portraits, entitled
'The *stanch* Patriot' and 'The Fair Hibernian'. The
former is not markedly recognizable as Charlemont,

while the latter, so far as I am aware, has eluded identification. An article in the series of '*Tête-à-tête's*' then
running, follows. 'We are happy', says the anonymous
author, 'to introduce to the world a character that is
indisputably allowed by all parties to be truly amiable.'
If the subsequent remarks were as readily intelligible
and as obviously true as this opening, we might know
something of interest. But the suggestions are cryptic
to a degree: there is mention of 'Dainty Daisy', 'Sir
Francis D——l', and 'Miss R——h', of whom the
second is perhaps Sir Francis Blake Delaval. Of the
lady we are told only that '. . . strange to relate, she has
escaped the observation of the amorous biographers of
the day'. The only things which serve to pin it to
Charlemont are the political allusions. There was probably no foundation for the article, which presumably
relied on an intentional vagueness to escape prosecution.

The triumph of 1782 was commemorated by certain
public undertakings of a ceremonial character—less
purely motivated than the Rockingham Library, and
more enduring than the feux-de-joie of the Volunteers.
During the Temple administration, George III con-
ceived the idea of founding an Irish order of knight-
hood, the Knights of St Patrick.[33] Charlemont was
among the first candidates whom Temple approached.
He asked for time to consider the matter, as he feared
that the institution might have undesirable political
effects. He feared also that if he accepted the honour,
he might find himself in bad company. Though the
Viceroy had assured him that 'the order was to be kept
as chaste as possible, and that, for this purpose, none
but earls were to be admitted', such chastity was not
the only consideration. 'It could not be very pleasing

to me to be one of an order which must be composed of
men who differed so essentially from me in every political
principle . . .' for, says Charlemont, he would be at
a loss to find seven earls 'with whom I would wish to
class myself'; and fourteen were needed. At the end of
three weeks he had not yet replied, and Temple pressed
for an answer.

Charlemont's main scruple was the fear of unpopu-
larity and resulting loss of influence. Wishing to take
Grattan's advice on this point, he had put off his decision; but Grattan was still away from town. He put his
dilemma, more or less candidly, to Temple himself, and
the latter ingeniously carried the matter by writing him
an open letter[34] which made the proferred honour an
endorsement of Charlemont's recent policy as a Volunteer leader. Charlemont so freely admits his love of
popularity that the corollary, that he loves it because
it gives him an instrument wherewith to serve Ireland,
carries conviction. Much elegant play was made during
this interchange, with the motto of the new order,
'Quis Separabit?',[35] a rhetorical question to which time
was not slow to give an answer.

'I had', he confesses, 'wished that in the offer made
to me of the ribband, and the manner in which this
honour was conferred, some difference should occur between the man of the people, the commander of the
Volunteers, and the other noblemen on whom the order
was bestowed . . . In this transaction lord Temple not
only acted handsomely but wisely also, since it was
certain that, had I refused, the order would have become unpopular, and possibly might have fallen to the
ground . . .'

Majesty itself was graciously pleased to occupy the
first stall in the Order. The Prince of Wales requested

the second stall, by custom occupied by a prince of the blood. But when it appeared that his Royal Highness expected to be allowed to go to Dublin for his installation, the combination of personal and national jealousy which commonly animated the King's breast, caused him to appoint Prince Edward instead. The remaining stalls were filled by the Duke of Leinster, and the Earls of Clanrickarde, Westmeath, Inchiquin, Drogheda, Tyrone, Shannon, Clanbrassil, Mornington, Arran, Courtown, Bective and Ely. The Viceroy was the first Grand Master, and Primate Robinson was the Chaplain.

The installation,[36] which Charlemont considered 'a badge and symbol of Ireland's newly rescued independence' took place in Saint Patrick's Cathedral on Saint Patrick's Day, March 17th, 1788. The Volunteers lined the streets, and were placed 'so that they became spectators, and, in some degree, a part of the ceremonial. This had a good effect, as it highly gratified them, and particularly distinguished me from my noble compeers, being saluted as general by the whole line, while the people, who were assembled in amazing crowds, received me everywhere as I passed with loud acclamations and shouts of applause.'

An installation feast followed in St Patrick's Hall, Dublin Castle. Horace Walpole intended at the time to suggest to Charlemont, and did in fact so suggest two years later, that the portraits of the knights should be painted in commemoration.[37] A painting was in fact already done by one John Sherwin; a poor enough piece, depicting the Knights as they arose to drink the King's health. Charlemont paid £7.17.6 to Sherwin for three copies of the engraving, and he notes on his receipt: 'I believe never delivered'.[38] William Drennan, later to be a founder of the United Irishmen, observed

that 'The collars of the Knights of St Patrick will in
time strangle the freedom of the nation'.[39] However
this may be, the banners of the Knights, including
those of the second and third Earls of Charlemont, have
hung in St Patrick's Cathedral undisturbed[40] since the
disestablishment of the Irish Church in 1869. They
have had as little effect on the nation as the nation has
had on them.

NOTES

1. H, I, 407.
2. HMC, I, 68; H, I, 134.
3. HMC, I, 413.
4. A great deal of information relating to the Volunteers is embodied
in papers by Robert Day and others in the *Cork Archaeological Journal*;
JRSAI and *UJA* 2nd series, and, more recently, in a series of contributions by T. G. F. Paterson to *UJA* 3rd series. I am indebted to Mrs Fayle,
daughter of the late Robert Day, for MS. material, and to Mr Paterson
for much verbal information. See also the Belfast Museum catalogue of
Volunteer, etc., Relics: pub. No. 120, 1938.
5. H, I, 408. Dobbs: op. cit., 1783, p. 37, bears similar testimony: 'The
Fair, also, materially served the Volunteer cause. Countrymen, from
being slovenly in their dress, and awkward in their manners, became
neat in their persons, and comparatively polished and refined.'
6. HMC, I, 405.
7. Ibid., 403.
8. Ibid., 99.
9. H, II, 59–60.
10. HMC, I, 101.
11. Lord Mansfield and Lord Abingdon were responsible for the
offences in this regard: HMC, I, 85, 423; ibid., 66, 67, etc.
12. Grattan: *Speeches*, 1847, 291.
13. Ibid., 96–97.
14. Lecky, VI, 337.
15. HMC, I, 392.
16. Ibid., 121 sqq. See also an extended character of the Earl-Bishop
by Charlemont in ibid., pp. 165 sqq.
17. Ibid., 428.
18. Ibid., 119–120.
19. He was hanged for sundry crimes at Castlebar in 1786. See *Fighting
Fitzgerald and other papers*, by Mary MacCarthy. Also Maxwell: *Country
and Town in Ireland*, Chapter I.

20. HMC, I, 125–126.

21. These facts are quite clear from Lecky, VI, 344 sqq., and from Charlemont's account in HMC, I, 123 sqq. Sir Jonah Barrington, in the *Historic Memoirs (Rise and Fall of the Irish Nation*, Duffy ed., p. 184) has simply misrepresented the known facts, to Charlemont's discredit.

22. HMC, I, 132, from which it appears that the Earl-Bishop was actually present at the last sittings, but held his peace. Barrington observes that 'Whilst Lord Charlemont gently descended into the placid ranks of order and of courtesy, the Bishop rose like a phoenix from the ashes of the Convention'. This is arrant nonsense, as the Bishop took no further part in Irish politics.

23. Except in so far as he happened to hold *some* views which the Government also held.

24. They did, however, continue to correspond until 1788.

25. HMC, I, 104.

26. RIA MSS., XIV, No. 3, Oct 22, 1783.

27. HMC, I, 106, Oct 23rd.

28. RIA MSS., XIV, No. 4, Feb 9th, 1784.

29. Ibid., No. 7, Feb 14th, 1784.

30. HMC, I, 158. See also, for Charlemont's high opinion of Temple; ibid., 85 sqq. and II, 66.

31. RIA MSS., XIII, 102. 'Sir John' is Sir J. Browne of the Neale, who married Charlemont's sister Alicia, 23 Apr, 1764. He was a baronet of Nova Scotia and was created Lord Kilmaine in 1789.

32. *Town and Country Magazine*, Dublin, Dec 1785, p. 625.

33. HMC, I, 151 sqq.

34. Ibid., 154.

35. In HMC, II, 404 sqq., is given a document which appears to be the secret constitution of an earlier 'order of St Patrick' of which Charlemont was Grand Master. It embodies some temperate restrictions on the convivial use of wine. The motto was 'for my country' and the secret sign was 'putting his right hand on his left breast under his waistcoat, denoting fidelity to his country, and immediately after raising it to his left shoulder, as an emblem that he has a musquet to support the rights of Ireland.'

36. H, II, 66 sqq.

37. HMC, II, 29–30.

38. RIA MSS., XIV, 41.

39. *The Drennan Letters* (PRO of N I), p. 400.

40. Save by an accidental fire in recent years, which destroyed half of them, together with the helms and swords over the southern stalls. Banners, helms and swords have since been restored in facsimile.

CHAPTER X

THE USES OF LEISURE

The household at Marino was, in the intervals of Volunteer expeditions, the very embodiment of the middle-class domestic ideal. The only touch of ceremonial was the gleaming new Casino. Even there, we may suspect, the ceremonial was more apparent than real. 'It is quite the fashion in Ireland', writes Lady Caroline Damer in 1778, 'to have a cottage neatly fitted up with Tunbridge ware, and to drink tea in it during the summer'.[1] This, however ludicrously inadequate as a description of the Casino, must be added to the other accounts of its purposes. When the Earl dates a letter from 'Marino' we may visualise him writing it in the tiny Zodiac room, perhaps more often than in the house itself. The Zodiac room was adapted to hold a considerable number of books: doubtless a selection of his most friendly volumes lined the shelves. And here, in the quiet years after 1783, he may have compiled the political memoirs addressed to his three sons, as well as the large body of verse translations which increasingly occupied his energies. Lady Charlemont, too, was fond of the Casino, and filled the other small room with chosen bits of china. As for the children, we may well wonder whether at this age they were allowed access to this delicate building. Very probably they were not.

This kind of architecture brings to the modern mind the reflexion that it depends very closely upon social circumstances which may never recur again. In general terms this is an obvious truism. But in particular physi-

See page 146

PLATE XII

THE MOY

from the Charlemont Fort. The early XIXth century Church stands on one side of the Square

cal respects it is even more strikingly true. No building
for the use of the many could afford so many vulner-
able small parts, on the exterior as well as inside. We
can, with an effort, imagine a state of society in which
admirable garden-houses could be erected in large numbers for the semi-private use of the public. But we cannot imagine the Casino surviving such usage. Most of
the detail would be broken off during the first six
months.

Nowadays a high wire fence entirely surrounds the
building. There was no such protection in the Earl's
time, though, as we read in an account of 1783 'The
utmost Liberality of Admission is permitted here; the
Inhabitants of *Dublin* may at all times amuse themselves with an agreeable Walk. This Liberty has never
hitherto been abused[2] . . .' The normal Irish demesne,
as every traveller is but too well aware, is entirely surrounded by a high stone wall. Charlemont's policy was
bold and public-spirited. It extended, of course, to the
grounds alone: he trusted to the native delicacy of
Dubliners where inhabited buildings were concerned.
In January 1789 *Exshaw's Magazine* reports that 'Last
week, the Temple of Marino, belonging to that worthy
nobleman the Earl of Charlemont, was stripped of
about 1,500 lb of lead, and several other articles, by a
set of nefarious villains, after whom the strictest search
is making'.[3] But we do not hear that he thought better
of his decision, for in March of the following year he
was robbed of six guineas in his own demesne. The mis-
creant, however, was caught by his Lordship's domest-
ics and immured in Kilmainham.[4] It was not the first
such incident. In 1774, on a September evening, 'As the
Right Hon the Lord Charlemont and his Lady were
walking before dinner, in his Lordship's inclosures,

o

Lady Charlemont, being weary, retired to rest herself
in the grotto, when a man, genteelly dressed, came up
to his Lordship, and, presenting a pistol, demanded his
money, which being complied with, the man walked off
through the wilderness, and made his escape. His Lordship, for fear of alarming his Lady, forbore to mention
the affair till they were both safe in the house'.[5] Exactly
two years later another person, also 'of a genteel
appearance' relieved him of watch and purse. When
captured he proved to be a former servant of the Earl's.[6]
In 1787 a 'daring footpad', armed with a case of brass-
mounted pistols, made off with two guineas and a half.[7]
Such incidents were not rare on the outskirts of Dublin;
but the Earl's advanced ideas of public spirit laid him
open to a peculiarly heavy tax in this direction. He
seems to have thought it worth the money.

While the general public might roam through the
grounds, individuals with suitable introductions were
entertained in the Casino itself. Of such, on at least two
occasions, was John Wesley; and it is instructive to see
what impression this pretty piece of paganism made on
the man of God. Wesley, it may be noted, had preached
in the precincts both of the Charlemont Fort, and of
Castlecaulfeild House. Of his visit to Marino in 1778 he
writes:

' It is one of the pleasantest places I have ever seen: the
water, trees and lawn are so elegantly intermixed with each
other, having a serpentine walk running through a thick wood
on one side, and an open prospect both of land and sea on the
other. In the thickest part of the wood is the Hermitage, a
small room, dark and gloomy enough. The Gothic temple, at
the head of a fine piece of water, which is encompassed with
stately trees, is delightful indeed. But the most elegant of all
the buildings is not finished: the shell of it is surprisingly
beautiful, and the rooms well contrived both for use and orna-

ment. But what is all this unless God is here? Unless He is known, loved, and enjoyed? Not only vanity, unable to give happiness, but vexation of spirit.[8]

Three days later he embarked on the *Prince of Orange* for England. Were his concluding remarks inspired by an observation that Charlemont was suffering from one of his recurrent fits of depression? or do they spring merely from the misconception that, because the Earl was unwilling to talk about religion, he therefore had none? His notice of another visit nine years later casts no light on these questions.

A few friends took me to Marino.... lovely mixture of wood, water and lawns, on which were several kinds of foreign sheep, with great plenty of peacocks; but I could not hear any singing-birds of any kind.[9]

Somewhat surprisingly, he notes the absence of song-birds anywhere near Dublin. Was it his imagination? At all events, 'In the evening I strongly enforced those awful words, "Strive to enter in at the strait gate" upon a numerous congregation ...' Few of his listeners were burdened with expensive miniature buildings, which might be difficult to fit through the needle's eye.

Arthur Young, a less imaginative traveller, visited both Charlemont House and Marino in 1776. Like Wesley, he soon diverges into his own particular enthusiasm. But before particularising the breeds of grass and clover grown at Marino, he has time to observe that the Casino 'ranks high among the most beautiful edifices I have anywhere seen; it has much elegance, lightness, and effect, and commands a fine prospect'.[10] This, from so stolid a soul, was a tribute indeed.

The view from Marino House was threatened during the 1790s by one Ffolliott, a house-painter and specula-

tive builder, who wanted to build houses on a plot near
the shore. Charlemont interviewed him without success,
and fell back on charging exorbitantly for the carriage
of materials through the toll-gate which he controlled.
But Ffolliott transported his materials by barge across
the bay, and took his revenge by designing the houses
as a handsome crescent which still stands. It succeeded
in spoiling the view from Marino House but does not
interfere with that from the Casino higher up the slope.

. At Charlemont House the Earl took on a more public
and more ceremonial character. There were visitors who
came, as to Marino, to see the house, the pictures and
the books. There were political emissaries from across
the water, such as Fox and Sir Philip Francis. There
were, from time to time, the party conferences of the
Irish Whigs. As far as possible, Charlemont kept the
Rutland Square house for this side of life. It helped to
protect Marino and preserve it as a personal retreat.
Sometimes, indeed, this neat division of life was
threatened from high quarters. In October 1785 the
Duke of Rutland, then Viceroy, drove out to Marino
unannounced, partly in order to see the place (for he
had a real interest in architecture), but partly also to
re-open a political discussion which had been shelved
at a point where differences seemed likely to crop up.
But the Earl was not at home, and Rutland was obliged
to return without gratifying his curiosity.[11] The ordinary citizen might enter at will whether the Earl were at
home or not; but etiquette forbade that the Viceroy
should linger in his absence. Political opposition complicated even cultural relations between Charlemont
and the Viceroy, and made it quite impossible for them
to call on one another in Town.[12]

. From time to time it would seem that Charlemont

carried ceremony to the length of keeping a private
chaplain. We hear little about these chaplains, but what
little we know is not altogether happy. There was the
Rev Dr Samuel Pullein, who had held the post as long
ago as 1759. As head of Charlemont's London household, he had dismissed a servant during his employer's
absence in Dublin. Dr Lucas, being on the spot, took
up the defence of the domestic against 'this haughty,
cruel priestling', apparently with success.[13] Dr Pullein,
it seems, was in some sort a protégé of Sir William
(then Mr) Chambers, and in 1763 the latter touches
rather coldly on something Charlemont has written
about the same Pullein.[14] By 1779 the position of Chaplain to the Earl had become more nominal in character.
The Rev Edward Ryan, who then held it, writes in
March of that year complaining of the loss of Charlemont's friendship for no apparent reason. The reverend
gentleman had had an uncle who was fond of his Lordship, but the nephew insinuates that he himself is at a
loss to account for such an affection. A week later Ryan
begs to relieve himself of 'the mock honour of your
Lordship's patent', and in resigning his post, encloses
also the portrait of Charlemont which the Earl had at
some time given him. Charlemont's draft reply protests
that Ryan's letter is unintelligible to him, and would
he kindly call to clear the matter up?[15] It seems quite
intelligible to us, so far at least as it goes, and if it is
true it leaves a slightly unpleasant taste in the mouth.[16]
But we know only one side of the story, and that im-
perfectly. It reminds us that Charlemont's relations
with his entourage were not invariably bland.

His relations with his men of business were strained
at times, to say the least. The very next letter in the
collection is endorsed by Charlemont 'Dogherty's last

letter', and a sorry tale it tells. Dogherty regretfully quits the Earl's service as attorney because he has not been paid. There follow a few letters on scholarly subjects, which incidentally reveal that Charlemont is still spending money freely on books. And in June Thomas Knox is dunning him for £4977.13.10.[17] Charlemont replies that he is indeed extremely sorry, but hopes that Sir Annesley Stewart may be able to help. When we remember that six years earlier a Government *catalogue raisonnée* of Members of Parliament had characterized Stewart thus:

> ... a relation of Ld Charlemont's by marriage Stewart is a banker and my Ld who is very necessitous owes him a large sum of money which makes Stewart independant.[18]

we realise that behind the prancings of the mighty ones on Volunteer parade-grounds, there lay a sad financial tangle. Four letters on financial matters between June 1776 and October 1778 were burned by the second Earl. It may be that they showed matters in an even worse light. And all the time he was spasmodically trying to realise the value of lands in the North, and to scrape together enough for the purchase price of Marino from his own landlord, Sir Francis Lumm.[19]

Yet apart from a few perfunctory asides in documents intended only for private perusal after his death,[20] there is little sign that these embarrassments weighed heavily upon him. Sometimes, like the rheumatism, they must have given him momentary twinges of pain, perhaps a few weeks of depression. Politics and pageantry formed an admirable diversion from such thoughts. But even upon these the shadow was cast. In the delirious days of 1782, a malicious rumour did not spare to assert that Grattan, having been voted

£50,000 as a free gift by a grateful nation, had refused to lend the General of the Volunteers a mere £5,000 of which, for all his noble attitudes and gestures, he stood sorely in need.[21]

In view of this, it is surprising that ruin did not overtake him, and still more surprising that his son lived to be a rich and prosperous landlord. The second Earl could afford to have the remaining lands surveyed, mapped and the maps expensively bound, and to carry through ambitious building schemes on his Northern lands. The explanation is probably that Charlemont, being a non-resident proprietor, was unable to extract much from lands which were rising in value all the time. It only needed a little application now and then to make them yield enough to get him out of a tight corner. And undoubtedly a timely bequest from an uncle who died some time before 1789, helped to ease the immediate pressure.[22]

Happily, these embarrassments did not cut him off from the enjoyment of taking part in the disbursement of public monies in the cause of architectural magnificence. When the appellate jurisdiction of the Irish House of Lords was restored in 1782, the problem of additional accommodation, which had already been discussed, became urgent. It was not so much the physical necessity for extra space, as the psychological necessity for an increase in the visible expression of inward political consequence. That this was so is evident from the fact that Gandon's design had been approved by the committee of the Lords before the political victory had been achieved.[23] Charlemont was on this committee, as were also Portarlington, who was Gandon's patron *par excellence*, and Tyrone, the brother of John Beresford of the Custom House. It was almost the only occasion on which Gandon was allowed to proceed un-. molested with an undertaking fully sanctioned at the outset.

The viceroyalty of Rutland, which lasted from February 1784 till October 1787, was a fortunate period for the arts in Dublin, and a particularly happy time for Gandon. While it lasted, the latter was comparatively free from those molestations which continually remind one of the tribulations of Wren himself. The first architecturally-minded Viceroy since the time of Chesterfield held office at a singularly happy time. He delighted in laying foundation-stones and in hastening the emplacement of coping-stones, he built fountains, and the square in which Charlemont House itself stood was named in his honour.[24] On this front at least, he cordially allied himself with the Irish gentlemen whose ambition was to raise themselves a series of monuments. When he died at the early age of thirty-three, a victim to the convivial commitments of his high office, he was sincerely mourned, and he lay in state in the Irish House of Lords.

The grandeur of architecture and ceremonial in the Irish Parliament and the Viceregal Court is constantly remarked by English visitors of the time, who contrast it with the relative poverty of London in this respect.[25] There was in Dublin no such jealousy of central authority as operated in England to scotch most schemes of magnificence. It was the Earl-Bishop of Derry, writing of the Church which he adorned, who put the matter in a nutshell: 'Let the Church', he said, 'decorate the country, if it cannot receive it, and let its steeple and spire make it the visible as well as the Established Church.'[26] Noble words indeed, and applicable with few alterations to the Irish Parliament: 'Let the Parlia-

ment decorate the country, if it cannot represent it . . .'
The monuments of this attitude are plain for the cir-
cumspect to see.

Although Charlemont was also of the committee
which unanimously approved Gandon's design for the
Commons extensions which balanced those of the
Lords, the petty persecutions of the architect had
begun again, and his plans were mutilated in the execution.[27] But the date, by then, was 1792, and political
disruption is reflected in the arts. Charlemont and Gandon, however, were always on good terms. During the
building of the Custom House, the Earl was in the
habit of frequenting, every Saturday, some sea-baths
near the new site, and he usually took the opportunity
of seeking Gandon out there or at his Mecklenburgh
Street house close by, for an hour or two's gossip on the
fine arts.[28]

There existed at this time in Dublin a 'Neosophical
Society' which was presided over by Dr Robert Perce-
val, the first professor of chemistry in Dublin University. At a meeting of this Society at the house of Mr
Preston the poet on March 29th, 1785, 'Dr Kearney . . .
intimated to the Society Ld Charlemont's approbation
of a scheme for establishing in Ireland a society for the
purpose of promoting Science, Literature & Antiquities[29] . . .' Such a society had indeed been founded by
the patriot William Molyneux in the late seventeenth
century, but it perished in the Williamite wars.
'Science', says Hardy, 'could only spring up, dubious
and languid, during the short intervals of our repose
from civic and religious contests.' He observes, on the
other hand, that the rise of civilisation tended to favour
the export of Irish genius and talent to England. But
the foundation of a permanent institution in Dublin

could do something to counteract this. There existed
already the Dublin Society, a European pioneer in its
own field, but it did not embrace any of the pure
sciences.

Charlemont was present at a meeting of the Neoso-
phists three days later, together with Lord Moira,
Colonel Burton Conyngham, General Vallancey, and
John Hely-Hutchinson (Provost of Trinity and Secretary of State). As a result, the first meeting of the Irish
Academy took place at Charlemont House on April
18th, 1785. There were thirty-eight original members,
including, besides those already mentioned, Lord Clanbrassil, the Primate and Bishops of Killaloe, Clonfert,
Waterford and Dromore, the Rt Hon Denis Daly,
Richard Lovell Edgeworth and Sir Joseph Banks (the
last-named an English corresponding member). Charlemont's friend Edmond Malone, and Richard Kirwan
the chemist, were also foundation members. Charlemont was unanimously elected President at the third
meeting, and it was resolved that the Eve of St Patrick's Day be the day appointed for the Annual Meeting
for the Election of the Council and of Officers. Charlemont was re-elected President every year until his
death. The fourth meeting was held at the Navigation
House in lower Grafton Street, long to be the Academy's home. At the fifth meeting Gandon, Grattan and
Hardy were elected members. At an extra meeting on
August 26th Charlemont proposed the Duke of Rutland, and he was admitted by a waiving of the ordinary
rules of procedure for this one occasion. The wisdom of
this move became apparent when on February 14th,
1786, the Royal Charter, which Charlemont had been
asked to seek for in the previous May, was produced
and read. The Royal Irish Academy as it now became,

had already a total of 101 members. By 1789 the figure
of 161 included almost every distinguished man in
Ireland.

Meetings were held rather more than once a month
during most of the year, and though some of the noblemen and prelates were largely ornamental, the enthusiasm had a hard core. Charlemont was nearly always in
the chair, and the quorum of sixteen members was rarely
lacking. Some of the more colourful entries in the minutes may be noticed. It is not difficult to visualise the
scene when 'A Large Vase was exhibited to the Academy by the Committee of Antiquities'. For many years
to come, the deliberations of the Academy were to
leave much to be desired from the viewpoint of archaeological science; but the heart was in the right place.
On the same occasion there was received for publication a 'Translation of an Erse Poem by the Revd Dr
Young'—apparently the same Young who figures in a
Neosophical Minute: 'Resolved that Mr Young be cen-
sured for playing the Devil.' Would that we knew more
of this.

In 1788 Charles O'Conor the antiquary was allotted
financial assistance to enable him to send the Academy
Irish manuscripts from the Vatican, and it was 'Resolved on the Report of a Resolution of Council, that a
Medal be directed to be struck in honour of the President by Mr Mossop'. A deputation was appointed to
wait on the Earl for his consent to this proposal. The
minutes in which this occurs are signed by Charlemont
himself. The medal was struck with his portrait in Volunteer uniform on one side, and an emblematic figure of
Hibernia on the other. It is still awarded.[30]

We find him depositing in the Academy collections
of objects found by the historian O'Halloran in a tumu-

lus in County Limerick, and a gorget of gold came accompanied by amateur antiquarian remarks from Lord Kenmare, a prominent Catholic peer. On June 28th 1788 it was 'Resolved that the Thanks of the Academy be returned to the Prelate Borgia, Secretary of the Congregation de Propaganda Fide at Rome for his Present of Prints and Inscriptions, and that the Secretary transmit the same to Doctor Troy titular Archbishop of Dublin'. The very fact that they dealt, however distantly, with that politic prince of the Church, serves to emphasise how far the Academy at least had moved from the simple erastian position of thirty years before.

Charlemont himself contributed four papers to the Transactions of the Academy: 'The Antiquity of the Woollen Manufacture in Ireland, proved from a Passage of an ancient Florentine Poet' in 1787, an 'Account of a singular Custom at Metelin, with some conjectures on the Antiquity of its origin' in 1790, 'Some considerations on a controverted Passage of Herodotus' in 1791–4, and 'Some Hints concerning the State of Science at the Revival of Letters, grounded on a Passage of Dante in his Inferno, Canto IV, v. 180' in 1797.[31] The scholarship displayed in these efforts is at least respectable by the standards of the time; but perhaps more to the point is the fact that they are admirably adapted for oral delivery, and must certainly have been interesting to listen to. On October 27th, 1798, he was in the chair for the last time, and had the happiness of seeing his second son Henry elected to membership, the eldest, Francis, having already been a member for some time past. During these last years the Academy offered an increasingly more congenial alternative to the parliamentary debates. It is hardly necessary to add that it

has continued to fulfil its purposes with increasing
lustre. Though the Committee of Polite Literature has
long since amalgamated with that of Antiquities, and
the Transactions no longer contain Irregular Odes to
the Moon, the gains have outweighed the losses. In
particular it has concentrated its energies on Irish
antiquities and language. It is pleasant to observe the
nascent interest in these matters during Charlemont's
term of office as first President.[32] Not only did it provide a focus for energy, but from the beginning it gave
that energy a specifically Irish direction. In doing so it
was of incalculable service to the cause of learning, the
more so as it arose in the very nick of time.

From about 1780 onwards, the number of letters per
annum in the Charlemont Papers increases enormously.
Those of later date have no doubt had the best chance
of survival, but this is not a full explanation. The volume of his correspondence became swollen with political communications from all quarters, but even this
does not account for all of it. His principal correspondents for the next ten years are Edmond Malone, Alexander Haliday, Burke and Baretti. Three of these are
members of the Johnson circle, and remind us that
Charlemont himself had, in the days when he had time
to spend in London, frequented their society. The
death of Topham Beauclerk, another member of the
set, in 1780, was a reminder that patriotism was inter-
fering with other ties which, at the best, would not last
for ever, and which could be kept in existence by letter-
writing, in default of social intercourse. As politics
lapsed into depression or, what was perhaps worse,
mere dullness, he turned increasingly to literary correspondence. 'Why', Beauclerk had written as long ago as
1773, 'should fortune have placed our paltry concerns

in two different islands? . . . . If life is good for any thing,
it is only made so by the society of those whom we
love.'[33] Charlemont was elected a member of the Literary Club in 1773,[34] and so much, in Beauclerk's opinion
at least, was he in demand that 'If you do not come
here, I will bring all the club over to Ireland to live
with you, and that will drive you here in your own
defence. Johnson shall spoil your books, Goldsmith pull
your flowers, and Boswell talk to you[35] . . .' But the
Club had been founded ten years earlier, and if we are
to believe Prior's *Life of Malone*, Charlemont was its
virtual founder.[36] He suggested the formation of such
a club to Reynolds, who passed on the idea to Johnson,
proposing the Earl as a foundation member. 'No', said
Johnson, 'We shall be called Charlemont's Club; let
him come in afterwards.' If this is true, it is a remarkable tribute. It certainly chimes in with what we know
of Charlemont's reputation in early life.

From Boswell we get only two glimpses of Charlemont in the Johnson circle. In 1778 Boswell and Johnson discuss the effects of travel on the conversational
range of the traveller. 'How little', says Johnson, 'does
travelling supply to the conversation of any man who
has travelled; how little to Beauclerk?' BOSWELL:
'What say you to Lord Charlemont?' JOHNSON: 'I
never but once heard him talk of what he had seen, and
that was of a large serpent in one of the pyramids of
Egypt.' BOSWELL: 'Well, I happened to hear him tell
the same thing, which made me mention him.'[37] On
March 30th, 1781, Charlemont, having heard a rumour
that Johnson was taking dancing-lessons of Vestris,
conspired with Boswell and others to ask the Doctor if
it were true. It required, as Boswell observes, the bold-
ness of a General of Irish Volunteers to make the at-

tempt. Johnson at first showed signs of irritation, but recovered and gracefully turned the question, 'For why should not Dr Johnson add to his other powers a little corporeal agility?'

We may presume that Charlemont kept off the subject of politics when talking to Johnson. Nearly half the Club were Irishmen, and though at least one unkind witticism of Johnson's at the expense of Ireland is on record, his treatment of Irishmen is not to be compared with that which he lavished on the Scotch. In 1772 we find Charlemont sounding Johnson, through the medium of Baretti, on the subject of political opinions. But the result was non-committal, for Johnson, in sending 'a thousand thanks for your kind words, yet wonders how you seem to think him of any party but yours, knowing, as he does, that yours is that of philosophy and virtue'.[38]

Malone was a much closer friend than Johnson ever became, yet even here, and though Malone was an Irishman, politics was a subject on which they did not always see eye to eye. The fact was that in spite of coming of a political family, Malone was unpolitical himself. He had settled in London in 1777, and thereafter he had a standing commission from Charlemont to collect old and rare books for him in London.[39] Most of their correspondence is on this topic, but they exchanged literary opinions and criticised each other's work. It was Charlemont who first suggested that Malone should edit Shakespeare,[40] and who urged him to enter the lists in the Chatterton controversy. Soon after Chatterton's death Charlemont was in Bristol, and a local Rowleian had engaged his interest in the matter of the disputed poems. Another enthusiast for authenticity is writing to him in 1778 and 1779, but it seems that Charlemont is wisely reserving judgment.[41] Malone himself sent him the pamphlets on the other side, while he promises his own effort, 'for I flatter myself your partiality will incline you to run your eye over it, notwithstanding your leaning to the other side of the question'. Finally, in 1782, when Malone had entered the field, Charlemont wrote to him: '. . . all the wit and genius is on one side together with some good argument—but the weight of proof seems yet to lie on the other.' The disagreement was amicable, and the Earl never came to close grips with the question.

Malone's attack on the Ireland forgeries is more closely linked with Charlemont's name. These impostures broke upon the world in 1795, and for a short time the pseudo-Shakespeare made as promising headway as the pseudo-Rowley had done. But Malone's victory was quicker and more complete on this occasion. When his four-hundred-page *Letter to Lord Charlemont* appeared in 1796, he had to explain away the fact that Charlemont had subscribed to Ireland's publication as follows: '. . . I am authorized by him to say that he subscribed to that work at the request of a gentleman who furnished him with a splendid prospectus of it, which he carried from hence to Ireland; and that if Lord Charlemont had known as much of it as he now does, he would not have given either his name or his money to the publication.' Charlemont himself writing to Malone, had observed rather ruefully, 'I subscribe whenever I am desired,'[42] but in saying so he certainly did himself something less than justice. How frequently he was desired we can judge from the number of extant publications which were dedicated to him. I have been able to trace some sixteen of these, and it is worth passing some of the more interesting of them in review. We

PLATE XIII

See page 174

CHARLEMONT HOUSE

The Rockingham Library, looking South (?). From a photograph
taken in 1865

have already noticed Skelton and Dunkin at an earlier
period, and of course the signal instance of Piranesi.
Then, in 1755, we have a Thomas Cooke,[43] a translator
of Plautus and victim of the *Dunciad*, who, according
to Dr Johnson, was notorious for living for twenty
years on the subscriptions to the Plautus, of which only
one volume of the projected ten ever appeared. Leland's
Demosthenes has already been mentioned. In 1759
Henry Brooke (author of the *Fool of Quality*) inscribes
to him *The Interests of Ireland . . . . particularly with
respect to Inland Navigation*. And in lighter vein, ten
years later, the *Fable of Hymen* on the occasion of the
Earl's marriage. The *Fable* depicts a Temple besieged
by women, and especially by a girl whom we identify as
the future Lady Charlemont. As for her destined mate,

> In him, by Science, Travel, Taste,
>   Be Nature polish'd, not defac'd,
> And set, as is the brilliant Stone,
>   To be, with double Lustre, shown.

The description is, of course, unmistakable, and so

> Your Suit, fair Creature, must miscarry
> Till CHARLEMONT resolves to marry.

Henry Brooke's daughter Charlotte was a pioneer in
Gaelic studies, and after her father's death in 1788 she
fell on hard times. We find her in 1787 or so writing
to Charlemont as 'the child of a man who was once
honored with your friendship', in the hope that he can
procure her the office of housekeeper to the Royal Irish
Academy. The Earl, torn between duty and kindness
of heart, was unable to further her cause, unable even
to fall in with the suggestion that an unpaid post should
be created for her.[44] It is a sad story, for Miss Brooke
died a few years later.

P

Baretti's *Manners and Customs of Italy* followed, also in 1769, and the receipt of it evoked from Charlemont the admission that 'I may love Italy as a mistress, while my native country claims from me the proper and just regard due to a wedded wife'.[45] Poor Baretti was shortly overtaken by a prosecution (happily unsuccessful) for murder, during which he was not a little supported by kind and anxious messages from Charlemont.

The Volunteer movement produced, as might be expected, a flow of military and political tracts, and Charlemont came in for his share of the dedications. More interesting is a two-volume *History of Ireland*, published at Strabane[46] by William Crawford, a local Volunteer Chaplain, to whom Charlemont lent books for his researches. 'To trace out and vindicate our national Rights is a principal Intention of the present Work', says the dedication; and it is not the Earl's fault if the book has not taken its place as a classic of scientific history.

In the archaeological field there was Walker's *Essay on Irish Dress*, which for long held its own if only for want of serious competition. Walker and Charlemont had other interests in common, for the former's book on *Italian Tragedy* was almost a collaboration between them.[47] In the sphere of science there was Richard Lovell Edgeworth, who in 1797 embodied his ideas 'on the tellograph and on the defence of Ireland' in a 'letter to the right hon. the earl of Charlemont'. In this case there is no doubt of the value of the work, for Edgeworth's system was, by the usual process, adopted by the Admiralty long after the immediate danger was past. It was not, we may remark, the first time that he and Charlemont had been concerned together in the

defence of Ireland, for through the stirring days of
1782-3 Edgeworth was the Earl's Volunteer A.D.C.,
in striking contrast to George Robert Fitzgerald who
attended the Earl-Bishop of Derry in the same capacity.

Dedications, to Charlemont as no doubt to many
others, could at times be an embarrassment. Thus when
in 1796 an 'intimate acquaintance and partial friend of
mine' took upon himself to publish an answer to Burke's
Letter to a Noble Lord, and addressed it to Charlemont
(not indeed by name, but recognizably), the latter
wrote in great concern to Malone. It was not that he
did not agree with the reply—and here, by the way, he
expects Malone to disagree with him—but that it spoke
of Burke in abusive terms, and this, for friendship's
sake, he deplored.[48] As for this last phase of Burke's
politics, 'what is human nature, when prejudice can
harden the best of hearts and pervert the most brilliant
talents!'[49]

We have left to the last the mention of poetical works
dedicated to the Earl, for the subject raises a melancholy problem. There were such people as Irish poets,
but only just. There was Thomas Atkinson, who in
1791 dedicated to Charlemont his *Hibernian Eclogues
& Miscellaneous Poems*. There was William Preston,
whose Sonnet to Charlemont begins

> Caulfeild, were mine the Chian father's vein,
> Or had I heir'd Tyrtaeus' lofty song,
> Then might I rise, to sing the patriot throng,
> And hail thee first amid that awful train . . .

and bears the date Dublin, Jan 16, 1781, but has no
other features of interest.[50] Preston was Charlemont's
tame poet *par excellence*, and tame he was in more

senses than one. Of the Volunteers we may too truly
say with Horace and with Pope, 'They had no poet,'
and are dead': They had, to be sure, Pleasant Ned
Lysaght; and he and George Ogle are the only live poets
of the time. Neither of them published books, and their
delightful songs and ballads circulated rather *viva per
ora virum*. As for the rest, there was the Volunteer
John Edwards, *The Patriot Soldier* of 1784 with his
Abradates and Panthea: a Tragedy; Mr Shepherd, the
parson of Celbridge and protégé of the Conollys; Mr
Anketell, the curate of Donaghendry and protégé of
Charlemont's friend James Stewart of Killymoon;[51]
Eland Mossom who translated *The Christiad* of Vida in
six books;[52] and many other names as dim or dimmer.
The fact that Edkins's *Collection of Poems* in 1801 has
a preface eight pages long enlarging on the fact that it
is 'exclusively composed of poetry strictly and purely
IRISH', serves only to reveal the poverty of the field.
In an age when Irish printing and binding were second
to none, there was no Irish literature to match. By the
time the literature first appears on the scene, it must
struggle against the handicap of a craft hopelessly
decayed by thirty years of Union.

Should we accept the explanation of mere accident,
we may glean some hint of what the poetry of Anglo-
Ireland might have been like, had Anglo-Ireland had
its poet, from the one noteworthy poem of John Philpot Curran. But in the recurring refrain of that most
Irish of poems 'Let us be merry before we go' we are
offered an explanation which is perhaps more likely.
The background was changing too quickly to favour
the production of more than the occasional graceful
anacreontic. Hardy implies the existence of a class of
Irish poets when, under the year 1755, he remarks that:

with Irish poets or artists Charlemont had then little
or no acquaintance.[53] He goes on to express surprise
that 'he, whose residence was afterwards more fixed in
Dublin, or near it, than that of almost any nobleman
in this country,' should 'for many years, feel himself
almost a stranger to it'. Hardy presumably accepted
the homogeneity of eighteenth-century Irish society at
its face value: Charlemont's wariness may have derived
from a perception that things in Ireland were not as
simple as they seemed. At this distance of time, it is
easy to detect in the exceptional qualities of Curran's
poem the reflexion of the fact that its author, though
a Protestant and Master of the Rolls, was partly native
and peasant in his origins. The fusion of these elements
in the mould of classical society could not happen
wholesale overnight: we are still waiting for it, and it
seems as far away as ever.

The Earl's own literary works, it must be admitted,
do little to save the situation. They are extant in four
folio volumes of manuscript,[54] nor is there any pressing
reason why they should be dragged from their obscu-
rity. One volume consists of epigrams, translated from
the Italian, French, Latin and Greek. They are mostly
competent, and this is perhaps the best of them, from
the Chevallier de Cailly:

> Whether Love's Fire, my pretty Nell,
> Inflames your Heart I can not tell;
> But, be your Heart inflam'd or not,
> Of this I'm sure—It boils your Pot.

(where the French has 'Il fait boullir votre Marmite')
or this, from the Greek anthology, into what is presumably intended for Mediaeval Scots:

> Devour'd by Bugs Sawney the Light blew out.
> Now seen me gif ye can, exclaim'd the lout.

It is, perhaps, interesting that in translating Catullus he uses an Irish idiom, that the law-courts appear as the Four Courts, and that in a version from Martial appears the phrase 'rich as John Scott' in allusion to Lord Clonmell, the Attorney-General, commonly known as Copper-faced Jack.

The remaining three volumes are occupied with translations of the Italian poets, from Dante onwards. They form, in fact, an illustrated history of Italian poetry. It is clear that this, like all his other literary undertakings, kept him occupied at intervals over a long period, for we hear that he resumed work on it in 1785, after the political climacteric was past, and he was still working on it as late as April 1799.[55] In this its chief value consists, as providing an outlet for energies otherwise threatened with disappointment, and a topic for consultation with friends. The section on Petrarch was published in 1822, 'at the desire of his nearest relative', and like the rest, it is scholarly, graceful and conscientious.[56] Dante, in the unpublished portion, he describes as 'this excentrick, excellent and ancient Bard ... I have sought', he goes on, 'to rise and to sink with him', and above all he has tried not to turn Dante into a 'modern fine Gentleman'.

This is perhaps the place to remark that Charlemont's literary taste was as robust and reliable as his taste in buildings. His occasional lapses are only to be expected, few as they are; and when he expresses a firm belief that *Jack Cade* is by Shakespeare, it is only fair to remember that his other dicta on the Shakespeare canon, though made at a time when the question seemed much more open than it does now, have been endorsed by later opinion. He recognised the merit of Maurice Morgann's *Essay on Falstaff* immediately on its appearance, and without knowing who the author was.[57] He admired Milton and Pope, and though we find him anxiously awaiting his copy of Erasmus Darwin's *Loves of the Plants*, we may give him credit for finding Hayley 'abominably dull' except in his *Life of Milton*.[58] We might expect him to enjoy Matthew Prior, as he does; and if we cavil at his description of Hesiod as 'certainly one of the best of Greek poets',[59] we are hardly likely to quarrel with his view of Dryden's prose style as 'one of the first in our language'.[60] He dislikes poetry which is full of 'clouds of sublimity by which the greater part of our modern poetry is, to me at least, rendered almost unintelligible'.[61] When we contemplate Mr Preston's effusions, it is easy to see what he means, though he was certainly too well-mannered to say so in particular terms. Above all, he is free from conventionalism. He recommends a certain Knolles, an 'incomparable Historian, whose Work is, in my opinion, the Test of english historical Style[62] . . .' Perhaps, in our ignorance, we do not know that Johnson, Southey and Hallam concur in this judgment. Finally we may add that he deprecated the use of rhyme even in lyric poetry; that he thought Chesterfield's *Letters* 'adequate to the purpose for which they were written— perhaps the only true criterion of literary merit;'[63] and that a faultless poem was, in his opinion, 'always a dull one'. Without making exaggerated claims on his behalf, it can be said that he put up a creditable showing for one who was, after all, only an earl.

NOTES

1. *Georgian Society*, V, 53.
2. Milton: *Views in Ireland*, 1783.
3. Exshaw (*The London Magazine*), Dublin, 1789, p. 52.

4. Ibid., 1790, p. 166.

5. *Gentleman's Magazine*, 1774, p. 442.

6. Exshaw, 1776, p. 669. Both robberies took place, oddly enough, on the 7th of September.

7. Exshaw, 1787, p. 334.

8. Wesley: *Journal*, July 16th, 1778.

9. Ibid., July 3rd, 1787.

10. Young: *Tour in Ireland*, Dublin, 1780, I, 4.

11. HMC, II, 25.

12. The technical term was 'closeting': if it got abroad that any opposition personality had had an unchaperoned interview with the Castle, his reputation stood immediately in need of strenuous vindication.

13. HMC, I, 254 sqq.

14. Ibid., I, 273: 'I shall not mention any thing your lordship has wrote about Mr Pullein.'

15. RIA MSS., X, 86, 88, 89.

16. Ibid., 90.

17. Ibid., 94, 95.

18. Bodkin in Procs. of RIA, XLVIII, C, 4, p. 177.

19. RIA MSS., X, 73–76, 84 (1776–1778). See also Gilbert: *Calendars of Ancient Records of Dublin*, XII, 90 sqq.

20. e.g. the epistolary preface to his political autobiography, addressed to his sons: RIA MSS., VII, *ad init.*

21. Letter from Lord Mornington to Charlemont, August 7th, 1782, partly given in HMC, I, 414. The sentences in question are in RIA MSS.

22. HMC, II, 104. The falling-in of leases no doubt helped.

23. Watson in *Dublin Magazine*, April–June, 1929, p. 14, gives the date as June 11th, 1782. The jurisdiction was restored in effect on May 27th. But it is easy to see that Gandon's plans must have been ordered well in advance. The matter had, in fact, been raised first in 1778: Watson, loc. cit., 13.

24. As first laid out by Dr Bartholomew Mosse, it bore the names Palace Row (North side), Granby Row (West) and Cavendish Row (East).

25. e.g. Wesley and James Malton.

26. Falkiner, *Studies in Irish History*, p. 73.

27. Gandon: *Life*, 112 sqq.

28. Ibid., 80 n.

29. This and subsequent extracts are taken from the minute books of the Royal Irish Academy. This first minute (the last of the Neosophers') is inserted loosely in the RIA minutes.

30. It is known as the Cunningham medal, from the testator whose bequest financed it.

31. RIA *Transactions*: I, III, V and VI.

32. Many of its most valuable Irish MSS. were acquired during Charlemont's presidency.

33. H, I, 330.

34. HMC, II, 359 n.

35. HMC, II, 360. He had earlier expressed a hope of visiting Ireland: ibid., I, 319.

36. Prior's *Life of Malone*, p. 88.

37. Boswell, May 12th, 1778.

38. HMC, I, 309.

39. Especially Shakespeare quartos, of which there was a fine collection at Charlemont House.

40. Prior's *Malone*, p. 51, *et alibi*.

41. HMC, I, 315, 340, 345, 395, 420. Charlemont's Rowleian correspondents were the Rev George Calcott and Francis Woodward.

42. HMC, II, 271.

43. See his letter in HMC, I, 207. Johnson's mention of him occurs in the *Tour to the Hebrides*.

44. HMC, II, 361, 366. See also ibid., 82.

44. Ibid., I, 293.

46. 1783. See HMC, I, 389, 415, 418. See also RIA MSS., XI, 79.

47. See especially a letter from Walker in 1799 (HMC, II, 345) in which he reproaches the Earl for not having published his own work on Italian poetry. There are many other letters from and to Walker both in HMC and in Hardy.

48. HMC, II, 271.

49. Ibid., 273.

50. *Poems*, Dublin, 1793, II vols. A beautifully printed book.

51. Stewart was a friend of Horne Tooke. See Anketell's very interesting Preface to his poems, Dublin, 1793.

52. HMC, II, 109

53. H, I, 84.

54. RIA MSS., I–IV. Vol. I contains translated epigrams, the remainder the history and translations of Italian poetry.

55. HMC, II, 349.

56. *Select Sonnets of Petrarch*, Dublin, printed by William Folds and Son, 1822. Including notes it contains 113 pages, more or less corresponding with RIA MSS., II, 365–512. It is an elegantly printed book, and represents almost the last effort of the old tradition of Dublin printing; though the tradition has run perceptibly thin.

57. HMC, I, 337.

58. Ibid., 197 and II, 272.

59. RIA MSS., VI, 209 n.

60. HMC, II, 278.

61. Ibid., 263.

62. RIA MSS., VI, 213.

63. HMC, I, 327.

CHAPTER XI

THE UNION

The graceful employments of literature, connoisseur-ship and the affairs of his Academy, contribute most to the tenor of the Earl's life during the years 1787 and 1788. But though political developments are increasingly able to manage without him there is less truth in the converse, that he could manage without them. Events will continue to march inexorably to-wards the Union, and Charlemont will be dead before that end is consummated. His intervention is no longer decisive, though it retains an interest as personal expression.

In July 1788 he is in Belfast 'as usual' reviewing his Volunteers.[1] They had fallen off in numbers since 1786, but they were still capable of drinking Charlemont's health over a cloth of Belfast linen, in which were woven his 'martial equestrian lineaments'.[2] Five years of life remained to them, before their suppression by proclamation in 1793. But barely a month before their end, he had written sadly of them: 'they are, alas! no longer what they were . . . I have indeed been their nominal general, but for many years past they have in no one instance asked my advice, nor have they ever taken it when offered unasked.'[3] He reviewed again in 1790, but by 1791 he is canvassing schemes for the erection of a memorial to their days of glory. He ob-jected to the suggestion that it should take the form of a statue of himself. The people of Armagh objected to Dungannon, the obvious site, because they, and Charle-

mont with them, divined that it would be used by the
local family of Knox to advertise their own grandeur,
and to set off their 'improvements' in the town of Dun-
gannon.⁴ Ultimately Sir Capel Molyneux erected on his
demesne near Armagh a conspicuous obelisk dedicated,
without distinction of persons, to the exertions of 1782.
It remains, so far as I am aware, the only such monument in the country.

The County of Armagh was already racked by dis-
tresses more severe than any since 1763. A clergyman
named Hudson, a frequent correspondent from now on,
and a presbyterian minister named Campbell, keep the
Earl informed of events. The judges, among whom was
the notorious John Toler, were evidently determined
to exacerbate existing frictions, and the liberal elements appealed to Charlemont to intervene. He arrived
in Armagh in late July 1788 and did his best; but this
time he had no lasting success.⁵ The protestant organisation of the Peep-of-Day-Boys, so named from their
nocturnal raids on the houses of their Catholic neighbours, who assumed the posture and the name of
Defenders, provoked and sustained a sanguinary catalogue of incidents in which they were abetted at first
by the demoralised and disintegrating Volunteers, and
finally, as was inevitable, by the military. In due course
there appeared in Armagh the Orange Society, the baleful genius of subsequent Irish politics, and with its
arrival the Ireland which Charlemont had known was
irrevocably doomed. 'With the History of Lord Charlemont', declares his biographer, 'it has nothing to do.'⁶
Nothing, in very truth; for it belongs to another world.
But its rise cast yet another shadow over his last years,
his correspondents report continually of it, till in 1798
Hudson writes from Co Antrim 'The "Orange" mania

has broke loose amongst us, and spreads with a rapidity almost incredible'.[7]

But before the bloody catastrophe which illumines the final ruin of the Irish parliament with the flames of civil war, there was to be one more occasion on which Charlemont and his fellow-senators could feel themselves acting as the spokesmen of a nation. In November of 1788, the King of England and of Ireland became incapable of discharging his royal functions. In the British Parliament began the celebrated contest between Pitt and Fox which was to end so damagingly for the latter. In the Irish Parliament there was an immediate accession of strength to the Whig opposition. The Whig argument, in Ireland as in England, was that the Prince of Wales had already become Regent,[8] and that it remained only for Parliament to call upon him, by Address, to take up his functions. The English Tories proposed that Parliament, acting as a Convention, should pass a Regency Act. The Irish Whigs would, if the second of these courses were adopted, find themselves necessarily in the position of having had their Regent elected for them by the British Parliament. It therefore followed that the sooner the Irish Parliament sent its Address, the more likely it was to forestall the British Act.

It was evident even to the Viceroy that the Irish Whigs had a safe majority, indeed an overwhelming one, on this question, such as Pitt's government in England did not possess. Accordingly, it seemed likely that they would win the race, and so they did. The Undertakers, the great borough owners and even many office-holders, had gone over to Opposition, presumably to worship what they thought to be the rising star, and for no worthier motive. But when Charlemont hears from one of his agents in London that 'the time is not very distant when those who have been steady will be well pleased at their own conduct',[9] we may be sure that he took it in the sense that virtue was its own reward. Whether it was true was another matter altogether.

If any feature in the English debates can be said to have approached, in its want of decorum, the bandying of Mrs Fitzherbert's name, it was the frankly party attitude adopted towards the medical reports on the King's condition. Charlemont saw that this could be turned to Ireland's account. The most dignified method of initiating proceedings in the Irish Parliament would be, he suggested, 'that the Irish state physicians should be permitted to visit his Majesty, and should in consequence make their report'.[10] That doctors differ is well known; how much more, then, if politicians are busily differing already?

On February 3rd, 1789, a meeting of the newly-swollen Opposition took place at Charlemont House. When Parliament opened on the 5th, there was a majority against Government. Grattan led it in the Lower, and Charlemont in the Upper House. On the 19th the Address, which they had both moved and carried, was presented to the Viceroy for transmission to the Prince. The Marquis of Buckingham refused to transmit it, on the grounds that the Prince had no regal status. Parliament passed a vote of censure against him, and cut off supplies for two months. It further appointed a commission of six to convey the address directly to His Royal Highness. The Lords appointed Charlemont and the Duke of Leinster, the Commons, Mr Conolly of Castletown, Mr O'Neill of Shane's Castle, Mr William Ponsonby and Mr James Stewart of Killymoon.[11]

They were graciously received by the Prince. The first gentleman in Europe enjoyed and retained the personal devotion of the gentlemen of Ireland. His intentions in the matter of the Order of St Patrick had been handsome; he was believed to entertain a special attachment to Ireland,[12] and he certainly tended to surround himself with Irish friends. On this occasion he exerted himself to captivate Charlemont in particular by the charm of his manner, and in this he succeeded perfectly. They had met at least once before, in 1787; and a little later it is certain that Charlemont had come to know him well.[13] The Prince saw to it that sundry graceful expressions concerning the Earl should come to the latter's ears, and the Earl, on his side, spoke and wrote with affectionate frankness of the Prince. If Royalty may be said to have interests, the Prince and Charlemont had at least one interest in common, for we find Henry Holland the architect making an appointment at this time to show Charlemont the plans of Carlton House.[14] And a little later the Earl is writing to thank His Royal Highness for the gift of a pocket-book; 'the contents of which must ever be dear to me, as a striking proof not only of his magnificence but of his taste, and as a lasting memorial of that palace'.[15] Holland or some other had perhaps been commissioned to furnish him with a memento of what Hardy calls 'this important and interesting scene'.

The immediate end of the story came with the recovery of the King. The Irish Opposition collapsed; some of the major actors, such as the Duke of Leinster, were deprived of valuable sinecures, and a wholesale creation of Irish peerages gave point to the Government's happy reprieve. Charlemont himself was personally unaffected by such measures, but we find him in June, back in Ireland, sitting at his desk in the Zodiac Room of the Casino, in full enjoyment of the Irish summer: 'Will this approaching comet never have done shaking his tail at us? It now rains as if it was just beginning, and I have twenty acres of meadow cut, and, what is worse, it is so dark that I must conclude my letter. Adieu, my dearest Haliday. For Heaven's sake be incessant in preaching Whig principles[16]...'

There was ample reason for foreboding. The part of Pitt had been taken in the Irish Parliament by John Fitzgibbon, who was now Attorney-General, and became Lord Chancellor and Baron Fitzgibbon immediately after the end of the Regency Crisis. The crisis had convinced him of the necessity of an Union, and he in turn spent the next ten years urging the measure upon his employers. Though it is dangerous to assign a single cause for any historical event, it may be allowed that Grattan's conduct of the Regency question did more than any other single thing to seal the fate of Grattan's Constitution. And Grattan's responsibility is also Charlemont's. Their policy did not indeed make the Union inevitable, but it turned the scales in the mind of an able and unscrupulous adversary who thenceforward set himself to make it so.

It is not in humanity to continue always in one mood, even in that of depression; and we find Charlemont admitting that in January of 1793 'I did indeed exult exceedingly, perhaps too sanguinely', when it seemed for a moment that a Reform Bill might be on the way.[17] But in July, when Fitzgibbon introduced a Bill against unlawful assemblies, Charlemont, who had himself presided over gatherings of equivocal legality, found, inevitably, that he 'had a nice course to steer between base acquiescence on the one hand, and dangerous irri-

tation on the other.'[18] The dilemma of the old party
was indeed inescapable, and Charlemont, by now quite
disabused of his heroic illusions, was painfully aware of
it. Saddest of all his many disappointments was the
heavy change which had come over Belfast. In 1791
the Belfast Whig Club had taken advantage of the
circumstance that the anniversary of the Battle of the
Boyne was closely followed by that of the Fall of the
Bastille, to celebrate both, laying the emphasis mainly
upon the latter. Charlemont's close friend Haliday (to
his left) and the future Castlereagh (to his right),
drank confusion to tyrants on this occasion.[19] The Earl,
though himself at the time at Bath drinking the waters
for his own health and that of his little daughter, could
so far have taken part without embarrassment. But by
January 1792, a mere six months later, he descants in
piteous tones upon his woes:

O Belfast, Belfast, dear object of my love and of my pride,
how art thou changed! Shall the prop of Ireland become its
battering-ram? Shall its best friends be compelled to wish for,
at least in the present instance, that loss of its weight which
you [Haliday] so wisely foretell from its dissensions? But no
more, the subject is too painful to be continued.[20]

The tears of the old testament prophet over the defaulting city of his choice gain an added poignancy from the
fact that by now his correspondent's views are perceptibly more radical than his own. Haliday's friendship
with Charlemont was in danger from the fact that the
Belfast doctor was on cordial terms with some of the
United Irish leaders.[21] The friendship survived the
strain, partly from its native strength but partly also
because Charlemont regarded Haliday much as the
Government had formerly regarded the Earl, as a sober-
minded man who might be able to restrain and influ-

RIGHT HON.ble Earl of Charlemont.

PLATE XIV　　　　　　　　　　　　　　　*See page 163*

'MARTIAL EQUESTRIAN LINEAMENTS'
From a Dublin Magazine of c. 1782

ence men with whom no direct official contact was possible.

The Reform Bill from which so much had been expected died untimely, smothered by the Catholic Question. Lecky considers that the Government deliberately fostered the latter at the expense of the former.[22] It is certain that Charlemont, who was genuinely anxious for reform, was opposed to the Catholic Relief Acts of 1792 and 1793, the second of which was a Government measure. But it was not that he feared the Greeks, even when they brought gifts; he feared even this particular gift from what quarter soever it might come. The English Government, and the English interest in Ireland led by Fitzgibbon, were actuated purely by policy. Pitt was determined on Emancipation, but he was hostile or at best indifferent to Ireland. Fitzgibbon, though he is generally written down as anti-Catholic, was in fact anti-Irish. In his own words, he 'would cheerfully give relief to the Roman Catholics, provided it should not extend to give effective situation in the State.'[23] And if policy made it necessary to relieve the Catholics to the point of endangering the stability of the State, then so much the worse for the State. The State must be re-defined. Ireland must be merged in a larger unit.

The procedure of defining the State to suit tactical convenience reached a *reductio ad absurdum* in 1921, and it is therefore interesting to examine an earlier application of the principle. Fitzgibbon's viewpoint was that the first essential was to create the form of an United Kingdom, in which Catholic Emancipation might be granted with impunity. Given the form, he believed that the reality would follow. And if the Catholics were obstinate enough to hold aloof, thus crippling

Q

the desired reality, at least the form would persist and could be backed up by force whenever it became necessary. We know now that the formal United Kingdom never became a reality, but it is not fair to blame Fitzgibbon or Pitt for that. We can, however, blame Fitzgibbon for devotion to an ideal which we ourselves find intrinsically repugnant.

It was on these last grounds that Charlemont took his stand. His argument was that the form of an united and independent Ireland was already in existence. He would, I think, have admitted that it was far from being the ideal reality. But he himself could remember occasions on which the spirit had filled the form and made it for a moment real. He held the conservative attitude that while the form was there, there was always the chance that the miracle might happen again; that the dry bones might live. As we have already seen, he thought it unlikely that Catholic and Protestant would easily grow together into a nation. But if other miracles could happen, this was not impossible, given fair conditions. 'Disappointment', he wrote to Haliday, 'is a never-failing source of anger, and possibly of tumult; and nothing is more wanting to us, both as a nation and as individuals, than peace and tranquillity.'[24] But all occasions conspired to deprive Ireland of peace, and to accumulate disappointment. His view of the Catholic question became more and more academic, and still he held it.

He held it partly because he saw the uses to which the unionists were putting the opposite side of the case. But cultural feelings weighed with him as perhaps with no-one else of his time. Emancipation would lead to a Catholic Ireland, and such an Ireland would not be the Palladian Senatorial Ireland of his day-dreams. 'As-

similation'—not, I think, doctrinal, but rather cultural
and political—was the end he kept in view. 'It could,
in my opinion, require a century at least of the best
education, before our semi-barbarians could be brought
to assimilate with their fellow-subjects, or to a capacity
of duly performing the functions of a citizen, before
they could possibly provide themselves with bare free-
holds of civilization.'[25] He asked for time, and time was
not forthcoming. His views may have been mistaken,
but at least they showed more true nobility than those
which would confine the 'barbarians' for ever in the
prison of electoral minority.

Haliday, who held views similar to Charlemont's
own, began in November 1791 to waver towards emancipation.[26] He tried to sound Charlemont on the matter
particularly of opening education to the Catholics, but
if there was a reply it has not survived. In December
he writes again, underlining the brute realities of the
situation, that the Catholics are now 'up at auction'
and the bidders are to be 'the government and the good
Protestant people of Ireland'. And again he repeats
that the gates of education must be thrown open,
though nothing else be done.

Charlemont replied in a long and very important and
interesting letter. The remarks already given are taken
from it; and on the last point, that of education, he has
much to say. He saw as clearly as the next man that to
sit and expect the Catholics to absorb traditional culture, while at the same time preventing them from
drinking at the official fountains of the same, was
grotesquely impracticable.

Certainly the laying open our schools and colleges will be
infinitely preferable to established Catholic seminaries, and
such was my meaning when I spoke of education . . . Semin-

aries common to all persuasions would, both in appearance and in reality, create and strengthen that cordial union among Irishmen, which it must be the wish of every honest man to cultivate by every method consistent with safety. Yet the Catholics I fear both think and wish otherwise . . .

But as for the other points, 'Complete your plan, and Ireland must become a Catholic country; but whether our masters will be as tolerant as we are may be matter of doubt . . .' 'There is no arguing from analogy between Ireland and any other country upon the globe . . .' Above all, the constitution must be preserved, for in spite of Paine's arguments, he persists in regarding it as 'the best that ever was devised, principally for this reason, among many others, that it exclusively possess the almost divine power of renovation and the innate faculty of repairing its defects without departing from its genuine spirit, but merely by a legal recurrence to its first principles'.

He was old and tired, depressed and half-blind. Little wonder that he wrote, 'My sight fails me, and my head is addled', and that, 'upon reading over, not without pain and difficulty', what he had written, he found it 'in every respect defective'. But he saw clearly enough in some directions. The Catholics were admitted to Trinity College by the Act of 1793, but in the following year Maynooth was established as a separate foundation; and from this step resulted that rupture of tradition which he had foreseen and dreaded. Protestant Ireland, thinking to seal off the Catholic seminary, had in reality sealed itself off from the life of the nation as a whole.

He stood almost alone among the Whigs in 1793. We are told by Hardy that the Catholics respected him and loved him none the less for his opposition.[27] On the

other hand, William Drennan wrote in 1791 'if Lord
Charlemont hates the Catholics, they detest him'.[28] But
there is no reason to believe the second half of this
statement any more than we believe the first.

By 1798 Charlemont had changed his attitude, and
was for emancipation. In that year he nominated
William Conyngham Plunket, a rising young barrister,
to a vacant seat for the borough of Charlemont. He had
at first offered the seat on condition that its occupier
should oppose Emancipation. In an interview between
them, Plunket refused to subscribe to this condition.
But Charlemont recalled him a little later, and offered
him the seat untrammelled by any such directive. It
was not long before, in another conversation with
Plunket, he admitted that he himself had come round
to the support of Emancipation. Plunket, on whose
authority we have this information, was unable to
remember afterwards the arguments which the Earl
put forward for his change of attitude, and he was even
uncertain whether it was 1798 or 1799.[29] But the author
of *Public Characters of* 1798, published in that year,
confirms the earlier date.

We can only guess at his reasons. We may conjecture
that they were less systematic than his earlier arguments, of which we know so much more. Very probably
the realisation that others thought his attitude illiberal
had induced him to think it illiberal himself. He spoke
to Plunket of having sacrificed a 'prejudice', and some
such instinctive motion of the heart must have been at
work. If the Irish Parliament were to perish, let its
dying actions be at least of a generous cast.

He had, with all other men of good will, shared in the
general consternation and dismay which greeted the
recall of Earl Fitzwilliam in March 1795. His successor,

Earl Camden, was an amiable man whose father had
been a friend of Charlemont's. But as a Viceroy he was
a man of straw. He called on Charlemont with every
mark of civility; but matters were rapidly progressing
to a point where such social graces were of no avail to
seal the rifts in the body politic.[30] As Grattan said a
little later, 'Two desperate parties were in arms against
the Constitution. I could not join the rebel—I could
not join the Government . . .' Or as Hudson wrote to
the Earl 'The only argument on the other side is, Will
you compromise with rebels? This seems to suppose
that all who are not entirely on the side of government
are rebels,' a supposition which is equally false and
dangerous.'[31] On the other hand it was of no avail for
an United Irish sympathiser, signing himself 'Amicus'
to address him with outrageous flattery as 'the Irish
Washington'; to say to him, 'My lord, this is not the
old contention of parties in Ireland. It is not the Whigs
against the Tories, or the 'ins' against the 'outs' . . . It
was of no avail to emphasise, as this correspondent did;
what the old man was beginning to realise with a sinking of the spirits and a sickening of the heart, that
'There is no middle way now; your lordship must either
be active in the service of the people, or take the
"Orange" oath of extermination'.[32]

The clarity of this analysis was not only brutal: it
was useless. Grotesque as it was to liken him to Washington, it was still more grotesque to expect him, at
the age of seventy, to re-emerge in his former character.
The mental vigour was wanting, and the bodily was on
the wane. A riding accident in July 1794 kept him in
bed for ten weeks, and his old infirmities, hitherto pre-
cariously kept at bay, began to encroach upon him,
taking advantage of the deprivation of air and exercise;

'those necessaries of life on which I live full as much as meat and drink'.[33] No more was he to be seen on horse-back in the Dublin streets, dressed for preference in his oldest clothes, and flinging his arms about so much that the street-arabs shouted after him 'My lord, my lord, where are you flying to?'[34] But by 1796 he had sufficiently recovered to be able to say that he could be found in town every day from two to five o'clock, should Earl Camden desire him to wait upon him at the Castle.[35]

He found some relief from public anxieties in the rising manhood of his two eldest sons. But even here his satisfaction was purchased by sorrow. In September 1793 his second son, James Thomas, died at the age of seventeen.[36] In 1795 he addresses a long letter[37] to his eldest son, Francis William, explaining at the outset that, to avoid the heat of argument, he is saying what he has to say on paper rather than by word of mouth. 'I have beheld', he continues, 'with the utmost anxiety the frightful dissipation in which you have been lately involved.' Francis had taken his B.A. from Dublin University in the previous summer, and social idleness held for him just those dangers which Murphy had seen surrounding his father. Wisely, therefore, the Earl bases his arguments to his son on his own shortcomings. The very exercise of writing calmed his spirits, for the 'frightful dissipation' is soon softened into 'the little defects which alarm me.... the time of dissipation is, I trust, nearly at an end, and I would rather alter your future than your present conduct'.

'In you', he tells the young man, 'the pure metal greatly preponderates. Your late conduct in Armagh was grateful to my soul; it was all a fond father could have wished.'

It would seem that when quite a child, young Francis was already something of a figure-head in local
Armagh politics. In 1797, though a petition of his drafting was rejected by the Armagh free-holders in favour
of another to much the same purpose, he was elected
member for the county. It had long been his father's
wish that he should succeed the amiable Brownlow,
who had died in 1794. In the interim he sat for Charlemont, and on his election to Armagh he left room, as
already told, for Plunket. On March 5th, 1798, he
spoke for the first time, greatly to his father's satisfaction. 'I feared', wrote the Earl, 'that the sheepishness
of the father might have been entailed upon the son.
For his first essay he was not deficient in matter nor in
manner, and he shewed a degree of bashfulness which
indicates that sensibility without which no man ever
yet succeeded as a speaker.'[38] With Plunket he was
equally pleased, and with Francis Dobbs, a curious and
lovable figure whom he had procured to fill the other
Charlemont seat. The youngest son, Henry, took no
part in politics, but established himself as a country
squire just outside Armagh, under the shadow of Sir
Capel Molyneux's Volunteer obelisk.

The Earl had thus a small but well-knit party to
fight his battles in the fateful Union debates. But before the grand question came to the test, the bloody
prologue to the tragedy was enacted. Close on the heels
of young Caulfeild's maiden speech came the Rising.
This grim episode impinges less upon the Earl's life
than might be expected. He was evidently in Dublin,
suffering from an attack of jaundice,[39] when the rising
in the south-east broke out on May 23rd. And though
his correspondents kept him well posted from day to
day, he seems to have been obliged to follow the course

of events in Antrim and Down from afar. His political
attitude remained what it had ever been, and it is needless to state that each item of news served only to aggra-
vate his distress. He shared in the universal patriotic
suspicion, which no subsequent research has succeeded
in entirely dissipating, that the Government viewed
the outbreak of armed violence with very mixed feelings indeed.

Though the rising did not touch him personally, he
cannot have remained unaffected by the harsh light
which it threw on the social relations which he took for
granted. The ugly rumours of floggings and half-hang-
ings in the riding-school of Tyrone House, by the orders
of John Claudius Beresford, son of the only begetter of
the glorious Custom House, must, one would think,
have disturbed the most complacent. And had the Earl
seen the spectacle of the sporting squire Thomas Coñol-
ly of Castletown, examining suspected United Irishmen
in his vast house, with 'wives all in tears before the
door',[40] he must have reflected somewhat disturbingly
upon the social order.

Worst of all, perhaps, was the fact that the ruling
class itself could not keep an united front. '12 Castletown servants & workmen', writes Lady Sarah Napier,
'have been taken up as house-breakers & United Irishmen. From the nearness of the connection one has with
servants, we have heard all the *ideas*, all the *complaints*
on both sides, & *both* are mad, & *both* are guilty, *both*
ought to be hanged for the general good of society. The
oppressor, the provoked to wrong, the revengeful, the
cunning & the seduced! These last indeed claim one's
pity most[41] . . .' The ducal house of Leinster suffered a
more serious division of sympathy. Lord Edward, the
Duke's brother, the most romantic of Irish revolution-

aries, had been the object of Charlemont's avuncular interest since 1793. In that year we have a picture of him bringing his wife, the celebrated Pamela, to see the library of Charlemont House. Pamela 'promised Lord Charlemont with great good humour, to assist him in keeping her husband in order'.[42] At the same time we hear that 'Leinster and Charlemont shed tears over [Lord Edward] to get an apology, but could not do much'.[43] Lord Edward was not to be kept 'in order', even by so powerful an alliance; and more and bitterer tears were shed at his death.

By none was he lamented more than by Lady Louisa Conolly, whose favourite nephew he was. She enlisted Charlemont's help in the attempt to protect Pamela and her children from the general act of attainder affecting Lord Edward's estate.[44] But though Lord Caulfeild presented the petition in the Commons, and Charlemont himself obtained leave from the Lords to testify in favour of Lord Edward before the lower house, the attempt was unsuccessful. Charlemont was neither well enough, nor sure enough of his ground, to affect a conclusion which was in any case predictable.

In the Autumn the rumours of Union became too insistent to be ignored. The new Viceroy, Cornwallis, had arrived in June, and in October or November Charlemont called upon him.[45] He alluded to the rumours, and warned the Viceroy that of the many reasons which he himself entertained against the measure, perhaps the most cogent was that it would infallibly lead to the ultimate separation of Ireland from England. Though Charlemont expressly disclaimed any wish for a reply, the fact that Cornwallis did not contradict the general report convinced him that it was true, and, as he wrote to Hardy, 'has put a finishing stroke to that misery of mind, with which every occurrence has, for some time past, contributed to afflict me'.

And so the heavy artillery of corruption was brought to bear upon the already unsound fabric of the Irish Constitution. Charlemont and his friends were impotent to save the situation, by the very virtue of their incorruptibility. The genuine anti-unionists were a small minority in parliament, because honest men are a minority everywhere. Even among the genuine opponents there were some whose opposition was founded on an outlook very dissimilar to the Earl's. Perhaps it was as well that he was now sometimes so ill that he could not even attend the debates on which so much depended.

Yet he was still capable of a flash of the old optimism, a moment's hope that the spirit of the country might yet escape the snare of English gold. On January 25th, 1799, he wrote exultantly to Haliday: 'We are yet a nation; the abominable project is defeated; I can think or talk of nothing else. This morning, at seven, there was a division in the house of commons on the agreeing to the union clause in the address to the king, when our friends divided 109 to 104, so the clause was rejected by a majority of five. This delightful event has braced my nerves, and added ten healthy years to my life.'[46] A government commentator said that he had never witnessed a debate in which so many votes were decided by the eloquence of the speakers, and especially by that of the Earl's nominee, Plunket.[47] The emphasis is significant. The Irish Parliament, where party was almost non-existent, excelled in eloquence but was normally ruled by interest. Fitzgibbon, now Lord Clare, and his friends straightway mobilised the resources of the British secret service fund, and when the Opposition in despair opened a subscription for counter-

bribery, he had the effrontery to allude to it in debate.
'I trust', he said, 'there is still sense and honour left in
the Irish nation, to cut off the corrupted source of
these vile abominations.'[48] Further comment is impossible.

. It seems that the Earl was not well enough to attend
the division which was to give him ten more years of
life. Maria Edgeworth left an account of a visit to
Charlemont House at this time, when the old man,
much shrunken and fragile in appearance, came tottering forward to lead her into his 'sanctum sanctorum'
and show her some of his treasures.[49] He was still able
to crawl to the House of Lords, but there he found no
sight more edifying than the complete ascendancy of
the insolent upstart Clare. In April he complained that
he could no longer climb to his bookshelves.[50] But his
friends came in numbers to see him while there was yet
time, until he could no longer receive them. Haliday
plied his friends with letters, fearing to tire the Earl
himself. But a month before the end he writes to hope
that 'that estimable bird of passage, Lord Wycombe'
has been to see him, as he knows no better prescription
than his lordship's society.[51] David Hartley the
younger, hearing that Charlemont intends to come over
for the waters, writes from Bath on July 9th, and ap-
pends to his letter a carefully-drawn map of the new
streets in that city, which he is sure the Earl will be
glad to see. But he was no longer capable of rising, even
to such a bait.[52]

All through July he continued to sink; his limbs
swelled and he lost his appetite. Lady Charlemont was
constantly employed bringing up buckbaskets full of
papers to his bedside, to receive his instructions for
destroying or preserving them. Three volumes of love-

letters, from a Piedmontese Contessa and a Roman
Marchesa, together with a mass of poems, rhymes and
political ballads—the last, we are told, more lively than
was seemly—perished during these days. Finally he
sank into a coma which lasted for several days, and on
August the 4th the inmates of the house were summoned to his bedroom. Dr Harvey came, and the foot-
curtains of the bed were opened. He appeared to be
sleeping. In fourteen days he would have been seventy-
one.[53]

The blinds of the great house were drawn upon the
Square, and the hatchments mounted on the portico.
In the large library the Volunteer banner hung with
leaden folds above the drum, and from the wall there
glowed the emblazoned resolutions of Dungannon.

A few days later, some English friends of Richard
Lovell Edgeworth arrived in Dublin, 'very desirous' to
see the statues and library of Charlemont House. 'The
old porter, who knew how intimate I had been with his
master, ventured to admit us silently into the library;
where I was not a little moved at seeing the chair, on
which he usually sat, in its accustomed place, his gloves
and snuff-box on the table; and Practical Education,
which he had been reading, lying open upon his chair.'[54]

A private funeral was intended, but the cortège was
accompanied to the Cathedral of Armagh by 250 horse
and foot, a large number of carriages, and 600 people
on horseback. Complete silence reigned, save only for
the tolling of the bell.[55] The Primate, Dr Newcome, a
Foxite Whig, conducted the service, and the Volunteer
Earl rests close by the burying-place of Brian Boru.

NOTES

1. H, II, 165.

2. HMC, II, 55.

3. Ibid., 211.

4. Ibid., 140–41. See also Dobbs: op. cit., 1783, p. 92.

5. HMC, II, 74. Early in 1791 a co-lieutenant of the County (Lord Gosford) was appointed without Charlemont's being consulted. In face of this direct insult from Government he sent in his resignation: HMC, II, 133 and H, II, 234 sqq.

6. H, II, 364.

7. HMC, II, 336.

8. This view was not pressed in its extreme form by Grattan. See the very full discussion in Lecky, VI, 416 sqq.

9. Burroughs to Charlemont: HMC, II, 93.

10. Charlemont to Forbes: ibid., 85.

11. H, II, 185–6.

12. He is said to have wished to come to Ireland as Viceroy to restore confidence in 1797. See HMC, II, 302, where is given the letter of the Irish party to the Prince (drafted by Charlemont) and ibid., 304, for the Prince's reply. 'What his royal highness' wrote Burke to Charlemont in 1789 'may be at bottom it is impossible for me to divine.' It is almost equally impossible for us.

13. HMC, II, 275. See also ibid., 369.

14. RIA MSS., XV, No. 37.

15. HMC, II, 374.

16. Ibid., 100.

17. Ibid., 210.

18. Ibid., 217.

19. Ibid., 141.

20. Ibid., 186.

21. Ibid., letter before. In ibid., II, 160, he meets Tone.

22. Lecky: VI, 565, 584.

23. Ibid., 565. As for his hatred of Ireland, Lecky, in Vol. VIII, p. 465, speaks of 'that burning hatred of Ireland' which was the 'dominant feeling' of Clare. This, to my mind the most interesting aspect of his character, has been strangely neglected by amateurs of psychology.

24. HMC, II, 183.

25. This and following quotations are taken from the very important letter to Haliday of Dec 15th, 1791, given in HMC, II, 181 sqq. See also ibid., II, 264.

26. Ibid., 160.

27. H, II, 298.

28. *Drennan Letters*, p. 72 (1791).

29. See *Life etc.* of Lord Plunket, and Falkiner: *Studies in Irish History*, pp. 204 sqq.

30. HMC, II, 264 and H, II, 352.
31. HMC, II, 315.
32. Ibid., 312.
33. Ibid., 247 and H, II, 342.
34. Prendergast in *Irish Times*, loc. cit., and J. G. Swift MacNeill in *Freeman's Journal*, Sept 12, 1899 (centenary.)
35. HMC, II, 282.
36. H, II, 315, and four letters in RIA MSS., XVII.
37. HMC, II, 268 sqq.
38. Ibid., 317.
39. HMC, II, 326.
40. *Drennan Letters*, p. 258, May, 1797.
41. Letters of Lady Sarah Lennox, 1901, II, 131.
42. Prior's *Malone*, p. 198.
43. *Drennan Letters*, p. 129. Lord Edward had described the Viceroy and his party as the King's worst subjects.
44. HMC, II, 334, 373, 375, and House of Lords Journals, 1798, Aug 22nd.
45. H, II, 412 sqq.
46. HMC, II, 344.
47. Lecky, VIII, 342 and note. R. Griffith was the hostile witness.
48. Lecky: VIII, 464. Few episodes in Irish history are more pathetic than this half-hearted attempt on the part of the Opposition to fight the government with its own weapons. Lecky observes drily that these denunciations come with a 'strange audacity' from Lord Clare.
49. Quoted in Frances Gerard's *Picturesque Dublin*. I have been unable to locate the original source. Among the 'treasures' was a carved gem (onyx) of the eighteenth century, which measured 3 inches across and portrayed Queen Elizabeth. See *Irish Times*, 1886, Sept 9th, which gives the Edgeworth visit and is presumably the source for Gerard, immediately speaking.
50. H, II, 424.
51. HMC, II, 355.
52. RIA MSS., XX.
53. The foregoing details are taken from Prendergast in *Irish Times*, loc. cit.
54. Edgeworth: *Memoirs*, 1820, II, 255. Edgeworth was, of course, himself the author of *Practical Education*, with his daughter Maria.
55. *Dublin Evening Post*, August 13th, 1799. A MS. note on a copy in the Armagh Public Library attributes the account, probably correctly, to 'Jemmy Stewart of Killymoon'.

EPILOGUE

The Irish Constitution did not long survive its most whole-hearted admirer. Charlemont House was the scene of the Opposition conferences, and the young Earl bore the part which all expected of him. Here, while they still had a country to lose, were met the keepers of the Anglo-Irish conscience: Grattan, O'Brien, Parnell, Foster and the Ponsonbys, Dobbs, Newenham, Parsons, Daly, Hardy, and Knox, Curran, Plunket and Charles Kendal Bushe, and country gentlemen of a less purely political cast, such as Edgeworth and Henry Brooke. But all was unavailing: on June 6th, 1800, the Bill finally passed, on August 1st it received the Royal Assent, and on December 31st, at midnight, the Irish Parliament ceased to exist.

With the Union, a grey veil is drawn over the history of Ireland. The weary and long-drawn misery of the nineteenth-century is rendered only more depressing by the many earnest efforts to substitute 'good government' for national self-respect. Even the ablest of the few able Unionist historians is constrained to admit that the era of Grattan's Parliament 'must always remain for the historian the grand period of Irish history'.[1] The immediate effect of the Union upon Dublin in particular was, as everyone knows, disastrous. The Parliament House made over to the money-changers, the great houses shut or sold or let in lodgings, the stuccodores and cabinet-makers and printers deprived at a blow of the market which supported them—all this is too familiar to need emphasis. But the Union has some redeeming features for the historian, and especially for the historian of taste. Thanks to it, there is no doubt, in Dublin at least, as to when the political eighteenth century ended. In matters of taste we have the normal Irish time-lag to reckon with; but this is almost exactly balanced by another factor. The impetus given by the great building period carries on for another twenty-five or thirty years, so that by the time it is spent Dublin settles down to stagnate as a complete Georgian city. Had it remained a political capital, we may be sure that it would have been tampered with. The historian of taste and of politics alike is presented with such a clean laboratory-experiment in classicism as he will not readily find elsewhere.

But before we generalise from Charlemont's own role to that of his caste, we may glance at the subsequent history of the family. In his will, the old Earl had left the 'house and temple' of Marino to his widow during her lifetime. He also exhorted his son not to disperse the library.[2] The dowager Lady Charlemont died in Marino House in April 1807, two months after a fire had caused some destruction in the northern wing.[3] The second Earl had less occasion for residence near Dublin, and devoted more attention to enlarging Roxborough in Co Tyrone. In 1825 Marino is spoken of as in a neglected state, but ten years later it was again put in order.[4] The third Earl, who succeeded his uncle in 1865, gave up Marino as a residence in 1867, though his first Countess is said to have been fond of it. In 1876 the estate was sold to the Christian Brothers, a teaching order who retained the house. An enormous redbrick school was built within a few yards of the Casino. The latter, neglected and despoiled—in particular of its lead roofing which was again stolen—had already

R

suffered irreparable damage to its upper storey when
it was rescued by the Act of 1930.[5]

In 1921 the lease of most of the Marino lands fell in.
The house was demolished and a housing-estate erected
on the southern half of the demesne. Cipriani's beautiful gates were dismantled and a small part of their piers
re-erected as gates to a seminary on the new Griffith
Avenue. They are difficult, at first sight, to distinguish
from a series of new gate-piers executed in imitation of
the original. Two of the chimney-pieces from Marino
House found their way into the National Museum.[6]

Most of the great town houses, as we have said, were
closed soon after the Union. Leinster House, sold to the
Dublin Society in 1815, was one of the last to be
vacated. But the second Earl maintained Charlemont
House intact throughout his very long life. He was
elected a representative Irish Peer in 1806; he was
painted by Lawrence; he was kindly mentioned by
Creevey; his wife was admired by Byron. Lawrence's
portrait, which hangs in the National Gallery of Ireland, shows him as a better-looking edition of his
father, with the same strong black eyebrows and suggestion of swarthiness. Creevey used to meet him at the
Brighton Pavilion, whither he resorted even before succeeding his father, and they talked about Ireland.[7] As
for the second Countess, the beautiful Miss Bermingham from County Galway whom he married in 1802,—
'I would', said Byron, 'to be beloved by that woman,
build and burn another Troy.'[8]

It was the second Earl who saw to it that every
religious denomination in the town of Moy was provided with a fit place of worship. He felt a coolness towards Plunket for 'the readiness with which he became *imperial*'[9] in spite of having opposed the Union,

and for the part he played in the prosecution of Emmet.
When other Irish landlords put up their rents, he
omitted to do so. In 1844 his sister-in-law met O'Connell and Davis, the right and left wings of the new
revolution, and O'Connell impressed upon her that 'the
only chance was for some person of high social position,
and who had claims on the confidence of the people, to
take the lead; that *the man* was Lord Charlemont . . .'
The role of a liberal nobleman was becoming uncom-
fortable when it exposed its player to appeals from the
leader of Catholic royalists. But it remained for the
third Earl to abandon, at long last and under grave
provocation, the family tradition.

He succeeded in 1865,[10] and the library was sold in
the same year. The doors and many of the chimney-
pieces were removed to Roxborough, and in 1870 the
house was sold to the Government and became the
General Registry. He employed the historian Prendergast to collect materials for an early history of the
family.[11] He rebuked the perpetual curate of Moy for
allowing his church to be 'bedizened with flags and
orange lillies' on the 12th of July. But, alas, in vain:
the parson would not even consent to a postponement
till the Earl should have left Roxborough for Marino.[11a]
When he was enlarging the Co Tyrone house, he took
the opportunity of embellishing it with busts of Glad-
stone, Bright and other Liberal heroes. But the Irish
Church was disestablished in 1869, and thereafter the
Earl performed an annual ritual of tarring the offending
heads. Politics and architecture are inextricably mingled
to the last. He died in 1892, and with him died the
posterity of the first Earl. Roxborough itself was demolished in the early nineteen-twenties.

If Irish history carries any lesson, it is a warning against facile generalisations. They are, of course, necessary as hypotheses upon which to act. The danger in a community which has never grown to unity, is that they will be formulated before the facts are ready to sustain them. When the discrepancy becomes apparent, the difficulty is got over by re-defining the terms to suit the needs of the moment. We have seen an integrated conception of the Irish state and of Irish civilisation disappear almost as though it had never been. We have seen Ireland turned into a province, a distressed area, a parade-ground for the British Army. We have seen the Anglo-Irish gentry degraded from a ruling class into mere hangers-on of British military snobbery, demoralised and disheartened, their libraries fossilised at the year 1800 because the need for ideas had disappeared. We have seen, in our own time, an idea of Irish civilisation arising, more arbitrary if possible than the former, because it does not even look adequate on the map. Irish history is a series of new beginnings, each claiming historical continuity, and each pretending that its predecessor never really happened. There is no good reason to suppose that the present mould will last any longer than the others.

The example of Charlemont is important, not because he was effective, but because he was more conscious of this problem than others. But we cannot use him as an example to prove anything, for this is to fall into the old trap again. There are two common misconceptions concerning the political context of Irish Georgian architecture. One—and this is still unfortunately the most widely held—is that it was erected by an irresponsible alien caste, that it is therefore not Irish, and furthermore that the plaster-work or any other

feature of merit was done by Italians or at best by
Englishmen. The other—and very much the more
attractive—is that the great builders were also the
great patriots, and that the Union put an abrupt end
to the golden age.

The first of these beliefs is the fruit of mere ignorance, and where it has needed specific disproof, abler
hands than mine have furnished it. As for the second,
John Beresford was determined on the degradation of
the capital he did so much to beautify. Lord Clonmell,
whose house, though like his eminence it was built of
shoddy materials, is among the finest, was of the same
party. Lord Belvedere, too, fell a victim to cupidity on
the eve of a division on the Union. Primate Robinson,
who first employed the greatest Irish-born architect,
was an unpolitical Englishman, while the edifying Earl-
Bishop of Derry, though political enough in all conscience, was English also and an exception to every law.

But there is something to be said on the other side.
Leinster, Charlemont, Moira and Mountjoy led alike
among the builders and the patriots. Much earlier in
the century, indeed, the Conollys at least entertained
the idea of embodying only Irish workmanship in the
building and furnishing of Castletown.[12] It is a pity,
from this point of view, that Charlemont, whose attitude was more consistently national, did not insist on
anything of the kind. The omission spoils what would
otherwise be a very pretty pattern. There were Irish
architects, Smith, Bindon, Ivory, the Ensors, Mack and
the Johnstons, and there were naturalised Irish architects such as Cassels, Cooley[13] and Gandon. But not all
these men were available to serve Charlemont's purposes. Some were dead, others had not come to matur-
ity, and many were occupied elsewhere. Gandon, in-

vited over by Lord Portarlington, settled here and
steeped himself in the spirit of Dublin. Or perhaps it is
truer to say that Dublin and Ireland became impreg-
nated with the spirit of Gandon. Whichever way we put
it, the advent of Gandon confirmed the already existing
individuality of Irish architecture. For this we are inevitably grateful to Lord Portarlington. But Charlemont, from the time that he first employed Chambers,
through his encouragement of Chambers's entry for the
Royal Exchange competition of 1769, was doing exactly the same thing. It is a mere accident that England
outbid Ireland in competing for Chambers's attention.
It was, after all, Cooley who won that competition[14]
and went on to build for the Primate in Armagh and
even to begin the Four Courts.

Yet there remains the impression that Chambers's
work for the Earl is not recognisably Irish architecture.
His work for Trinity College (carried out by a resident
Irishman)[15] is more consonant with Dublin than the
earlier English work on the West front, by Keane and
Saunderson. But Charlemont House is less of its time
and place than any comparable building. It has not
suffered the sea-change which Professor Richardson
notes as coming over Palladianism and the Adam style
alike, when both are planted in Ireland.[16] As for the
Casino, it is entirely free from time and place alike. It
would not be English in England, French in France,
nor even Italian in Italy. The most we can say is that
in China it would be European.

In a small country like Ireland, where one man—be
he politician, patron or artist—can count for so much,
the imponderables of national style have an almost
personal value. Gandon, with all of Chambers's delicacy,
had a daring which is his own. Irish architecture, dom-

inated as it is by Gandon, is most Irish when it is most
daring, when it echoes the heroic bravura of the age of
Grattan's Parliament. Or, to widen the field somewhat,
there is the salient note of the urban vernacular: a
brooding cliff-like reticence, relieved by the warmth of
brick, lightened by the breadth of the streets. As for
the country, when there is as much space as thinly-
wooded Ireland has to give, the note changes. Who
does not know those bleak abrupt Irish houses, which
shot up out of the bog any time after 1690, stood for
two hundred years or so with a faintly perplexed, faintly
defiant expression on their faces, and are even now
falling under the hammer, one by one?

It is idle to say that this is not the 'real Ireland'—as
though there ever was such a thing!—and idle, too, to
point out that this was not quite the effect the builders
intended. As Miss Elizabeth Bowen so admirably puts
it, 'The settlers had built their houses out of the stones
from ruins; their descendants now built a society out of
another ruin.'[17] They started, in this sense, with a clean
sheet. But architecture, like everything else, grows by
its own laws when it is transplanted even to an untilled
field. It produces results which surprise even those who
thought they had arranged everything. Nor can there
be any doubt but that the roots of this new growth
went deep into the soil of Ireland. We have, again, Miss
Bowen's word for it that, for the Anglo-Irish themselves, 'the grafting-on had been, at least where *they*
were concerned, complete.'

This element of extravagance, of daring, is lacking
in the Earl's buildings. In the first place, he lived always
in or near Dublin, and was never subjected for very
long to the disturbing influence of the Irish landscape.
In the second place, his political character, as all

authorities agree, was distinguished by a certain tim-
idity. Is it then surprising that he should have chosen an
architect who, for all his incomparable elegance and
grace, was himself inclined to play for safety?

When we turn to interior decoration, the same contrast can be traced. Irish plaster-work is perhaps even
more distinctively Irish than any external treatment.
In particular it delights in naturalistic forms, especially
of the birds, the birds, if you will, of Aengus which
return to Ireland whenever the political auspices are favourable. More than one critic has remarked upon them:
'birds peacefully feeding their young or rising with clam-
orous wing from the staircase walls, stridently shrieking
at the passer-by; they circle the ceilings in graceful flight
or with fierce beak and talons engage in death grapples
with dragons.'[18] This sort of thing, we may take it, was
too much for the Earl; and in his buildings we will find
nothing of the exuberance, so insistent as almost to
become oppressive, which we see in the Rotunda
Chapel, the saloon of Carton, or the much later work in
Belvedere House. We, who know how much magnificent work was done in Ireland by Irishmen, even before Charlemont began to build, can find no other
explanation for the fact that he found himself 'much
distressed'[19] with his workmen. Among these workmen,
in the opinion of the best-informed modern authority,
Mr C. P. Curran, were two Irishmen, the brothers
Thomas and Charles Clarke, who worked for Chambers
on the Somerset House ceilings. They are the only
Irishmen whom we can attempt to connect by name
with the Earl's buildings.

If the term classicism in art can bear any meaning at
all, we may suggest that it involves the ideal of leaving
nothing to chance. Charlemont and Chambers, as we

have seen, exercised a closer supervision of detail than
any other patron and architect of whom we know.
They concentrated on purity and refinement of line
and colour, conformity to an exacting canon. But other
patrons, without anything approaching Charlemont's
interest or taste, let the men on the spot have their
head. As a result, they have left us buildings not indeed
better than his, but much more characteristic of their
time and place.

The emphasis upon refinement is a constant feature
of every tribute to the Earl's influence upon the society
in which he lived. It is, in fact, largely owing to him
that there was any polite society in Dublin in his time.
One can read very deeply in the memoirs of the period
without being made aware that Dublin contained any
but gamblers, rakes, spendthrifts and duellists. With
some reason, Charlemont House has been called 'the
Holland House of Dublin;'[20] and the need for such a
centre was great indeed. We can forgive him, under the
circumstances, for cultivating polish at the expense of
exuberance.

Inevitably, our picture of the man suffers from the
part in which he is cast. Nobody, for example, has left
a record of an informal conversation with him. We
know that there was a simple man behind the public
figure, and in his letters to Malone and Haliday we can
savour his amiable melancholy humour. He will begin
a letter to Grattan with 'My dear Harry', or refer to
'my poor little daughter' when she is ill, but he is never
really off his guard for more than four words at a time.
Instantly he is back again playing his part, a man who
has had the position of *arbiter elegantiarum* almost
thrust upon him. There was no Horace Walpole at hand
in Dublin to calendar his unbuttoned moods. The most

that happens is that sometimes there escapes from his pen some such observation as this: 'The age is, I fear, already too much refined, and our manners even too polished. ... Too much polishing, I speak to you as an artist, has, I fear, well nigh effaced and worn out the great strokes, the characteristic touches of the master.'[21] In letting out one secret, he has allowed another to escape on its tail. 'I speak to you as an artist . . .' Much later, writing to his son, he complained that 'almost incessant study . . . did not place me where I ought to have been in the ranks of literature'.[22]

Long years before, his acute old tutor Murphy had 'observed two appetites constantly predominant' in his pupil: 'the love of pleasure, and the love of well-founded praise.'[23] He himself admitted the second at least, in writing. But conscious of having done little in literature to merit praise, he did not claim it. He did not even claim that which was legitimately his due as a patron of the arts. He left among his papers 'My own Epitaph',[24] more remarkable for what it omits than what it includes:

> Here lyes the Body of James
> Earl of Charlemont.
> A sincere, zealous, and active Friend
> To his Country.
> Let his Posterity imitate him in that alone,
> And forget
> His manifold Errors.

We need not suppose from this that he wished to stand before posterity as a politician. If love of country be interpreted in its widest and richest sense, there are few today who will not find in the Earl's life something to imitate. The errors which he bids us forget, we may forget; for is it not certain that whatever mistakes we make will be all our own?

Dublin
October 3rd, 1946

NOTES

1. C. Litton Falkiner: *Studies in Irish History*, p. 190. I do not count Lecky as a Unionist historian because if he is so, it is only in retrospect: Falkiner, one feels, would have been Unionist at the time.

2. *Gentleman's Magazine*, Vol. LXIX, p. 899 (1799).

3. *Gentleman's Magazine*, 1807, Pt. I, p. 269.

4. Brewer: *Beauties of Ireland*, 1826. I, 195 D'Alton's *History of County Dublin*.

5. In the restoration, which took place from 1931 onwards under the direction of H. G. Leask, the large bedroom was restored in verifiable facsimile, and the ceiling of the saloon made structurally sound. A little restoration was also necessary in the latter case. No attempt was made at reproduction by guesswork, and any necessary substitution (e.g. of balusters) is made quite evidently new.

6. Where they are labelled as being from 'a house at Marino'.

7. *Creevey*, ed. Maxwell, I Vol., 1912, pp. 147, 148, 150, 666. See also the *Diary* of Thomas Moore.

8. See Gerard: *Some Fair Hibernians*. Byron, Works, 1832, VI, 362 and II, 268. A stanza in the first edition of *Don Juan* celebrated her beauty, but was later expunged at the request, it is said, of her husband.

9. *Monthly Review*, Vol. XI, June 1903: 'Charlemont House Memoirs' by the Hon Mrs Caulfeild of Hockley, wife of Henry Caulfeild, and mother of James Molyneux Caulfeild, third and last Earl of Charlemont. Edited by C. Litton Falkiner. I have been unable to trace the original MS., said to be much fuller than the printed extracts. It is not among the Falkiner papers in RIA. From this source comes also the interview with O'Connell.

10. The second Earl died Dec. 26th, 1864, at Charlemont House.

11. The results (except so far as they are embodied in the JRH & ASI article already cited) have disappeared, but Maj. Burges of Parkanaur possesses the autographed cover in which they were formerly contained. From other indications it seems that Prendergast acted as secretary to the third Earl.

11a. MS. letters preserved in the Public Library, Armagh.

12. Bishop Berkeley: *Letters to Percival*, ed. Rand, 1914.

13. I am informed by Miss Eleanor Butler that there is some reason to suspect that Cooley's ultimate origins are Irish.

14. And Gandon who was awarded second prize. Gandon's *Life*, pp. 26–35. Possibly Chambers never actually entered the competition. See

HMC, I, 291 and 292. From the latter it would appear that the drawings were sent.

15. Meyers: see HMC, I, 350, from which it is clear that Chambers did little more than furnish some general suggestions. Meyers was an architect in his own right and must be credited with most of the final effect.

16. *Monumental Classic Architecture in Gt Britain and Ireland,* 1914. In this monumental and classic work may also be found some pertinent observations upon Gandon's influence on subsequent Irish architecture.

17. *Bowen's Court,* pp. 95 and 117.

18. C. P. Curran: 'Dublin Plasterwork' in JRSAI, March 1940, p. 34.

19. HMC, I, 283 (1767).

20. By Falkiner in *Monthly Review,* loc. cit.

21. HMC, I, 327.

22. Ibid., II, 269.

23. Ibid., I, 220.

24. RIA MSS., VII, *ad init.*

ALEXANDER CAULFEILD

George = Martha Taverner

SIR TOBY, 1st Baron
d. unm. 1627

WILLIAM = Mary, dau. of Sir John King of Boyle Abbey, Co. Roscommon
2nd Baron *d.* 1640

ROBERT, 4th Baron
d. unm. 1642

TOBY, 3rd Baron
d. unm. 1642

WILLIAM = Sarah Moore, dau. of Charles, 2nd Visc. Drogheda
5th Baron
1st Visc. *d.* 1671

WILLIAM = Anne, dau. of William Margetson, Archbishop
2nd Visc. *d.* 1726 | of Armagh & Primate of all Ireland

John, of Donamon, Co. Roscommon

Rev. Charles

John = Catherine, dau. of Thomas Burgh of Oldtown, Co. Kildare
(*C*)

JAMES = Elizabeth Barnard
3rd Visc. | who *m.* 2ndly
d. 1734 | Thomas Adderley
& *d.* 1743 leaving
1 dau. by 2nd marriage

JAMES, 1st Earl = Mary Hickman (*B*)
d. 1799

Alicia = Sir John Browne
of The Neale,
Co. Mayo

Francis

James Eyre   Eleanor (*A*)

Henry = Elizabeth
Margaret Browne

Elizabeth
d. unm. 1831

James

JAMES MOLYNEUX = *1stly,* Elizabeth
3rd Earl *d.* 1892 | Jane
Somerville
dau. of
Lord
Athlumney
2ndly, Anna
Lambart

and daughters

(*B*) Sir Edward O'Brien
= Mary Hickman

Sir Lucius   Edward = Charlotte Hickman
(sister of
1st Countess of
Charlemont)

FRANCIS WILLIAM = Anne Bermingham
2nd Earl *d.* 1863

Emily
Charlotte

Maria
Melosina

William
Francis

James
William
('Lord
Caulfeild')

[all died *aet. circa* 20-22]

[no children from either marriage]

(*A*) married 3rd Earl of Wicklow
(*B*) See inset
(*C*) The 7th and 8th Viscounts Charlemont are descended from the 2nd Viscount, the Earl's line having died out.

259

EXTRACT FROM CHARLEMONT'S MS. ACCOUNT
OF HIS TRAVELS
RIA MSS., Vol. VI, pages 29–32

Having heard much of the peculiar Charms, and irresistible
Attractions of the Ladies of this Island, as well as of their unequal'd Kindness and Condescension, particularly from the
report of a late Traveller, *Dr Askew*, who boasted that, during
a short Abode in this Land of Love, he had enter'd no less than
fifteen times into the holy Bands of Matrimony, and declared
that no Women upon Earth were in any degree comparable
to the fair and all-accomplish'd Miconites, We cou'd not avoid,
in Quality of accurate Travellers, to use our Endeavours towards verifying this curious Fact, in order to the advancement
of natural Knowledge—*Frank Burton* therefore, who in matters
of this Nature was usually the Agitator, and was indeed in
such Researches the keenest of all Naturalists, set himself to
work, and soon discovered a skillfull and friendly Coadjutor
who promised that our laudable Curiosity shou'd be amply
gratified, but warn'd us that, as the Town was now full of
Levantis, one of the Captain Bashaw's Squadron lying at that
time in the Harbour, it wou'd be neither prudent nor safe to
attempt our Interview, or to perform our Experiments in the
City, but that, if at Night we wou'd walk with him a little way
into the Country, He wou'd take care to fix us in a proper and
secure Station, where we might remain in perfect Safety 'till
He shou'd conduct to us such a Damsel as wou'd surprise and
please us, and fully verify whatever wonderful Reports We
might have heard—With the utmost Alacrity We accepted the
Proposition, and accordingly, as soon as the old Folk, who,
fond of and bigoted to the Knowledge of their own Day, are
naturally averse from new Experiment, were gone to Bed, We
sallied forth with our obliging Mercury, who led us at least two
Miles out of Town, and stop'd at a sort of ruin'd old Castle,
into which He bad us enter, and there wait his Return, which

he assured us shou'd be speedy—In this wretched uninhabited
Mansion there was but one Room; if such it may be call'd,
which had any covering, and that too by no means sufficient
to keep out the Rain; It was perfectly unfurnished, the Walls
crack'd in various Parts, and apparently ready to fall into
Ruin—Here We waited with some Degree of Patience for
above an Hour, when at length We began to be weary of our
Situation, and not a little alarmed at the probable Consequences of our Adventure—To attempt a Return wou'd have
been Madness—We were totally ignorant of the Road; The
Night was dark and dismal; We doubted not but that these
formidable Levantis, of whom We had heard such terrible
Reports, were straying about the Country, and We had been
foolish enough to bring no Arms, concluding that, for our Purpose, *those We usually carried about with us were fully sufficient.*
—Calling therefore a Council of War, after due Deliberation
We concluded that it wou'd be most prudent to keep Garrison
where We were, and to wait the Approach of the Morning,
which We doubted not wou'd find us here, in the mean time
fortifying our Castle as well as we cou'd; and for this purpose
strongly barricading our Door, which had no fastening, and
was by no means *Foot-proof*, with Beams, Boards, and great
Stones, which we collected from among the Ruins—Having
thus in some measure secured ourselves from any sudden
Attack, We sat down on the Ground in pitiful Plight, cursing
at once the Doctor, whose Information had seduced us, our
mercurial Friend, who had conducted us, our unlucky Gallantry,
and our unknown Mistress—In this disagreeable Situation
We had not remain'd above half an hour when We were addi-
tionally alarmed by a most violent Thumping at the Door, and
upon our calling out to know who it was that knock'd so furi-
ously, We were answer'd by our Mercury, who, in the greatest
seeming Agitation, beg'd, for Heaven's sake, and as we valued
our Lives, that we wou'd forthwith come out, and betake ourselves to Flight as our only Resource—He informed us, with a
Voice interrupted by Fear, that, in returning to us with the
Nymph, He had been overtaken by a desperate crew of Levantis, who had beaten him cruelly, and taken from him the un-
happy Maiden, who was at this Instant probably ravish'd by

a Dozen at the least—that He had with Difficulty escaped out
of their Hands, and had evaded their Pursuit by the Darkness
of the Night, and his superior Knowledge of the Country; But
that They were even now at his Heels, and that, if They found
us, we were all dead Men!—Without requiring a second Bidding, We instantly evacuated the Garrison, and follow'd our
Guide, who ran at full Speed, over Hedge and Ditch, thro'
miry Cross Roads, and Passages hardly passable by Daylight—
We however, for fear of being bewilder'd, were oblig'd to keep
up with him, and nothing surely cou'd be more truly ludicrous
than the Figure we made upon this Occasion—Poor Frank
especially, whose Body, any more than his Soul, was never
form'd for Flight, exhibited the most exact and the most
humourous Representation of Sir John Falstaff's precipitate
retreat from Gadshill—Out of Breath with running, and
scarcely able to keep up, He damn'd the Levantis, the Pimp,
the Whore, the Greeks, and the Turks!—'Is it not better to
have one's Throat cut than to burst one's Wind?'—'I can not
stir an Inch farther—Let them come and be damn'd—Zounds,
I'm in a Ditch—up to the Neck by Jove! What the Devil
brought me a Whoring in this unchristian Country? Stay for
me—Let me recover Breath—Zounds Man, Stay!'—In this
Manner after having ran several miles, weary, wet, and
splashed up to the Eyes, We at length regained the wished-for
Town, and reached our Habitation as perfectly free from all
amourous Inclination as if We had return'd from an Interview
with Doctor Askew's fifteen Wives—A little Rest however
having repaired our Courage, We began to be vex'd at our
Disappointment, and in a Day or two after We prevailed upon
our Friend, partly by Promises, and partly by Threats, to obtain for us an Assignation with the Lady, who had cost us so
dear, insisting however that this Interview shou'd be in Town—
With great Difficulty We prevailed, and how much soever it
may grieve me, I am compel'd by that Truth, which shall ever
be inseparable from my Narration, to declare that this *Teter-
rima Causa* was rather more fit for the Arms of the Levantis,
than for our more refined and sentimental Passion!

NOTE: They subsequently found out that their 'Mercury'
had been servant to Askew during the latter's stay on Micone,

and on questioning him were told that he had never touched
a woman—or at most perhaps one. 'Such' says Charlemont,
'was the Doctor's boasted Harem, and such are the Stories of
Travellers!'

SIR WILLIAM CHAMBERS'S *TREATISE OF CIVIL ARCHITECTURE*, 1759, AND THE CLONTARF CASINO AS IT EXISTS

In the plans reproduced from Chambers's *Treatise* there are certain small differences from the building as erected. In the basement, the four angle columns are not shown descending through the vaulting, as they in fact do. Their position can be gauged by mentally superimposing the 'Principal Floor' upon the 'Cellar Story'. It is not conceivable that the architect should not have intended them to carry through to the foundations from the outset. The inference is that they are omitted from the plate in the interests of clarity, or perhaps even through carelessness.

Nine steps, instead of eleven, are shown as leading up to the north front. The steps which flank the small central area on the south front are omitted altogether. Here we have, presumably, a change of plan, and a change for the better.

The false doors in the saloon, which gave both owner and architect so much trouble, are visible in 1759, but were finally abandoned. The small closet opening westward off the Vestibule does not, as executed, communicate with the room marked 'Bedroom' in 1759. In the latter room the formal solution of 1759 was not adopted. A shallow alcove was created at its northern end (lower on the page), thus displacing the secondary axis of the remaining space in a southerly direction. This remaining part was then treated symmetrically, and by consequence a small part only of the window was used internally. A similar modification was adopted in the study.

This change, and the fact that a ground-floor room is labelled 'Bedroom', seems to link up with a remarkable discrepancy between this plan and the (north) elevation which was simultaneously published. The plan represents a later stage in the evolution of the design than the elevation, for in the latter the pairs of columns to east and west, and the pedi-

ments over them, are omitted entirely. This suggests very
forcibly that the original intention was to have a much less
extensive upper storey, or even perhaps none at all. When it
was decided to extend the north-south attic to east and west
under the pediments, the small rooms thus created were per-
force at a lower floor-level than the bedroom over the saloon.
Thus the ground-floor west room, no longer necessary as a
'bedroom', was robbed of its original height. Had it not been
replanned as described above, the window would have been
nearly square, and other formal complications would have
arisen. We may presume that they did in fact arise, as they
were certainly solved by the shifting of the axis and consequent
transformation of the proportions.

Some documentary evidence in support of these conjectures
is supplied by an undated water-colour drawing of the Casino
by Thomas Sautelle Roberts, in the National Gallery of Ireland. Here, the building is shown apparently complete and in
occupation. But where the western pediment should be, there
is a balustrade, and though the north and south attic walls
with their urns are shown (as in Chambers's elevation of 1759)
there is nothing between them. Roberts, in fact, depicts it as
a one-storey building. The weakness of this evidence is that the
drawing is meticulously inaccurate in particulars as to which,
had the artist been working with the building standing before
him, he could hardly have gone wrong. On the other hand, as
he embodies features—or rather the lack of features—which
we can deduce from the discrepancies of 1759, it seems likely
that we have here a garbled but not quite worthless version of
what the Casino was intended to be at some stage in its evolution. The marvel, and the final tribute to Chambers's dex-
terity, is that no-one would suspect from the finished article
that it had been the fruit of anything but a single flight of untrammelled inspiration.

APPENDIX IV

SOME CHARACTER-SKETCHES OF THE VOLUNTEER EARL BY CONTEMPORARY AND LATER HANDS.

HENRY GRATTAN (in *Answer to a Pamphlet of Lord Clare,* 1800).

In the list of injured characters, I beg leave to say a few words for the good and gracious Earl of Charlemont; an attack, not only on his measures, but on his representative, makes his vindication seasonable. Formed to unite aristocracy and the people, with the manners of a court and the principles of a patriot, with the flame of liberty, and the love of order; unassailable to the approaches of power, of profit, or of titles, he annexed to the love of freedom, a veneration for order; and cast on the crowd that followed him, the gracious light of his own accomplishments; so that the very rabble grew civilized as it approached his person. For years did he preside over a great army, without pay or reward; and he helped to accomplish a great revolution without a drop of blood.

Let slaves utter their slander, and bark at glory which is conferred by the people; his name will stand. And when their clay shall be gathered to the dirt to which they belong, his monument, whether in marble, or in the hearts of his countrymen, shall be resorted to as a subject of sorrow, and an excitation to virtue.

JOHN PHILPOT CURRAN (in *Speech at the Newry Election,* 1812).

Never was a more generous mind, or a purer heart; but his mind had more purity than strength. He had all that belonged to taste, and courtesy, and refinement; but the grand and the sublime of national reform were composed of colours too strong for his eye, and comprised a horizon too outstretched for his vision.

WILLIAM DRENNAN (in a letter of 1792).

He is the Fayette of Ireland, honest but narrow-minded . . . he retains a character merely because it has never been put to the proof.

EDMUND BURKE.
.... he was indeed a man of such polished manners, of a mind so truly adorned, and disposed to the adoption of whatever was excellent and praiseworthy, that to see and converse with him should alone induce any one who relished such qualities, to pay a visit to Dublin.

SIR JONAH BARRINGTON (in *Historic Memoirs of Ireland,* 1809–1835).
From the first moment that James Earl of Charlemont embarked in Irish politics, he proved himself to be one of the most honest and dignified personages that can be traced in the annals of Irish History. The love of his country was interwoven with his existence—their union was complete, their separation impossible ...

His view of political objects, though always honest, was frequently erroneous; small objects sometimes appeared too important, and great ones too hazardous: though he would not actually temporize, he could be seduced to hesitate, yet even when his decision was found wandering from the point of its destination, it was invariably discoverable that discretion was the seducer.

Had the unwise pertinacity of England persisted in her errors, and plunged his country into more active contest, his mildness, his constitution, and his love of order, would have unadapted him to the vicissitudes of civil commotion, or the energetic promptitude of military tactics ...

Around this nobleman the Irish Volunteers flocked as around a fortress; the standard of liberty was supported by his character, the unity of the Empire was protected by his wisdom; and as if Providence had attached him to the destinies of Ireland, he arose, he flourished, and he sunk with his country.

(later in the same work)
. A cautious attachment to regularity and order, a sincere love for the people; a polished, courtly respect for the aristocracy, with a degree of popular ambition and a proportion of individual vanities were the governing principles of Lord Charlemont during the whole of his political conduct. But,

unfortunately, these were accompanied by a strong taint of
that religious intolerance which has since been proved the
interruption of Irish tranquillity.

No man in Ireland could do the honours of a review better;
and though his personal courage was undoubted, no man in
Ireland was likely to do the duties of a battle worse ...

(*on the Convention of* 1783)

In his weak and virtuous mind, pride and patriotism were
ranged on the one side; but imbecility and a sense of incapacity
to meet the crisis, blinded him to the nature of that insidious
conduct, which on this, and perhaps the only occasion of his
life, he meditated against his benefactors ....

Whilst Lord Charlemont gently descended into the placid
ranks of order and of courtesy, the Bishop rose like a phoenix
from the ashes of the Convention.

(*on the anti-Union meetings of* 1799)

No man in Ireland was more sincere than Lord Charlemont.

W. E. H. LECKY (in his *History,* 1877–1890).

... one of the purest as well as one of the most prominent of
Irish patriots ...

... he brought back [from Italy] a great taste and passion
for art, a wide range of ornamental scholarship, and a very
real earnestness and honesty of character.

... in addition to his great social position, he had personal
qualities of a kind which often go further in politics than great
brilliancy of intellect, and he was one of the very few prominent
Irish politicians who had never stooped to any corrupt traffic
with the Government.

... He was a Whig of Whigs—with all that love of compromise; that cautious though genuine liberality; that combination of aristocratic tastes and popular principles; that dislike
to violence, exaggeration, and vulgarity; that profound veneration for the British Constitution, and that firm conviction that
every desirable change could be effected within its limits,
which characterised the best Whig thought of the time.

... He was a man, in his best days, more eminent for his
accomplishments than for his abilities.

DR. R. B. McDOWELL (in *Irish Public Opinion*, 1944).

It might be said that the earl was the type of man who oscillates inconclusively between making omelettes and smashing eggs.

INDEX

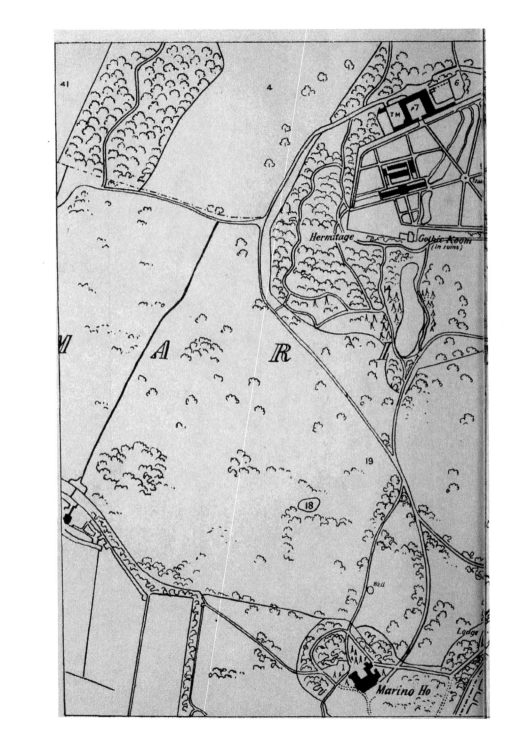

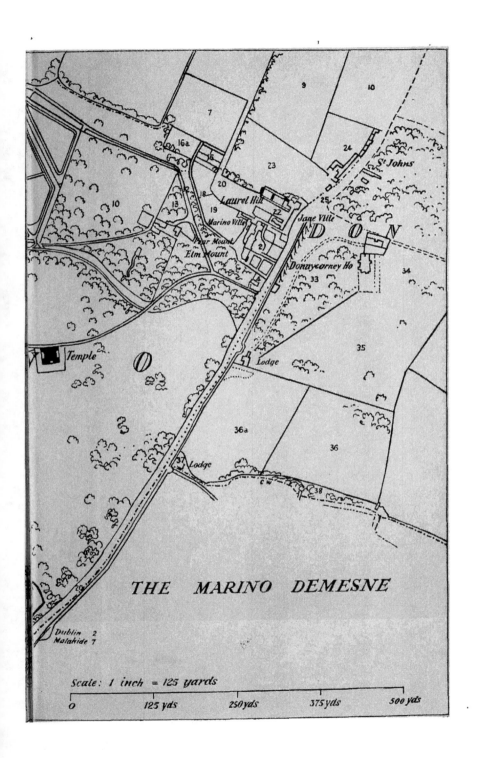

THE MARINO DEMESNE

Scale: 1 inch = 125 yards

| 0 | 125 yds | 250 yds | 375 yds | 500 yds |

CPSIA information can be obtained
at www.ICGtesting.com
Printed in the USA
BVHW051042270223
659294BV00010B/340